STEPHEN BEAUMONT'S
GREAT
CANADIAN
BEER GUIDE

• THE BEST BEERS • THE BEST BREWERIES • THE BEST BREWPUBS •

Canadian Cataloguing in Publication Data
Beaumont, Stephen, 1964-
   Stephen Beaumont's Great Canadian beer guide

ISBN 0-7715-9031-8
1. Beer - Canada.   2. Brewing industry – Canada – History.
I. Title.   II. Title: Great Canadian beer guide.

TP573.B43 1994 641.2'3'0971 C93-095491-2

Macmillan Canada wishes to thank the Canada Council and the Ontario Ministry of Culture and Communications for supporting its publishing program.

Macmillan Canada
A Division of Canada Publishing Corporation
Toronto, Canada

1 2 3 4 5   98 97 96 95 94

COVER AND BOOK DESIGN: Brant Cowie/ArtPlus Limited
PAGE MAKE-UP: Heather Brunton/ArtPlus Limited
COVER PHOTO: Peter Paterson

Printed in Canada

Dedicated to Christine. You are not only my love, but my best friend as well. Without your support in so many ways, this book never would have been written.

Acknowledgments

My deepest gratitude to my friends and family who made the research of this book so much easier, including my mother and father, Rick, Angela, Cathy, Shawn, Kathleen, Jeff and Delia in Montreal, Alastair, Laura, Kevin and Louise in the Soo and, of course, Christine.

Thanks also to all the brewers, brewery owners and representatives who assisted me with their time and knowledge.

Finally, a special thank-you to Peter Goddard who, back in '91, had the foresight to recognize the potential a regular newspaper column about beer had to offer.

Foreword: It's About Heritage

It would be easy to begin this book with a lengthy treatise on the magic of brewing or the wonderful complexity of beer. But I suspect you will probably feel that you get enough of that for the remainder of this odyssey through the successes and failures of Canadian brewing, past and present. Instead, let me start by asking, and answering, a simple question: why are you reading this book?

It's likely that your first reaction to the above question was that you want to see how the beers of Canada stack up and perhaps, how your favourite brew fares against those of the rest of the nation. I know that would be my first response.

However, if you dig deeply enough into the Canadian psyche, you will probably realize that there is something to this great country's brewing industry that makes Canadians feel that a beer is more than just a cold drink on a hot day. In some vague and curious way, beer forms an essential piece of Canadiana. In fact, along with back bacon, winter and hockey, beer practically defines Canada.

Beer has been a major part of Canada's identity since long before Rick Moranis and Dave Thomas donned their toques to become the "hosers" Bob and Doug Mackenzie. It has bolstered business empires like those of the Bronfmans and E.P. Taylor and has led to the establishment of some of the country's most colourful historic figures such as John Molson, John Labatt and, much more recently, the West Coast brewing rebel Ben Ginter.

Can anyone imagine a stereotypical Canadian without a beer bottle in his or her hand? Has any Canuck not had an American friend comment on how great the beer was "up here"? Is there a patriot in the country who, regardless of whether or not they drink it, does not feel a little pride in how Canadian beer is seen as being better than Yankee brews?

So you turn to these pages as more than a search for a new brand or an exercise in comparative shopping. Whether consciously or not, you also want to gauge the health of the brewing industry in Canada because, after the Charlottetown Accord and Free Trade, you want to see at least one important aspect of Canadiana showing good form.

I do not think you will be disappointed.

Despite constant pressures from the monstrous American brewers and the seemingly continuous shrinking of the market, the Canadian beer industry is alive and well in the 1990s. Oh sure, it is not exactly fit enough to run the four-minute mile, but it can get around on its own and, as long as it doesn't try to push too hard too soon, the prognosis is generally good. The reason for my optimistic assessment in the face of such adversity is the trend over the last decade toward the consumption of less, but better, beer.

Ten years ago, a Canadian beer guide would have been a very boring affair indeed. Although there were three rather than two major breweries at the time, those three ruled the national beer industry with an iron fist. A few regional brewers like Pacific Western, Drummond, Northern and Moosehead rounded out the field, but they were not brewing anything too terribly different than what the Big Three were churning out. In short, the life had left our breweries.

Today, Canadians are returning to their roots in great numbers, with more beer drinkers opting for the traditional styles of their parents and grandparents. While it is true that porters, stouts and ales are not exactly supplanting the domestic lager as the choice of millions, the movement has begun, and regardless of what the big breweries say publicly, the trend is being noticed in even the highest offices of the industry.

Not that it is going to be totally smooth sailing. The next few years will likely see a great deal of turmoil in the Canadian brewing business, some of it with good results and some culminating in disaster. In the long run, however, I am sure that Canadians' tastes for a characterful beer and a sense of their history will rule the day.

So uncap a bottle, pour the brew slowly and leisurely, sit back, relax and enjoy this ride through the breweries of Canada. You may find yourself discovering a sense of Canadian nationhood along with a good beer. Cheers!

CHAPTER ONE

A Little History

Why write a book about Canadian beer?

To begin with, how about the fact that over the past decade, Canadians have sipped, gulped, savoured and chugged an average of two billion litres of brew per year? Or that despite the recent spate of major brewery closings, there are now more than twice as many breweries in Canada as there were in 1982? Or even that specialty beers form one of the very few alcoholic beverage markets that continues to grow well into the 1990s?

The question should not be why, but rather, why has it taken so long?

What I like to call the "natural beer renaissance" has been under way in Canada for over ten years now and in full bloom since 1985. At first, the going was tough and tiny breweries blossomed sporadically across the country, taking many different forms. As time passed, however, and people's tastes adjusted to the new flavours of beer flowing out of the micro-breweries, brewery growth accelerated until, in 1993, there existed craft breweries or brewpubs in all but four provinces and one territory.

With this kind of relative stability in the industry, I decided that the time had come to offer my views on this metamorphosis of the Canadian brewing industry. The beers are rated—from the exceptional to the mundane—and, perhaps more important, the stories behind the breweries are presented for the record.

To fully appreciate those stories and reviews, however, it is important to have a sense of the roots of this industry that is so much a part of Canada.

Canadian historians have long been frustrated with the blasé attitude their countrymen have toward our nation's colourful past. Canadians have grown convinced as a people that the history of their country is not exciting. Indeed, the average Canadian seems to know more about the American Declaration of Independence than the Canadian Constitution.

Unfortunately, but not surprisingly, Canada's brewing background often gets treated with the same indifference. I have frequently encountered major- and micro-brewery salespeople or management who are blissfully unaware of the storied background of their industry and in some cases, their own companies. With that kind of an attitude within the industry, how can ordinary Canadians be expected to know anything about the brewing past of their country?

The following history is not, nor is it meant to be, a definitive chronicle, for there are many good books on the market that are totally devoted to the subject. Rather, it is a short background piece designed to place the remainder of this book in perspective and perhaps serve as an incentive to the reader to delve further into this fascinating field.

I've divided the history of beer in Canada into four separate eras that I refer to as: Traditional Brewing, Prohibition, the Decline of Distinction and the Renaissance.

Traditional Brewing

The first period of brewing in Canada began virtually as soon as the land was first settled in the early 1500s. French and English explorers alike did not happily do without their beer, and it is safe to assume that a good deal of brewing was done in those early years using any materials available. When one remembers that the glorious marriage that results in beer is essentially the pairing of fermentable grains and yeast, it becomes easy to imagine the voyageurs boiling up pots of whatever cereals they could find and flavouring them with whatever else was handy, including the prolific spruce tree.

Credit for the first organized brewery, however, goes to Louis Prud'homme, a Montrealer who was granted a royal decree to operate Canada's earliest brewing establishment in 1650, a scant eight years after the founding of that city.

Others soon followed Prud'homme, and as Canada stretched slowly westward, the brewers followed the explorers, albeit at a respectful distance. In fact, if we are to believe the writings of the day, the lag time between pioneer and brewer was a bit too much to bear for some settlers. As Catherine Parr Traill noted in her diary of 1854, "There is nothing that the new settler complains more feeling of than the want of good beer and ale."

By the dawn of the twentieth century, there were dozens upon dozens of breweries scattered across the young nation. One brewing historian's estimate put the number of breweries in the 1880s at 80 or more in Ontario alone.

Each of these establishments—of minute size even by today's microbrewery standards—served their own communities with draught beer from one or occasionally two or three taverns. It is a safe bet that virtually every small town or village had a resident brewer, official or otherwise.

According to Toronto beer historian Larry Sherk, most, if not all beer consumption during that era was confined to elegant public houses where men would while away the after-work hours dressed in their finest clothes and standing in front of elaborate and ornate bars of mahogany or oak. The Wild West image of swinging doors, player pianos and barroom brawls may have existed to a certain degree in western Canada, says Sherk, and even in Ontario, as well, but the norm was a dignified and respectable pub.

When the bottling of beer first commenced in the 1890s, it did little to change the situation, says Sherk. Perhaps it was the chore of carting heavy crates of quart bottles that dissuaded the men from drinking at home or, as the temperance crusaders avowed, the bar acted as a ready means for men to avoid their wives, but the public house continued in its glory well into the twentieth century.

Ironically, by the dawn of the twentieth century, the popularity of the pub was proving to be its own undoing as, citing drink and the pub as agents of the family unit's collapse, the advocates of temperance spread their message across the continent. As the history books tell us, they eventually got their way and Prohibition took hold of Canada.

Prohibition

One may be forgiven for thinking that Prohibition might well be described as a period of non-brewing, but that was actually not the case.

The Temperance movement played out its hand slowly across Canada through the early 1900s. The first move was to establish something known as the Local Option, which allowed towns and cities, upon the completion of a successful referendum, to ban alcohol outright. Frequently the effect of this option was that one town would go dry while a neighbouring community would stay wet and reap the profits of the entire area's drinkers.

Thus, the Local Option proved to be really no option at all and it was soon replaced by new legislation designed to be even more powerful. Before long, Prohibition hit Canada.

Coming into play in different areas at different times, Prohibition had hit nearly every drinker in Canada by 1920, the only exception being— bless their souls—the people of Quebec. Even total Prohibition was not total, however, and allowances were made in many constituencies for the continued sale of "temperance brews" of around 2.5% alcohol or less. In 1924, this level rose a little over halfway through Prohibition with the legalizing in Ontario of "Fergie's Foam"—beer of 4.4% alcohol named in honour of the premier at the time, G.H. Ferguson.

Although it was more successful in Canada than in the United States, the history books show that Prohibition was an overall failure. The legacy of the "Noble Experiment" includes books full of bootlegging lore and some of the most romanticized figures of this century. Even the breweries and distillers that survived the dry era such as Seagram and Sleeman have tended to subtly work their illegal pasts into their modern advertising campaigns.

One thing that Prohibition did accomplish, on the other hand, was the virtual gutting of the Canadian brewing industry. In the long run, however,

Prohibition's effect would prove to be nothing in comparison to the job that one E.P. Taylor did over the next few decades.

The Decline of Distinction

Canadian Breweries was a post-Prohibition company that was formed by Taylor on the back of Brading's Brewery (see entry under Molson for more history). Taylor's apparent goal was to buy as many breweries as he could, thereby effectively shrinking the market dramatically.

Over the course of a little more than two decades, Taylor gobbled up close to thirty breweries, and according to one report, reduced the number of available brands associated with those companies from 150 to eight. His position, albeit one that was never proven in court, was that the market would be more profitable in an oligopolistic state than in one of open competition.

It should be noted here that although Taylor was the worst offender, he was not the only company head to be buying out other breweries. All across Canada, breweries were being absorbed, purchased and closed, or forced out of business entirely by other, usually larger breweries.

When, in the 1970s, all this buying, selling and closing had at least slowed down considerably, only a handful of breweries remained on the market. Given that these survivors were the ones with the superior business, if not necessarily brewing, acumen, it comes as no surprise that their next step was to begin dropping the brands that were marginal in sales but superior in character.

Meanwhile, those brands that remained were allowed to drift more toward a median taste, thus making the market depend more on advertising and less on the character of the brew. For reasons that will be explained more fully in the next chapter, Canadian beers continued to become more similar in flavour throughout the second half of the 1970s, and especially in the 1980s. By the middle of that latter decade, a handful of entrepreneurs decided that they had endured enough of what they thought was bad beer and took matters into their own hands.

The Renaissance

The roots of the renaissance in the brewing industry are to be found in the fog of San Francisco where a young Fritz Maytag, heir to the appliance family fortune, came to the rescue of a floundering brewery in the 1960s. Selling his interest in the family business and investing it in beer, Maytag took the small brewer of the distinctive Anchor Steam Beer and made it into a national success that has likely launched more breweries than Helen of Troy did ships.

Maytag's most important accomplishment was that he demonstrated that it was possible to brew specialty beers and still compete in a market dominated by increasingly less distinctive, mainstream lagers. That lesson was not lost on the early micro-brewers of Canada.

It was a few years coming, but the return of distinction and taste in natural beer was well under way by the late 1980s and the overall reaction of the Canadian beer drinker was that it was about time. The early micro-brewers took off and while they may not have been making a lot, or even any, money, they were receiving critical acclaim from all quarters. It was clear that a change had begun and that it was destined to be every bit as decisive and telling as that which took place after Prohibition. It was indeed a Renaissance.

This latest period of Canadian brewing history is still comparatively young at less than ten years old and it is difficult to say where it is headed in the next several years. However, one fairly safe and welcome prediction is that we will likely never have to go back exclusively to the carbon-copy brewing methods of the past. As with every great renaissance, this one has marked the beginning of a new era.

CHAPTER TWO
The Shape We're In

After a taste of where we've been, the next logical question should ask where we are and where we are going.

Unfortunately, brewing in Canada is no longer the universally romantic and meritorious occupation it once was. Big business, huge volumes and high-profile advertising have, in many cases, reduced the noble brew to little more than a commodity. Even among some small, craft breweries, the infernal bottom line has begun to dictate styles and tastes. I remember a brew master at a small brewery once saying to me that he crafted a particular beer according to the specifications given to him by the marketers at the company. That, to paraphrase an old song, is no way to treat a beer.

Fortunately, we still have craftspeople among our brewers who care more about designing a wonderful recipe than making a standard beer that will please everyone. And, as for the others, one can hardly blame them for brewing what sells. After all, we all have to put bread on the table.

Yet all of this ignores the question posed at the beginning of this chapter: where are we now? For the answer, I think it best to start where 90 to 95 percent of all Canadian beer drinkers do—the Big Two.

The Big Two Breweries and Their Development

It should come as no surprise to any beer drinker that the brewing industry in Canada is virtually controlled by two companies—Molson and Labatt—known collectively as the Big Two.

It is tempting for someone analyzing Canadian beers for taste to summarily dismiss the majority of brands produced by the Big Two as being overly similar, lacking in character and singularly unimaginative. Tempting, yes, but not smart.

For, to throw aside all Molson and Labatt brands would be to ignore the fact that the vast majority of all Canadian beer drinkers choose from these two companies for their personal favourite. Ignore this reality and one risks ignoring what has been essentially the main driving force in the national beer market for the better part of the last century.

As I mentioned in the brief history of Canadian brewing, E.P. Taylor was a key player in the post-Prohibition swallowing-up of small breweries by larger ones. Consequently, some of the more distinct brands and styles began to disappear from stores and bars as Taylor and others shut down many of the operations they bought and altered others to better serve the needs of their larger companies. The result was that there remained far fewer available beer brands and styles and those that were left began to taste increasingly similar. The killer blow to the characters of Canadian brews, however, did not occur until the 1970s.

The Lifestyle Ad

It began inauspiciously enough: a helium balloon floating among the clouds and the simple ditty, "Labatt's Blue smiles along with you." That harmless balloon, though, heralded the beginning of so-called "lifestyle" advertising in the Canadian beer industry.

Prior to the balloon campaign, beer ads in Canada had no qualms about emphasizing the qualities of the brands being promoted, although federal advertising codes did prevent them from going too far in trumpeting their tastes. In the decade where style over substance became a virtual calling card for a generation however, the "beautiful people having a great time while drinking beer" approach quickly caught on and rose to dominate the industry. Even today, lifestyle beer advertising remains very much in vogue.

With the advent of this superficial style of promotion came the reduction in the importance of a distinctive taste for beer. After all, why bother spending a lot of time and money on a new flavour when your market research shows you that young adults (the target market of the day) are just looking for a brand with which they can identify? Why indeed.

Through the 1970s and early 1980s then, Canadian brands began to resemble one another more and more, even to the point that there were (unproven) accusations that the major breweries were marketing the same beer under several different names.

While it is highly unlikely that the Big Three (as they were known prior to the Molson-Carling merger) were, in fact, duplicating brands, there is little doubt that two of their main practices were contributing to that perception. Those practices were, and are, blending and high gravity brewing.

Blending

The process of blending functions exactly as it sounds: two separate brands are blended to form a new brand. While this may seem like a somewhat sleazy way of entering the market with a new label, it is actually a time-honoured practice in certain brewing nations. Some Belgian ales, for example, are the result of blending separate ales, or young and old ales, to form the finished product. The difference is that it is only very seldom that each constituent brew is marketed singularly, as well.

Rumours abound as to how many actual brews are produced by the Big Two; some say as few as five per brewery, making the majority of Canadian brands the products of blending, while others maintain that there is, in fact, very little blending going on in the industry. As the majors steadfastly refuse to reveal any of their brewing formulations, it is unlikely that the truth will ever be known, although I feel that the reality probably lies somewhere between the two extremes.

High Gravity Brewing

The second practice, that of high gravity brewing, is quite simply a fact of life in the big brewery field worldwide. In high gravity brewing, a beer is brewed so as to produce a higher concentration of flavours and strength in the resultant product. This high-alcohol beer then has sterile water added to it, which results in greater volumes of a normal-strength beer.

In some cases, this may result in more than one beer being the product of the same brew. For example, a particular beer may be brewed at 7% alcohol and then watered down to 5% for the standard product and further diluted to 4% for the light. In these cases, the brands other than the basic 5% beer are known as derivative brands.

While high gravity brewing per se is not explicitly detrimental to the taste of a beer, the risks of the process were expertly summarized in a story told by a Canadian brew master. This brewer, while working for a brewery that will remain nameless, was put under pressure from the plant production managers to experiment with high gravity brewing as a means of reducing costs. The first experiment, using a slightly higher gravity, produced a beer that, when watered back down to the normal alcohol level, displayed no discernible difference between it and the original, non-high gravity beer. They therefore proceeded with subsequent tests, each using a slightly higher gravity and each being rated against the previous try. By the time they reached a gravity 50 percent higher than the original regular gravity beer—in a brew that finally satisfied the bean counters—it still, after being watered down, displayed no discernible difference from the final product of the prior test.

What the brewer in question noticed, however, was that the final beer was never tasted against the original, non-high gravity brewed beer, a trial that would have no doubt resulted in some very telling differences of flavour.

Thus, through marketing, blending and brewing "advances," we have reached the state we are in today. Yet the question remains as to whether the Big Two have been manipulating our tastes or whether they have simply been responding to market demands. Again, the reality very likely lies somewhere between the two views.

Whose Tastes?

The Big Two speak with one voice when they say that they are brewing strictly to satisfy consumer tastes and they inevitably point to the extensive research that goes into each brand prior to its launch. As someone who has, in his student past, participated in numerous beer focus groups for agencies contracted by the majors, I can add that it has been my experience that these groups almost inevitably target the marketing aspect of the brew rather than the taste. Of course, that is only my experience, but it does lead me to believe that the "image over taste" approach is alive and well in the research to which the two big breweries so frequently refer.

Even without the need to qualify the breweries' background work, there is still the question of whether the Canadian consumer has independently chosen a sweet and creamy lager or been led to that style by the breweries themselves. There are indeed many arguments on both sides of this issue, but over the last decade, the North America-wide explosion of micro-breweries and brewpubs—with their more distinctive and flavourful beers—leads one to believe that there has been at least a little unsolicited guidance by the larger brewing powers in the latter half of this century.

There is no doubt that beer tastes in Canada are changing; this fact is reflected by some of the new brands being designed and released by the Big Two. For the time being, however, Canadian, Blue and other brands like them remain the mainstays of the national beer drinking public. Whether you consider this good or bad—and your viewpoint will undoubtedly reflect your own personal choice of brands—it is likely to remain the case for some time to come.

The Other Players

When the micro-breweries entered their renaissance in Canada, it was easy to pick them out from the rest of the market. Quite simply, micro-brews were the brands that harkened back to European beer styles that had not been brewed commercially in Canada for many years. To the average beer consumer, that put them on the same playing field as the imports.

There was no mistake about the focus on this section of the market either. Early brewers and brewery owners from Jim Brickman of Waterloo's Brick Brewing to Kevin Keefe of Halifax's Granite Brewery have all said that their original intent was to bring to their markets styles of beer that were either available only as old and stale imports or not accessible at all. It was a good strategy and one that proved to be quite successful.

Then the market shifted a bit and some of the new brewers decided that they wanted to beat the majors at their own game. A lager that tasted like the major brewery brands but, as opposed to the national bestsellers, eschewed preservatives and pasteurization, could, the thinking went, capture enough of the market to keep a small brewery afloat and even turn a tidy profit. And that strategy also worked.

By the dawn of the 1990s, the market, especially in areas like southern Ontario and Vancouver, was beginning to get a little crowded with micro- and not-so-micro-breweries. Some came and went, usually as a result of sloppy planning or inconsistent beer, but enough stayed around that it became time to permanently redefine the Canadian beer market. The problem was that nobody knew how.

In the summer of 1993, the beer industry in Canada remained in a hopelessly confused state. Where the early micros brewed only 5,000 to 10,000 hectolitres (hl) (1 hectolitre = 100 litres) as compared to the millions of hectolitres being brewed by the majors, some micro-breweries had grown in size to 100,000 hl or more and did not wish to be called micros any more. On top of that, there were also mini-breweries with production capabilities of a few thousand hectolitres or less that defied categorization, micros that were brewing major brewery-style beer and vice versa and, just to complicate matters, contract brewing was on the rise.

Contract brewing is the production of a specialty label for a bar, restaurant, hotel chain or another company that is a brewery in name only. Often a small scale contract brew will just be a minor variation of an existing brand already produced by the brewery or simply a relabelling of another brand.

Nevertheless, there are a lot of beer brands scattered across the nation these days and, when one is handed a good ale or porter, the question arises as to whether it matters if the brew comes from a large, medium or small brewery.

So let the brewery owners bicker about who is what and why. There are only two things that should concern a consumer: variety and quality. The former characteristic should be prized because it is something we have not had for a long time in the Canadian beer market. The second factor, on the other hand, should be at the heart of what any customer expects from any purchase. As with all things gastronomical, the bottom line with beer is taste.

BOPping in Canada

On the subject of taste, one new wrinkle that seems to be changing the way Canadians view their brew is the recent rise of a new phenomenon known as the brew-on-premises, or BOP, store. The methodology of the BOP shop is as simple and straightforward as its reason for existence: customers brew their own beer, and the reason is that people are fed up with paying such high taxes on their case of commercial beer.

The BOP movement began in British Columbia and very quickly spread to Ontario in the mid-1980s. Yet only a handful of shops existed for the first several years of the industry's life and it was not until the early 1990s that the concept really began to take off. By 1993, there were hundreds of these shops across Canada, largely concentrated in Ontario but also spreading rapidly across the nation.

Brewing in a BOP is a uniquely Canadian exercise spawned, as already mentioned, by high taxes and clever entrepreneurship, which is now beginning to be exported to other nations including the United States and Australia. The way it works is that a space is set up with several small brewing kettles of about a 50-litre capacity, each with additional room set aside for the bottling and fermenting of the brew. The customer then pays a set fee based on the style of beer (pilsner, ale, porter, etc.) they wish to make and is then allowed to brew their very own beer following directions supplied by the house recipe book, a process that can take from one to two hours. Following fermentation, customers return for about an hour to bottle their brew and leave with the equivalent of six cases of 24 bottles of beer for a little over one half the price of commercial brands.

In 1993, certain BOP owners made this process even simpler by providing the option of brewing the beer in advance for their customers, who are then only responsible for adding the yeast to begin fermentation (five minutes) and bottling their finished beer. While this new spin takes away some of the mystique and enjoyment of brewing one's own beer, it has apparently been embraced by people without the time to spend brewing and serves to reinforce the price motivation behind this industry.

I conducted an informal survey of several dozen of the estimated 200-plus Ontario BOPs in early 1993 and found that, virtually without exception, each owner pointed to the cost advantage they have over commercial beer as their main selling point. However, the owners were equally unanimous in adding that, by the customer's third or fourth batch, the price usually became less of a consideration and the motivation was instead directed to experimentation with the brewing process itself.

This latter point gives rise to an interesting and often overlooked aspect of the BOP industry's impact on the commercial beer market: the beer education factor. The typical BOP customer, again according to every BOP owner surveyed, enters the store with a mind to replicating their favourite domestic beer brand, be it a Molson or Labatt product. After a few tries at cloning mainstream lagers, the average BOPper will become curious about some of the other available beer recipes and perhaps try an English-style ale or Czech pilsner rather than their normal brew. Another three or four brews later, that same customer who walked into the BOP with a Canadian or Blue in mind is now buying a micro-brewery brand when they do purchase commercial beer (because BOPpers seem to inevitably run out of their own beer before the next batch is ready). And that transition in taste occurred entirely because of the brew-on-premises.

In this manner, the BOP acts not only as a method of tax protest, but also as a training ground for broadening beer tastes.

The Taxation Factor

In its spring of 1993 budget, the Ontario government responded to the popularity of BOPs and the corresponding decline in beer tax revenues by adding a 26¢ per litre tax to the beer brewed at the stores. It is suspected that this tax, which took effect in November of that year, will thin out the plethora of BOPs in Ontario or, at least, control the industry's outrageous growth by making the economics of the operation less enticing.

My hope is that the tax will have the positive effect of weeding out some of the unscrupulous operators who are tarnishing the industry's image through improper brewing conditions and outright bootlegging. Regardless of its effectiveness on that point, however, I suspect that the tax will not have its desired effect of restoring a significant percentage of the nation's lagging beer sales because it does not address the original reason for the BOP's existence, that being the high price of commercial beer.

In the Brewers Association of Canada (BAC) newsletter of March 1993, the organization reported that it had completed a study of beer taxation policies throughout the world and found that Canada tied with Norway for the highest beer taxes anywhere, based on a percentage of the total retail price. According to the survey, 53 percent of the price Canadians pay for beer goes to the government, compared to an overall average of 32 percent and examples of 29 percent in Belgium, 18 percent in the United States and 13 percent in Spain.

The powers that be will tell you that the purpose of these taxes is to discourage over-consumption and alcoholism, but beer drinkers across the nation have long been of the mind that the taxes serve only to gouge more money out of the public. This debate has raged for years and will likely continue for many more to come, but regardless of who is telling the truth, that taxation rate will undoubtably remain, to continue separating the Canadian beer consumer from large amounts of his or her money and keeping the BOP industry hopping indefinitely.

CHAPTER THREE

The Basics of Beer

It is true what they say: all you really need are water, barley, hops and yeast to make beer. In fact, even hops are relatively new additions to the at least 5,000-year-old brewing process. It is estimated that the first hopping of beer took place some time around A.D. 1000.

But beer is so much more than the sum of its parts. It is experimentation with new ingredients, the archaeology of old recipes, the delight of discovering an ingredient combination that works and the joy of realizing a new taste. All this, and more, is contained in every bottle of beer.

Aside from these romantic notions, exactly what physically makes up a beer? The short answer to that question is back in that first sentence— water, barley, hops and yeast. However, as it so often does in things beery and in life in general, that short answer leads to a much longer one.

What Goes Into a Beer?

THE REINHEITSGEBOT

Brews that do use only the four ingredients can, and all too frequently do, claim to be brewing according to something called the *Reinheitsgebot*, the ancient Bavarian Purity Law of 1516 that was designed to prevent the adulteration of the local beers. While the old *Reinheitsgebot* is great for identifying a pure and natural beer, some members of the micro-brewing community seem to be trying to convince the beer drinking public that adherence to the law is synonymous with the making of quality beer. This is rubbish.

I have tasted numerous *Reinheitsgebot* brews that are very good and approximately an equal number that are not so good. Conversely, some of the great beers in the world do not come close to making the Purity Law grade while other tremendous brews would pass without problem. So what is the big deal about this German word most which many English-speaking people cannot even pronounce?

For the most part, the law has been invoked to differentiate between truly pure beers and "all natural" brews. Those of the latter, non-*Reinheitsgebot* class may contain such ingredients as sugar syrups, rice, corn and other adjuncts which, when used too liberally, may spoil the full flavour of a beer. When you drink those of the former group, on the other hand, you can at least have confidence that your beer has not been totally diluted of its flavour—a truly difficult task in a *Reinheitsgebot* brew.

THE OTHER STUFF

The flip side of the *Reinheitsgebot* controversy are the 105 ingredients, preservatives, stabilizers and other agents allowed into beer by the Canadian Food and Drug Act.

The reason that some breweries employ some of these unusual additions is that they are deemed to be necessary to offset the effects of modern brewing methods. In other words, the bigger the brew, the greater the chance for problems, and therefore, the greater the need for tools to eliminate those problems. From hop oils to foam enhancers and stabilizing agents, they are all used to help control the making of beer.

If one takes the government duty to protect its citizens at face value, then one must believe that none of the 105 ingredients and agents are in any way physically detrimental. At the same time, the question is raised as to why any of the 105 should be consumed when in the strictest sense, none of them are necessary.

The important thing to remember, though, is that it is not necessarily what goes into a beer that makes it good or bad but how it is all put together. The brewer's art is exactly that—an art—and no one should suppose to tell artists how they should construct their work. As with all artists, however, the brewer must be aware that the final product will have to face the final test of the consumer.

Further Divisions

TOP OR BOTTOM

Beyond ingredients, there is one basic differential in the beer world and that is whether the beer is top-fermented or bottom-fermented.

Ask anyone who has brewed beer and they will tell you that the process is similar to that of making soup. Simply put, malted grain and boiling water make the "stock" while hops or, occasionally, other flavouring ingredients act as the "spices." Where the resultant brew, known as wort, and Mom's chicken noodle soup differ, however, is when the magic microbe yeast pays a visit to add alcohol to the beer.

Without getting deeply into microbiology, top-fermenting simply means that the yeast rises to the top of the vessel during a fermentation that is conducted at relatively warm temperatures. The flip side, bottom-fermentation, occurs at colder temperatures and the yeast—you guessed it—sinks to the bottom of the vessel.

Structurally speaking, top-fermented beers are of the very broad category of ales, while bottom-fermented brews are of the lager class. And beyond those two divisions lie a host of other styles.

Most beer neophytes automatically assume dark beers are heavy ales while lighter-coloured beers are lagers and therefore lighter in taste. This is simply not the case; the body of a beer is determined by the amount and types of ingredients used, not where the yeast ends up. The smaller but more popular category of bottom-fermenting beer contains some dark and heavy-tasting styles like bocks, some dark but not heavy types such as German dunkels, light-coloured but robust pale bocks and North American lagers that are light in both taste and colour.

At the top of the fermenting vessel, the categorization becomes a bit more complicated. On the light side are wheat beers, which essentially have a classification all their own due to their unique character derived from the use of a percentage of wheat in the preparation of the wort, and North American light and cream ales. On the decidedly dark side lie stouts and porters in addition to all sorts of ales and bitters, including strong barley wines and Trappist ales.

One final twist on the fermentation road is a process known as bottle-fermentation. Extremely rare in Canada, this is the process through which a second or third fermentation is instigated by adding a dosage of yeast prior to bottling. Its effect is to increase the alcohol content slightly, spritz up the beer and, of course, modify the taste. While bottle-conditioning may be done in numerous styles of beer, it is most suited to, and common in, wheat beers and certain ales.

The bottom line for taste in all this is that one should not be chased away from tasting an ale or a dark beer because of the impression that it will be heavy. Often, enchanting surprises are found in those ebony brews.

GRAIN OR EXTRACT

A second distinction in brewing and one that is especially useful for this book, is the one between full-grain and malt-extract brewing.

Anyone who has brewed at home or in a BOP will be familiar with malt extract. It is the gooey syrup that you load into the boil in place of any real grain. What may come as a surprise to you—if you think that extract is for home brewing only—is that your favourite brewpub might well be using that same stuff.

The telltale sign of an extract brew is a candylike sweetness in the taste and especially in the finish. It is a taste that BOP users will be well familiar with but for which they may not wish to pay full price in a pub.

Numerous brewpubs have malt extract breweries; the reason for this is often that they were the only products on the market when the pub was starting up. Other brewpubs, however, have somewhat more questionable reasons for using extract.

Unfortunately, certain extract breweries come about simply as a result of ownership or management that does not concern itself too greatly with the quality of the beer. Often these people will respond to the question of whether they would be willing to go full grain with a shrug and an indication that it would be too much bother. Fortunately, these characters do not constitute the majority, or even a healthy minority, of brewpub owners.

Full-grain brewing is exactly that: brewing with all barley and/or wheat malt and no added extracts. While it too may result in a terrible brew at times, the taste of a basic all-grain beer will beat that of a standard extract brew nine times out of ten.

This is not to say that malt extract cannot produce good beer. I have sampled several extract brews that were indiscernible from full-grain brews and were of excellent quality. For this to happen, however, the extract must be handled properly and be of good quality. All too often, this is sadly just not the case.

How to Taste a Beer

A good beer, like any other good food, is enjoyed with the eyes and nose as much as with the mouth. To deny the aesthetics of a beer is to refuse a healthy part of its enjoyment.

APPEARANCE

There is no arguing that a cold, frothy beer on a hot summer's day is a sight that would set most beer drinkers' mouths to watering. And yet, when that sight could be a deep burgundy-coloured bock with subtle purple tones nestled into a snifter, we ignore the look of our beer and instead dump it unceremoniously into a pint glass or straight-sided tumbler.

We must slow down to taste beer, and the first step is to admire its appearance. Take note of the tones, choose a stylish and appropriate glass, watch as the head rises, making sure it goes no higher than an inch or two at the maximum; these are the preliminaries to true beer appreciation.

AROMA

The next step is to take in the aroma, or "nose," of your beer. Aroma is a vitally important and yet often underemphasized factor in the taste of a beer. The reason for its importance revolves around the same old saw that has graced the pages of countless wine books, namely that a human being's sense of smell is far more acute and discerning than his or her sense of taste. What we smell is quite often what we taste.

If you question the importance of aroma in a beer, try the following test. Have a friend blindfold you, serve you two beers that are significantly different and plug your nose while you taste them. Chances are that unless you have a very good palate, you will have a difficult time discerning between the two brews.

Many brews have marvellous aromas with all sorts of fruit, spice, nuts and even wines showing up without any of those things being among the ingredients. I have found beers with pineapple, papaya and perhaps oddest of all, Christmas pudding aromas. But you will never find these unless you are prepared to stick out your nose and breathe in deeply.

TASTE

The biggest factor in a beer is, of course, taste. It is also the area likely to cause novice beer tasters more problems than any other.

I am regularly asked how I manage to pick out the various flavours of the beers I taste, and my answer is always the same: practise, practise, practise. Though it may sound trite, the hard fact is that it is true.

Of course, a little background never hurts so that a person might know what to look for in the flavour of a particular beer style. Generalizations are always dangerous, but in the most general of terms, bottom-fermentation tends to result in crisper, drier beers with more bitterness, while those that ferment at the top of the tank will have a more fruity and sweet character.

There are quite naturally exceptions to these rules across the board and regardless of what else I propose in this chapter, everybody with a mind to exploring the world of beer will find some brew that will contradict what I write. Instead, I will suggest that hard concentration on what you are drinking and a little crossreferencing with friends and other beer drinkers will be your best tools for educating your palate.

Most of all, just remember that the golden rule for tasting beer is the same as for any other skill: the more you practise, the better you will become. And of course, in this instance, the practice is not without its enjoyment.

CHAPTER FOUR

The Ratings

Breweries are about much more than the mere production of beer; they are also about history, tradition, mystery and alchemic magic. They are at once products of our environment and catalysts for our culture. Most of all, especially in Canada, as already mentioned, they are an integral part of our national identity.

While it is true that the commercial brewing of beer is indeed a business designed to turn a profit, it does not stop there. For, to brew purely for commerce and without regard for the mysticism of the craft is to lose the very soul of the beer. The result would be like a four-star chef flipping burgers at a greasy spoon; the food would be edible but the action would constitute a tragic loss of purpose.

So, because breweries are so much more than simple businesses, I decided at the outset of this project that there had to be more to the reviews than whether or not I liked each particular beer. If I was going to offer the "complete picture," I felt that the whole story behind each brewery would be an essential part of each entry. Therefore, I have divided each brewery's entry into three parts: the Stats, the Story and the Scoreboard.

Of course, the final aspect of the reviews was their organization and it is one which, I suspect, some people will question. While for the most part, the breweries have been grouped geographically, there are a pair of exceptions, those being the pairing of the Territories with the Prairies and the Maritimes with Quebec. With apologies to the residents of those regions, the entries were organized this way only because neither the Maritimes nor the Territories could claim enough breweries to garner a section of their own. Hopefully, when the time comes for a second edition of this guide, that situation will exist no longer.

THE STATS

The first portion of each listing consists of the basic factual information on the brewery: name, address, phone and fax numbers, key personalities, brewing data and the names of the brews offered by the company. All these details are current as of July 1993.

Two areas in the entries which may cause some confusion are the Brewing Capacity and Consulting Brewer categories. The definition of brewing capacity I have used is the maximum amount of beer a given brewery could produce annually if it were to operate at peak efficiency. The figure is given in hectolitres. One hectolitre is roughly the same amount of beer you would find in 12 cases of twenty-four, 341 ml bottles.

The consulting brewer is the person or company responsible for assisting the owner in the setup and commencement of the brewing operations.

Occasionally this is the same person as the brewer or, more frequently, a company professionally contracted as specialists. Two such companies which crop up frequently are Cask and Continental, systems professionals who were virtually the only players in the game back when the craft brewing industry was just getting started.

THE STORY

The second part of every entry consists of the story behind the brewery. These tales are based on personal interviews with at least one high-level individual connected with the company, be he or she brewer, owner, marketing manager or otherwise. I have attempted to report these business histories as nonsubjectively as possible, letting the story tell itself rather than goading the tale along .

Because the details of the brewery backgrounds are based on information supplied by brewery representatives, who quite naturally want to present their companies in the best possible light, some of the stories may inadvertently hide some blemishes and embellish more positive aspects of the company's history. Despite my best efforts to crossreference all the stories I heard while researching this book, the fact remains that many of these businesses are quite simply too young or too small for there to be a wealth of accessible information on them. The histories, therefore, are unfortunately subject to minor omissions and embellishments.

THE SCOREBOARD

The final piece of each brewery account is a very subjective review of every beer brewed by that individual company. In order to maintain some kind of reasonable scope, however, I had to place certain limitations on which beers warranted review.

For bottling breweries, every attempt was made to review all brands: seasonals, specialties and regular listings. The exceptions to this rule fall into three categories: derivative brands, temporarily unavailable brews and, in the case of the majors, certain regional and fringe labels.

Derivative brands, as explained in chapter three, are literally watered-down versions of other beers. Since reviewing these would effectively constitute two evaluations of the same basic brew, I have chosen to review only the normal (5% alcohol) strength version. The only exceptions to this rule are Labatt 50 Light and Coors Light, the former because it is actually better-tasting than the 5% beer and the latter because it is the top-selling light beer in Canada. All other listed light brands are unique formulations.

As for the other two categories, it was obviously impossible to conduct tastings on the unavailable brands and I quickly found that a cap had to be put on the number of regionals I included in this book, lest it become a catalogue of Molson and Labatt brands.

The beers that I reviewed from the brewpubs had two limitations, one unavoidable and the other imposed. The unavoidable limitation was the same one faced by the bottling breweries, namely availability. If a brewpub was out of a specific brand because there had just been a run on that beer, then the beer unfortunately had to be skipped. It wasn't the fairest way to treat the smallest members of Canada's brewing community, but it was either that or countless cross-country trips to try to sample every brew.

Due to the tendency of certain brewpubs to keep a file of up to three dozen or more recipes that they occasionally brew, I felt that, in the interests of fairness, only the regularly featured brews would be tasted for review. The result of this is that each reviewed brewpub brand is guaranteed to be on tap at least 40 to 50 percent of the time, or at least that was the case as of the summer of 1993.

Not included in these entries are the members of a new wave of what I can only call "ferment-pubs." These are establishments that use a crack in the Ontario brewpub legislation—I know of no others outside of that province—to present a house beer without actually having a brewery on site. The way they accomplish this seemingly impossible task is by having the unfermented brew, called wort, prepared by an outside contractor and brought to the pub so that it might ferment in-house. By finishing the beer on-site, they abide by the letter, if not the spirit, of the law and are able to claim to have a house brew. There is even a business called Mr. Beer that specializes in this sort of thing.

While it is true that the actual production of alcohol does not begin until fermentation and certain beers produced in these "ferment-pubs" are indeed relatively high in quality, I fail to see how a location in which there is no brewing activity may be called a brewpub. For this reason, at least at present, these establishments have been omitted from these pages.

CAVEAT EMPTOR

This brings me to one final point before the explanation of the four-star rating system, and it has to do with the time frame of this book and the nature of the brewing industry.

People change, breweries change and beers change; these are facts of life in the beer business. Even rigidly controlled brands like those of the Big Two go through occasional evolutions of taste and I can present no guarantee that a beer you see reviewed in this book is not going to taste better or worse by the time you get to it. Nor, for that matter, can I even assure you that any particular brewery or brewpub will still be around. Stable this industry is not.

The Rating System Explained

While I have never been reticent to laud a great beer or skewer a terrible one, I have always been uncomfortable with the concept of rating a product that, like beer, so thoroughly depends upon an individual's tastes. To this end, I have always placed a greater emphasis on a description of the colour, aroma and flavour of a brew than on a judgmental rating system.

If, for example, I were to write off a beer with a score of four out of 100 because I found that it was extraordinarily sweet for its style, I might unintentionally put off a potential drinker who prefers sweetness to style adherence simply because that person read the number instead of the review. Thus, I am not the guide who tells you, the reader, what to drink. Rather, I provide the map with a few suggested stops.

Alas, a book such as this is expected to provide some sort of rating system, and for that purpose, I have fallen back on the same practice I use for my personal notes. The ratings run from one to four stars, with a half star being reserved for a brew with some serious technical flaw such as yeast contamination, and four stars being a virtually unattainable standard.

The four-star system is not a perfect one and it differs greatly from the common route of scoring out of 50 or 100. For example, the four-star fails to note small differentials of taste that would be glaringly obvious in a score out of 100. The latter system, on the other hand, does prompt one to wonder what benefit there is in knowing that Beer A scored a 76 while Beer B merely rated a 74, or a whole two percent worse.

One quirk to the four-star system is that it is more difficult for a beer to gain stars when it has a high original rating than when it starts low. The effect this oddity has is that the one-star tier becomes very crowded while the four-star level is, in Canada's case, bereft of inhabitants.

Which brings up a final point about the rating system, namely, its inherent toughness. The beers in this book have been evaluated on a par with the best and worst brews the world has to offer. This means that competition is much broader than just among the beers presented here and, as such, the evaluations more stringent. True, there are no four-star beers in the following reviews, but that does not mean that there are none in the world.

The Rating System

★—Standard but unimaginative and, therefore, unlikely to inspire

★★—Well-brewed and worthy

★★★—Thoroughly enjoyable, what the brewer's art is all about

★★★★—A classic in every regard, a world-beater

CHAPTER FIVE

The Big Two

Between the two national breweries in this country there exists more than 400 years of history, including the comparatively short past of Carling O'Keefe. The amount of interesting and anecdotal information contained in those years is enough to fill volumes, much less a chapter of a book.

It would not, however, be fair to simply ignore the stories behind the two oldest and largest breweries in Canada by hiding behind the enormity of their pasts. So, in trying to accommodate the issues as best I can, I have resorted to that most Canadian of tactics—compromise.

Rather than engage in a lengthy pontification on the beginnings of the two Johns, Molson and Labatt, I have chosen to present thumbnail sketches of how Canada's two national breweries came to be. It is my hope that, by not even attempting to do justice to the colourful pasts of both businesses, I may offer readers just enough information to allow them to understand the composition of these two breweries.

In defense of my plan, I must add that it was my query for information that motivated both breweries to begin construction of short histories of themselves, thus proving that their pasts are so broad that not even the individual breweries had attempted to document them in a short and concise format.

As always, these reviews encompass every available beer with the exception of the derivative brands. Sharp-eyed readers may note the absence of one or two regional or draught-only products and, for those omissions, I apologize; ours is a large country with many beer brands. As for the national brands, all the reviews are based on the Ontario-brewed version of that brand.

In order to help locate the majors' brands, I have used a coding system to identify in which provinces each brew may be found. The key to these codes is as follows: N = National; B = British Columbia; A = Alberta; S = Saskatchewan; M = Manitoba; O = Ontario; Q = Quebec; F = Newfoundland; V = Nova Scotia; W = New Brunswick; P = Prince Edward Island; T = Territories.

Labatt Breweries of Canada

LOCATIONS:

(Executive Offices) Labatt House, 181 Bay Street, P.O. Box 786, Toronto, Ontario M5J 2T3
(Breweries) 210 Brunette Street, P.O. Box 580, New Westminster, British Columbia, V3L 4Z2

Labatt's

	(Columbia Brewing) 1220 Erikson Street, P.O. Box 1950, Creston, British Columbia V0B 1G0
	4344—99th Street, Edmonton, Alberta T6E 6K8
	1600 Notre Dame Avenue, Winnipeg, Manitoba R3C 2N3
	150 Simcoe Street, London, Ontario N6A 4M3
	50 Resources Road, P.O. Box 5050, Terminal A, Etobicoke, Ontario M9N 3N7
	50 Labatt Avenue, Lasalle (Montreal), Quebec H8R 3E7
	(Oland Breweries) 3055 Agricola Street, Halifax, Nova Scotia B3K 5N4
	Leslie Street, St. John's, Newfoundland A1E 3Y4
PHONE:	*(Executive Offices) 416-361-5050, (fax) 416-361-5200*
	(Customer Service) 1-800-268-BEER
	(Breweries) 604-521-1844, (fax) 604-521-8409 (British Columbia)
	604-428-9344, (fax) 604-428-3433 (British Columbia)
	403-436-6060, (fax) 403-462-0099 (Alberta)
	204-633-9286, (fax) 204-632-9088 (Manitoba)
	519-663-5050, (fax) 519-667-7304 (London)
	416-248-0751, (fax) 416-235-2201 (Etobicoke)
	514-366-5050, (fax) 514-364-8005 (Quebec)
	902-453-1867, (fax) 902-453-3847 (Oland)
	709-579-0121, (fax) 709-579-2018 (Newfoundland)
OWNERS:	*John Labatt Ltd.*
PRESIDENT:	*Hugo Powell*
EXECUTIVE VP OF OPERATIONS (BREWING):	*Larry Macauley*
CAPACITY:	*9,770,000 hl*
TOURS:	*Available at certain breweries, call for information*

Labatt's is the younger of the Big Two by about 61 years, having been founded just outside of London, Ontario, in 1847 by an Irish immigrant farmer.

According to the Labatt archives, John Kinder Labatt arrived in Canada in 1833 and began farming some 200 acres of land at the age of 30. He wrote to his wife of his interest in brewing in 1847 and purchased a brewery later that same year with his partner and brewer, Samuel Eccles.

A short six years later, Labatt assumed full ownership of the brewery and it was rechristened John Labatt's Brewery soon after. As Canada expanded, so did Labatt's, using the newly established Great Western Railway to open up distribution across southern Ontario.

During that period of expansion, the first John Labatt died and was replaced at the helm of the company by his son, also named John Labatt. The second generation led the brewery into further expansion through the latter half of the 1800s and into the twentieth century. By 1900, Labatt's had offices in Toronto and Montreal and was reportedly one of the larger breweries in the country.

The third generation of Labatts took over the brewery in 1915 when another John Labatt assumed the presidency of the company after his father passed away. His welcoming present was not a nice one— Prohibition hit Ontario in 1916.

Through the brewing of Prohibition-strength beer (less than 2.5% alcohol) for the domestic market and full-strength beer for export, Labatt's was able to weather the storm through the temperance years. In fact, it was the only one of the 15 Ontario breweries to survive Prohibition that was guided by the same management after the act's repeal.

By going public in 1945 with a reported 900,000 shares, Labatt's was able to raise enough money to branch out from their London operation for the first time in almost 100 years. The expansion came with the purchase of the Copland Brewing Company of Toronto in 1946.

In 1950, Labatt Breweries came under the control of a non-family member for the first time when Hugh Mackenzie took the reins from a retiring John Labatt. It is rumoured that Labatt never completely recovered from the trauma suffered when he was kidnapped for a week in 1934 and that effectively Mackenzie had been running the company for years prior to his official ascension to the presidency.

On the heels of the 1951 launch of a new brand called Pilsener Lager Beer and known simply as Blue, Labatt Breweries continued its expansion with several out-of-province brewery purchases over the following years. Among the purchases were Shea's in Winnipeg, Lucky Lager Breweries in British Columbia, Saskatoon Brewing and the Bavarian Brewery in Newfoundland. A new brewery was also constructed in Montreal during those growth years.

The brewery that now bills itself as the nation's only Canadian-owned national brewery was almost denied the opportunity to make that claim when the American brewer Schlitz, riding high at the time, tried to buy 39 percent of Labatt's in 1964. While brewing historians like to play up the idea that national pride in our breweries put a stop to the sale, it was actually the United States government that halted the deal over concerns as to its effect on the competitiveness of the U.S. market.

At about the same time as the Schlitz purchase furor, John Labatt Ltd. was formed as a parent company for the brewery. It has, of course, become much more than that through the years. John Labatt now owns 90 percent of the Blue Jays baseball team, cable television's *The Sports Network* (TSN) and its French language equivalent *Le Réseau des Sports* (RDS), along with several other entertainment interests.

Since the 1960s, John Labatt Ltd. has acquired and disposed of several breweries and other businesses, the disposals having taken place predominantly in the early 1990s as the Big Two both try to slim down for increased international competition in Canada. Among its more successful acquisitions have been Moretti Brewing in Italy, where the beer market is exploding, and Pennsylvania's Latrobe Brewing, producers of the trendy Rolling Rock Beer.

It has been almost a century and a half since the first John Labatt opted for brewing with barley rather than the growing of the grain. Although the company that still bears his name is but a comparatively small player on the international brewing scene, utterly dwarfed by such giants as Miller and Anheuser-Busch, it is known by virtually every Canadian and has its beer in 39 countries worldwide. In retrospect, it would appear that John Labatt made the right choice.

SCOREBOARD

(Note: Included in this Scoreboard are labels brewed by the Oland and Columbia brewing companies, both owned and operated by Labatt.)

Alexander Keith's IPA (W,V,P—5% vol.)

Light gold-coloured with a fresh, sweet and malty nose holding lots of sugar and notes of lightly fruity grain. The start is fairly dry but with a sweet grassiness leading to a sweet and sugary body with butterscotchy malt and a slightly sour, rooty tang. The finish is slightly bitter but sugary with notes of faint, woody hop. ★

Blue (N—5% vol.)

Pale to light gold in colour with a sweet, perfumey nose tempered by earthy tartness. An acidic and sour start leads to a grassy, sweet-and-sour body containing hints of citrus toward an acrid finish. ★

Blue Star (F—5% vol.)

Light gold in colour with a thick and malty aroma holding strong notes of sweet grain, canned corn and some sour, rooty hopping. A sweet-and-sour start with forceful grassy notes leads into a very creamy body of grass, grain and root with hints of bitter nutshell. The finish restores some of the original sweetness before ending with a trace of alcohol. ★½

Budweiser (5% vol.)

Pale gold in colour with very grainy and sweet aroma holding light custard notes. The bittersweet and very grassy start has a slight rootiness leading into a still-grassy body with touches of saccharine and a distinct creaminess. The light flavour is completed with a sour (bordering on tart) and acidic finish. ★

Carlsberg (B,O,Q—5% vol.)

Light to medium gold in colour with a light rye bready aroma holding some grassy notes. A strong, bittersweet start moves to a sour, almost acrid body with grainy and rooty notes and a very tart, rooty finish. ★

Club (A,M—5% vol.)

A light gold-coloured lager with a very sweet and sugary nose. The body is candied and acidic with a sugary start and a sour, rooty finish. ★

Columbia Extra Malt Liquor (B—5.6% vol.)

Light to medium gold in colour and strong in aroma with notes of fresh-mowed grass punctuated by confectionery sugar. A candied lemon and grain start precedes a full body with caramel, light butterscotch and sour root flavours. Some alcohol rises in second half and it finishes with light cherry and apricot notes. ★½

Crystal (M,O—5% vol.)

Pale gold-coloured with a light, sugary and slightly floral aroma. The slightly sour and earthy front leads to a mild body with notes of sugar, corn, grass and lemon with a sour, orangey finish. ★

Duffy's Draught (B,O—5% vol.)

Rusty brown in colour with a slightly hoppy nose containing a touch of woodiness. A light and thin start leads into a well-carbonated and slightly vinegary body with notes of ash, wood and citrus. The finish is somewhat chalky and bitter with woody notes. ★

Extra Dry (N—5.5% vol.)

Light gold-coloured with a very soft and sweet "bubblegummy" aroma. The start is carbonic and broadly neutral with a light graininess. The sweetness hits in the body with its alcoholic plumminess and slight sweet-and-sour, grassy edge leading to a fairly quick finish that is cardboardy with some lingering sugar. ★

50 (S,M,O,Q—5% vol.)

Light gold in colour with a sweet and slightly hoppy nose. The earthy start sweetens in the body with sugar and a hint of sour orange. Bitterness rises through the finish with lingering woody and rooty flavours. ★

50 Light (Q—4% vol.)

Pale to light gold with a sweet but woody aroma holding sucrose and subtle apricot notes. The moderately sweet front has significant carbonation, which partially obscures the candied fruit notes. The sugary body holds, like its parent brew, a touch of sour orange leading to a thin, slightly rooty finish. ★½

Guinness (N except F—5% vol.)

Very dark brown in colour with a lightly sweet, roasted malt aroma holding sweetened coffee notes. A dry, coffee bean start heads into an astringent body with sour espresso and light licorice notes before a very bitter and astringent, burnt wood finish. ★½

Ice Beer (N—5.6% vol.)

Medium gold in colour and very sweet in aroma with strong notes of fresh, wet hay and candy sugar. A forcefully sour and grassy start lead to a bitter-sour body of dried leaves and root with the occasional spot of icing sugar creeping in. The finish is sourly alcoholic on top with cloying sugar underneath. ★

Jockey Club (F—5% vol.)

Light to medium gold in colour with a thick and mildly sweet nose featuring a combination of grain and slightly smoky wood aromas and a hint of saltiness. The fairly dry and slightly oaky start precedes a woody body with light traces of fruit (orange, peach) before ending with a touch of alcohol in a dry, tobaccoey finish. ★★

John Labatt Classic (B,A,S,M,O,Q,T—5% vol.)

A medium gold-coloured all-malt brew with a caramelly, malt aroma. The start is thick but light-tasting and leads to a body which, although it could use more malt and hop, is relatively full with some toffee flavours combining with a very woody hop. The finish is fairly dry but with a tart and slightly candied edge. ★¹/₂

John Labatt Extra Stock (O—6.5% vol.)

Light to medium gold in colour with a toasted grain and brown sugar nose. The very sugary body starts sweet and confectionery with a creamy, caramelly and mildly alcoholic middle. The finish mixes slightly burnt sugar with oaky alcohol. ★¹/₂

Keith's Dry (V,P—5.5% vol.)

Light to medium gold-coloured with a lightly sweet aroma carrying notes of fresh-cut grass and sweet hay plus very light, rooty hop. A carbonic and caramelly start precedes a sweet and grassy body with notes of sour woodiness and a faint hint of citrus. The finish is fairly quick, woody and dry, although with some lingering sweet malt. ★¹/₂

Kokanee Glacier Pilsner (B,A,S,T—5% vol.)

Light gold-coloured with a sweet, grassy grain nose holding very faint floral hop notes. A very sweet candied start leads to a fairly thin, grassy and sweet-and-sour body with a very light touch of woodiness. The dry and acidic finish holds some perfumey and floral tastes. ★

Kootenay True Ale (B,T—5% vol.)

Light to medium gold in colour with a very soft aroma of fresh hay and licorice notes. The malty, slightly maple-edged start heads into a thick body of caramel and candied orange malt and lightly nutty hop. The finish is sweet and somewhat walnutty. ★¹/₂

Labatt Genuine Draft (B,A,S,M,O,Q,V,T—5% vol.)

A light gold lager brewed without preservatives or pasteurization. The sweet, grainy nose carries a few light hop notes. Some further hop flavours exist in the front, but they are quickly overpowered by a sugary sweetness leading into a sweet, citric finish. ★

Labatt Lite (N except Q—4% vol.)

Pale straw-coloured with a sweet-and-sour grain nose. The largely neutral start turns to a sweet, almost fruity grain body touched with some rooty sourness and acidity before a light, confectionery finish. ★

Lucky Lager (B,S—5% vol.)

Light gold, almost straw in colour with a soft and sweet corn aroma. The sweet and very sugary start leads to a similar body with buttery notes and very faint and sour grassiness. The sugariness continues in the finish with a strong icing sugar flavour. ★

Oland Export Ale (W,V,P—5% vol.)

Light gold-coloured with a sweet and grassy aroma holding very faint, plummy notes. The sugary and carbonic start carries a sour grain edge prior to a body that is also sweet and sugary but cut with a very light, woody hop and more sour grain. The finish is fairly quick and mixes caramel malt with some woodiness to dry it out. ★

Porter (Q—5% vol.)

Very deep purple in colour with a slightly chalky, sweet chocolate aroma. An extremely sweet start with strong notes of grape juice leads into a body that is a mix of icing sugar and sweet molasses with more grape notes. Candy sugar and chocolate notes round out the sweet finish. ★

Schooner (O,W,V,P—5% vol.)

Light gold-coloured with a sweet and very grassy aroma. A very carbonic, sweet-hay start heads into a light, thin and sugary body of malted grain leading into a quick, dryish finish with a lingering hint of grain. ★

Wildcat (A,S,O,Q,T—5% vol.)

Pale to light gold in colour with a sweet and very grainy aroma holding some light hay notes. The very sugary start precedes a thin and sweet body of sugar, grain and grass. The quick finish tastes predominantly of corn syrup with some light, grassy notes. ★

Molson Breweries

LOCATIONS:

(National Office) 175 Bloor Street East, North Tower, Toronto, Ontario M4W 3S4
(Breweries) 1550 Burrard Street, Vancouver, British Columbia V6J 3G5
10449—121st Street, Edmonton, Alberta T5N 1L3
1892—15th Street SE, Calgary, Alberta T2G 3M2
1300 Dewdney Avenue, Regina, Saskatchewan S4R 1G4
77 Redwood Avenue, 2nd Floor, Winnipeg, Manitoba R2W 5J5
1 Carlingview Drive, Etobicoke, Ontario M9W 5E5
1 Big Bay Point Road, Barrie, Ontario L4M 4V3
1555 Notre Dame Street East, P.O. Box 1600, Montreal, Quebec H2Y 3L3
131 Circular Road, P.O. Box 5308, St. John's, Newfoundland A1C 5W1

PHONE:

(National Office) 416-975-1786, (fax) 416-975-4088
(Customer Service) 1-800-565-8800
(Breweries) 604-664-1786, (fax) 604-664-1840 (British Columbia)
403-482-1786, (fax) 403-482-5799 (Edmonton)
403-233-1786, (fax) 403-237-0227 (Calgary)
306-359-1786, (fax) 306-757-3011 (Saskatchewan)
204-586-8011, (fax) 204-586-4883 (Manitoba)
416-675-1786, (fax) 416-675-6717 (Etobicoke)
705-722-1786, (fax) 705-721-7296 (Barrie)
514-521-1786, (fax) 514-521-6951 (Quebec)

	709-726-1786, (fax) 709-726-2382
	(Newfoundland)
OWNERS:	*Molson Cos. (40%), Foster's Brewing*
	(Australia, 40%), Miller Brewing
	(United States, 20%)
PRESIDENT:	*Bruce Pope*
VP BREWING:	*Walter Hogg*
CAPACITY:	*12,910,000 hl*
TOURS:	*Available at certain breweries, call for*
	information

The best and perhaps only accurate way to describe Molson Breweries is as an amalgam of past Canadian breweries. Of course, more than 250 years of history is a lot of time for purchases and takeovers.

On the Carling O'Keefe half of the company alone are listed the names of more than 30 brewing businesses that have fallen into the fold over the years. When this number is combined with the Molson side of the ledger, a total of more than 40 breweries have been acquired in the eventual makeup of the modern company.

With that many breweries involved, it is easy to see where Molson's history can get a little complicated. In order to simplify the matter, it is best to split the brewery's background into two parts: that of Molson and that of Carling O'Keefe.

The Molson arm of the brewery was begun by John Molson in 1786. It is, according to the company's documents, the oldest continuously operating brewery in North America and Canada's second oldest business after the Hudson's Bay Company.

Molson Breweries was born just outside of Montreal, Quebec, and for more than 150 years the company was unable to expand beyond those boundaries, not for the lack of trying, though. The Molson family reportedly made their first attempt to crack the Ontario market in 1850 but were thwarted by Toronto city council, which refused to issue them a permit to build in the city. One hundred and five years later, the Fleet Street brewery opened in Toronto.

During the time between the two stabs at the Toronto market, Molson had become a driving force in the Quebec brewing industry. So great was the company's strength, in fact, that it acquired an additional seven breweries within seven years of the Fleet Street opening, including the five western operations of Sicks' Breweries (Lethbridge, Regina, Edmonton, Prince Albert and Vancouver) as well as facilities in Winnipeg and St. John's.

Molson's final domestic brewery purchase prior to the merger with Carling O'Keefe came in 1974 when the company took over the Formosa Brewing Company and their nearly new Barrie, Ontario, brewery.

The Carling O'Keefe story is a most complex one that ironically derives its point of origin from neither the Carling nor the O'Keefe breweries. Instead, it all begins with E. P. Taylor and the Brading's Brewery.

Taylor's post-Prohibition control of Brading's gave him a position from which to launch his well-known acquisition drive of the 1930s and 1940s. His buying splurge began in 1930 when he formed the Brewing Corporation of Canada, later to become Canadian Breweries Limited.

By the end of 1930, Taylor had already purchased nine breweries, all but two of which were located in Ontario. The oldest of the nine, Carling Breweries, dated back to 1840, while most of the others began operations in the mid- to late-1800s, and the youngest, Regal Brewing in Hamilton, had only existed in that form for scant months.

Taylor's plan in all of these acquisitions seemed designed as much to shut down the competition as to expand his own brewing capacity. While nothing to this effect was ever proven in court, one wonders how else Taylor could explain the purchase of two breweries in the small Hamilton market during the same year or, similarly, the acquisition of two other operations in the equally small Manitoba market in 1930.

The Canadian Breweries spending spree continued virtually without pause right up to 1952. Taylor apparently concentrated on Ontario for the first several years with his purchases including O'Keefe Brewing in 1934 before he entered the Quebec market in 1951 with the purchase of National Breweries Limited.

National, better known by the brand names of Dow and Dawes, had curiously enough been developed much the same way that Taylor had guided the growth of his company. At the time of the takeover, National was composed of at least six older breweries including the Dow Brewery of Montreal. Not wanting to lose his regional appeal in *la belle province*, Taylor grouped all of his operations in Quebec under the name of the Dow Brewing Company.

Following a handful of further purchases through the 1950s and 1960s, Canadian Breweries was itself bought by Rothman's of Pall Mall in 1969 and renamed Carling O'Keefe Limited in 1973. Carling was then, in turn, purchased by Foster's Brewing of Australia in 1987 and the stage was set for the now-famous merger.

Molson and Carling joined forces in 1989 with the new company's ownership being evenly split between Molson Cos. and Foster's Brewing. The result, aside from several redundant breweries and a dramatically shrunken work force, was the new leader in the Canadian brewing industry.

To gain a toehold in the United States, Molson effected one more deal in early 1993 by selling a piece of the company to Miller Brewing of Milwaukee, Wisconsin. The sale gave Miller complete ownership of Molson's American distribution wing and 20 percent of the company, while Molson Cos. and Foster's each gave up one tenth of the ownership and gained hundreds of millions of dollars.

Not content with merely shaking up the industry financially, Molson followed the Miller deal with the unprecedented move of eliminating preservatives in all of their beers and introducing a new series of all-malt brews in the fall of 1993. The new brands, known as the Signature Series, introduced traditional beer styles to the Molson line-up and marked what the brewery called a return to their roots.

Molson's public position since the Miller deal has been that they are now prepared to butt heads with the American majors or any other breweries that wish to land upon our shores. While only time will tell on that score, one can scarcely doubt that, with more than 40 Canadian breweries in their past and two foreign ones in their present, Molson has plenty of ammunition for the battle to come.

SCOREBOARD

Amstel (B,O—5% vol.)
Light gold in colour with a soft aroma of grain, fresh hay and faint, leafy hop. The taste starts dry and lightly woody before moving to a bittersweet body blending sour root, faint tobacco and sugar cane notes. The finish is sweet-and-sour with some grassy notes. ★¹/₂

Black Horse (F—5% vol.)
Light gold in colour with a light, bittersweet and tobaccoey aroma. The carbonic start is slightly fruity (peach and pear) while the body is of lightly roasted, malted grain, sour grass, hay and very faint pear notes. The finish tastes of sweet-and-sour grain with a light, earthy and bitter hopping. ★¹/₂

Black Ice (N except S,W,T—5.5% vol.)
Light gold in colour with a soft aroma of fragrant grain, candied orange peel and faint alcohol. A light, sweet, fresh hay start leads into a sweet-and-sour body with the predominant grassy and sugary notes mixing with sour root, a hint of fruitiness (orange) and light alcohol. The fairly dry finish is woody and mildly alcoholic. ★

Black Label (B,A,O,Q,T—5% vol.)

Light gold in colour and light in aroma with an earthy grain nose holding soft florals. The sweet and very sugary start leads to a sweet-and-sour body of perfumey and sweet grain and grass, with icing sugar notes. The finish is bittersweet with bitter root notes and a drying hint of alcohol. ★

Bock Reserve '93 (seasonal; B,M—6% vol.)

Cherry-rust-coloured with a rich, malty and somewhat alcoholic nose carrying cherry and caramel notes. A very cherry and slightly medicinal, semisweet start leads to a mildly alcoholic body with fruity brandy and dark chocolate notes. The sweet-and-sour finish has a stronger alcoholic bite along with some candied tartness. ★½

Brador Malt Liquor (O,Q,W—6.2% vol.)

Pale gold-coloured with a sweet, roasted and faintly smoky nose. The soft and malty start gives way to floral body with hints of raw sugar before a slightly bitter caramel finish with sweet-and-sour notes. ★

Canadian (N—5% vol.)

Pale to light gold in colour with a very sweet nose of slightly vinous grain with mild sugary notes. A mild, slightly sweet and carbonic start leads to a floral sweetness in the body with cane sugar, grain and grass notes along with some acidity. The finish begins sugary and ends woody and slightly bitter. ★

Canadian Ice (B,A,S,O,T—5.5% vol.)

Light gold-coloured with a very sweet and perfumey malt nose holding light orange brandy notes. The sugary and carbonic start precedes a sweet, almost candy-like body with a light grassiness and sweet lemon and orange notes. A hint of alcoholic "heat" shows just before and during a sweet finish that holds some sour, grassy notes and evident sugariness. ★

Carling (S,M,O,Q—5% vol.)

Light gold-coloured with a strong and lightly sweet cereal aroma cut by some metallic hopping. The soft and carbonic, creamed corn start moves to a sweet and sugary body of grain, grass and acidity. The sweet and lactic finish has a faint touch of sour root. ★

Carling Ice (O—5.5% vol.)

Light gold in colour with a sweet, grainy aroma carrying slight wood and pronounced alcohol notes. The very sweet start displays a distinctly sugary character before it leads into a sweet-and-sour body of grass and grain with evident "hot" alcohol notes. The quick finish shows a flash of refined sugar prior to settling into a faintly alcoholic aftertaste with light, bitter hopping. ★

Coors (N except M,F,W—5% vol.)

Light gold in colour with a sweet, lightly fruity (orange) and perfumey nose. A sweet and mildly acidic start with notes of licorice leads into a very sweet and very creamy, sugary body. Very light notes of sour grass rise before the faintly spicy, honeyish finish. ★

Coors Light (N—4% vol.)

Pale gold in colour, the aroma is actually more perfumey than Coors due to the reduction in the sweet fruitiness. The lighter body results in a less sweet beer than its parent with a similar character except for the finish, which loses all spicy elements and is instead more acidic. ★

Durango (O,Q—4% vol.)

A line of "beer coolers" in five different flavours, all of which taste strongly of their flavouring ingredient. There is shockingly little to do with beer in these products. Unrated.

Export Ale (S,O,Q,W,V,P—5% vol.)

Light gold-coloured with a sweet and slightly hoppy, hay nose. The start is carbonic and fruity (canned peaches) leading to a sweet body of some faintly metallic hop, grassiness and light fruity (peach, apricot) notes. The finish bitters slightly with woody hopping but has a sugariness as well. ★

Foster's Lager (B,A,O,W,V,T—5% vol.)

Light gold in colour with a sweet, wet hay aroma holding grassy notes. The light and carbonic start is confectionery in its sweetness with just a hint of underlying root. The rootiness grows slightly in the body, becoming more acidic as it does, and is joined by sweet hay flavours and a note or two of citrus before a sour and grassy finish with significant acidity. ★

Golden (A,O,Q—5% vol.)

Light to medium gold in colour with a sweet-and-sour aroma containing unrefined sugar and petrol notes. The start is rather thin, acidic and sweet with candied lime notes. The body combines a light fruitiness (sweet lemon-lime) with a sour grain taste before moving to a finish that starts sugary and ends with bitter grass notes. ★

Laurentide (Q—5% vol.)

Light tending to medium gold in colour with a very soft aroma of light grain and caramel notes. The taste begins light and carbonic with a dry grain character before becoming slightly fuller in the faintly fruity (peach, orange), sweet-and-sour grain body. The finish is sweet and thin with some astringency and a note of saline. ★

Löwenbräu (O,Q—5% vol.)

Light gold in colour with a fairly dry aroma holding a hint of corn syrup alongside the predominant woody and leafy hop. The dry, salty start leads into a sweetish body of sour root, sweet hay and sugar cane. The finish holds a touch of kelp along with off-dry, grainy flavours. ★

Miller Genuine Draft (B,A,S,M,O,Q—5% vol.)

Light gold in colour with a petrol, grain and hop nose. The acidic start holds sour and tangy root notes along with some sugariness before the very earthy body carrying a saccharine-like sweetness along with sour, vegetal notes leading into a finish that begins dry and acidic but ends with a lingering sugariness. ★

Miller High Life (M,O,Q,F,W—5% vol.)

Light gold-coloured and sharp in its acidic, sweet grain aroma with light metallic notes. The start mixes a slightly fruity (orange) sweetness with a rooty bitterness before leading to a creamy and sweet body with soft petrol notes, some astringency and a sour tang in the second half. The finish is confectionery. ★

Miller Lite (O,Q,F,W—4% vol.)

Light gold in colour with a soft, sweetish grain nose holding peanutty notes. The soft and lightly creamy, sweet grain start has a light astringency that builds in the papery, bittersweet body with light butterscotch notes. The finish has a butter-like sweetness and evident woodiness. ★

Milwaukee's Best (O—4.5% vol.)

Pale to light gold-coloured with a sweet and slightly lemony aroma containing notes of grass, refined sugar and grain. The moderately sweet start has lemon peel notes leading into a light body of sour grain, grass and creamed corn. The quick finish is faintly sweet and holds some acidic citrus notes. ★

O'Keefe (O,Q—5% vol.)

Light gold in colour with a sweet, peachy aroma holding soft floral notes. The start is very sweet and fruity (orange) with some icing sugar notes while the body is similarly sweet and malty with candied lemon, orange, peach and apricot flavours along with the sugariness. The finish dries out slightly and has a faint hint of anise. ★½

O'Keefe Extra Old Stock (N except O,W—5.65% vol.)

Medium gold-coloured with a moderately sweet and caramelly aroma. The sweetish and butterscotchy start has some bitter, woody hopping prior to a somewhat alcoholic body that is full and malty with notable fruitiness (orange, peach). The soundly alcoholic finish carries sweet malt that is partially neutralized by the light, bitter and earthy hopping. ★½

Old Style Pilsner (B,A,S,T—5% vol.)

Light gold-coloured with a sweet and creamy grain nose holding a hint of sour hop. The carbonic, sour grass start leads into an astringent grain body with a sour and bitter character and notes of metallic hopping. It sweetens markedly in the finish with confectionery sugar and more grain notes. ★

Old Vienna (A,S,M,O,T—5% vol.)

Light gold in colour, the sweet aroma is of perfumed grain with very light florals. The start is sweet with grain, light butterscotch and creamed corn flavours. The body remains sweet but with an underlying sour root taste and fresh hay notes. The finish bitters and sours with light mustard seed notes and acidity. ★

Signature Series Amber Lager (O—5.3% vol.)

Light copper-coloured with a midly sweet and fruity (berry, apricot) aroma holding faint florals. The start is bittersweet with toasted grain flavours and a faint chalkiness. The relatively dry and bitter body contains notes of dried apricot, orange, burnt toast and very faint clove before a finish of roasted grain with bitter, nutty hopping and a hint of fruity sweetness. ★★½

Signature Series Cream Ale (O—5.1% vol.)

Light to medium gold in colour and moderately sweet in the nose with slightly caramelized, roasted malt aromas and faint, fruity florals. A lightly burnt start holding fresh hay and grain notes leads to a bitter-sweet, nutty body with more roasted grain notes and a very faint hint of cherry. The finish is bitter with mild tobacco notes and a light floweriness. ★★

Special (B,S,M,O—3.3% vol.)

Light gold-coloured with a cereal nose holding some light, sour hopping. The very light and astringent start leads to a soft, bittersweet and grainy body with light floral notes and high acidity. Notes of caramel malt show just before the relatively dry finish holding light hints of sugar. ★

Special Dry (N—5.5% vol.)

Pale gold in colour with a sweet and sugary, cotton candy nose. The creamy and rather neutral start leads into a very sweet body with strong sugary notes and hints of lemon and orange. The finish remains sweet overall but adds a bit of vegetal sourness. ★

Stock Ale (O—5% vol.)

Light to medium gold in colour with a soft, dry and fairly hoppy aroma carrying light grape notes. The sweet and lightly sugary start holds some faint plummy notes before leading into a very fruity body with notes of plum, blueberry and sweet apple alongside some tinny hopping. The bittersweet finish carries some mild, remaining fruit and metallic hop. ★★

Toby (B,O—5% vol.)

Copper-coloured with a rich and malty aroma of demerara sugar and caramel. The brown sugar start has light molasses notes and leads to a sweet and lightly chocolatey body with faint, earthy hopping. The finish develops some woody bitterness and espresso notes. ★¹/₂

CHAPTER SIX

Micro-Breweries and Regionals

British Columbia

Granville Island Brewing

LOCATION:	*1441 Cartwright Street, Granville Island, Vancouver, British Columbia V6H 3R7*
PHONE:	*604-688-9927, (fax) 604-685-0504*
OWNERS:	*The International Potter Distilling Corp.*
PRESIDENT:	*Ian Tostenson*
PLANT MANAGER:	*Mark Simpson*
BREWER:	*Mark Simpson*
CONSULTING BREWER:	*Rainer Kallahne*
BREWING CAPACITY:	*25,000 hl*
TOURS:	*1:00 & 3:00 p.m., 7 days, or groups on request*
BRANDS:	*Island Bock, Island Lager, Island Light, Lord Granville Pale Ale*

One of the biggest tourist attractions in Vancouver is Granville Island, an island attached to the mainland and located beneath the Granville Street bridge. It has all the amenities one expects from a tourist mecca: shops, craft studios, restaurants and bars. It also has something few other such spots can boast: a micro-brewery.

The first modern micro in Canada, in fact.

In many ways, says Granville head Mark Simpson, the development of Granville Brewing mirrored the emergence of Granville Island. Following the opening of a public market and a government-financed redevelopment scheme on the Island in the 1970s, Simpson says, the whole focus of the area was changing from industry to arts and crafts in the early 1980s. And what blends art and craft better than a small brewery?

Granville Brewing was the brainchild of Mitchell Taylor who, following a tour of the Bavarian beer country of Germany, became convinced that there was an unfilled niche for traditionally brewed beer on the West Coast.

According to Simpson, who was not with the company at the time but has schooled himself in its history, the Island location was chosen both for the image that the area presented and for its reasonable proximity to the middle- to upper-income young adults who formed the brewery's target market. By 1983, the construction to convert an old warehouse into a showpiece brewery had begun.

Of course, being the first bottling micro-brewery in Canada, Granville also had to figure out what licensing was needed and lobby the government to pass and amend the necessary legislation that would allow them to exist. All of this paperwork reportedly took Taylor two years and, for this reason if for no other, the rest of the British Columbia micros should be grateful to Taylor for blazing the trail.

In June of 1984, the first German-style lager was sold out of the new Granville Island Brewing Company and the craft brewing industry in Canada was reborn.

The first dramatic change in the structure of Granville Island Brewing was the decision to go public on the Vancouver Stock Exchange through a share exchange agreement with the Quantum Energy Corporation on October 1, 1985. Quantum, now the owner of the brewery, then changed its name to the Granville Island Brewing Co. Ltd. and, through the deal, needed capital was added to the brewing operation.

Aside from the new company structure coming into place, 1985 to 1986 were also busy years for the brewery as several, originally unplanned maneuvers took place in those years. These included the expansion of the brewery's beer store to include local wines and ciders, the start of draught beer production, the introduction of Island Bock and the development of Island Light.

Although, by all reports, the brewery was doing quite well, 1989 saw another dramatic move take place when Granville was purchased by International Potter Distilling, the then parent company of Pacific Western Brewing. While there have been industry rumblings that this move had a short-term negative effect on the brewery, Simpson strongly denies this suggestion and adds that he believes Potter to have been a strong and supportive owner for as long as it has held the brewery.

One definite impact the Potter ownership has had on Granville was the commencement of a licensing agreement with Ontario's Brick Brewing (see separate entry) and the transfer of the brewery's bottling facilities to Kelowna in the summer of 1993.

When Potter shut down its Pacific Brewing in St. Catharines, Ontario, a deal was struck with Brick to allow for a mutual licensing arrangement whereby each brewery could brew the other's labels. As of the summer of 1993, Brick still lacked the brewing capacity to produce any Granville brands but it was expected that Granville would soon begin brewing Brick's Amber Dry and Henninger Kaiser Pilsner.

Another result of the Pacific closure was the relocation of the brewery's equipment (including bottling and canning lines) to Potter's Kelowna, British Columbia, facility. It was expected that sometime during the summer of 1993, the bottling of Granville's beers would move to Kelowna where it can be done on the newer bottling line, although kegging continues at the original brewery.

Not that all this activity has had any profound effect on the day-to-day operations at Granville. According to Simpson, the brewery remains strong, and its status as Canada's first micro has provided it with a solid brand awareness and national image. He sees further growth occurring over the next five years and envisions Granville Island Brewing rising back to its former status as the top-selling micro-brewery in British Columbia.

With, no doubt, the tourists well in tow.

SCOREBOARD

Island Bock (6.5% vol.)

Deep black cherry-coloured with a chocolatey malt aroma. The slightly sugary and plummy molasses start leads to a chocolate and cherry body with some bitter, earthy hopping. The finish is alcoholic and somewhat port-like. ★★$^{1}/_{2}$

Island Lager (5% vol.)

Medium gold in colour with a soft aroma mixing woody and slightly nutty hop with faint, sweet grain. A bittersweet malt start leads to a medium to lightly hopped body with leafy and woody bitterness along-side some cereal grain. The finish is sharply bitter with woody hop. ★★

Island Light (4% vol.)

Medium gold-coloured with a very full and floral hop nose holding sweet caramel malt notes. The start is of sweet, slightly butterscotchy grain and heads into a medium-hopped body with a minor cereal char-acter and grassy hop notes along with faint hints of citrus. The finish is dry and mildly bitter with some rooty hop and light notes of lemon and hay. ★★$^{1}/_{2}$

Lord Granville Pale Ale (5% vol.)

Of deep copper colour with a fragrant, floral hop nose holding light caramel notes. The sweet and slightly candied start with soft fruity notes precedes a bittersweet body that sees the fruity malt mixing with nutty hopping and some light alcohol notes. The bitter and acidic fin-ish has sour cherry and nutshell flavours. ★★

Horseshoe Bay Brewing Company

LOCATION:	*6695 Nelson Street, Horseshoe Bay, British Columbia V7W 2B2 (expected to move early in 1994)*
PHONE:	*604-921-6116, (fax) 604-921-8110*
OWNER:	*David Bruce-Thomas*
PRESIDENT:	*David Bruce-Thomas*
BREWER:	*Tom Digustini*
CONSULTING BREWER:	*John Mitchell*
BREWING CAPACITY:	*2,750 hl*
TOURS:	*On request*
BRANDS:	*Bay Ale*
	Specialty brands brewed seasonally and for specific pubs and restaurants

The story of the Horseshoe Bay Brewing Company is, in many ways, the story of the birth of craft brewing in Canada.

It is also one of the more confusing tales in our national brewing lore.

Although Spinnakers in Victoria (see separate entry) is frequently given credit as the site of the natural beer renaissance's origins, it was actually at Horseshoe Bay that it all really began. The principal in either case, however, was most definitely John Mitchell.

Mitchell was guided by a love of beer to lobby the British Columbia government for a change in that province's liquor laws in order to permit the sale of house-brewed beer on-site. While he was successful in the long run at Spinnakers, the first step resulted in a little less than he had expected.

What the government was willing to allow was the sale of house beer as long as the brewing facility and the selling establishment were kept separate. The result of this legislative quirk was that Horseshoe Bay Brewing was born in a different building than that which housed the Troller pub where the brew was served, although both establishments were equally close to the Bay ferry terminal.

This odd but functional arrangement worked from March 1982 until some three years later when Mitchell and his two partners had a falling out, resulting in Mitchell's leaving the company. This left the remaining two to run the business until after Vancouver's Expo '86 when the partners decided to close down the brewery but maintain the pub and restaurant.

Enter David Bruce-Thomas.

After Mitchell had left the company, Bruce-Thomas had begun brewing for Horseshoe Bay and continued to do so until the operation was shut down. At the time of closure, the partners approached Bruce-Thomas with regard to the possibility of his buying the business but, unfortunately, the asking price was so high that he was forced to refuse the opportunity. That did not, however, dissuade him in his desire to own the business.

As it happened, Bruce-Thomas knew the owner of the scrap yard where the brewing equipment was eventually deposited, and arranged to buy back the works, renegotiate the lease and reopen the brewery at a fraction of the original, or even the secondhand cost.

This move obviously did not sit well with the owners of the Troller pub, so, when he restarted brewing in the spring of 1987, Bruce-Thomas had to look for a new place in which to sell his ale. He found this in Ya-Ya's Oyster Bar, located just up the dock from the brewery.

In both physical size and brewing capacity, Horseshoe Bay Brewing is still among the tiniest micros in Canada, but it has been growing slowly and steadily through the 1990s. Bruce-Thomas and brewer Tom Digustini now boast four accounts for their "bulk delivery" system, whereby the finished ale is tanked to a 200-gallon serving vessel in the establishment, and an additional dozen or so draught accounts.

As well, the company's bottle-conditioned ale is beginning to make an impact on the British Columbia micro-brewery scene; their seasonal specialty draughts (such as their Easter Ale) have developed a strong following; Bruce-Thomas is exploring export opportunities in New York and Japan; and the brewery is supplying the strong ale that is blended into FBI Foods's juice-based Shandy.

All in all, a fair bit of business for a brewery that almost ended up on the scrap heap.

SCOREBOARD

Bay Ale (5% vol.)
Hazy from its bottle-conditioning, it is copper-rust coloured with a very bready aroma holding some fruity (bing cherry, black current) notes. The soft and lightly acidic front with faint sweet molasses notes leads to a leafy, bitter body with slight yeasty tang and apple notes. The finish is well hopped and woody with light floral notes. ★★$\frac{1}{2}$

Nelson Brewing Company

LOCATION:	*512 Latimer Street, Nelson, British Columbia V1L 4W4*
PHONE:	*604-352-3582*
OWNERS:	*Paddy Glenny, Deiter Feist*
PRESIDENT:	*Paddy Glenny*
BREWER:	*Deiter Feist*
CONSULTING BREWER:	*N/A*
BREWING CAPACITY:	*2,000 hl*
TOURS:	*By appointment only*
BRANDS:	*Old Brewery Ale*
	Silverking Premium Lager

Books on how to start a successful micro-brewery generally point to the merits of establishing yourself close to a metropolitan area, the sageness of having a plan that allows for expansion and the practicality of enlarging your sales district through direct distribution.

Then again, the people who write such books have never spoken to Deiter Feist or Paddy Glenny.

To say that Nelson Brewing has gone against the conventional wisdom of micro-brewing is like saying that Babe Ruth was pretty handy with a bat. Feist and Glenny have cut against the accepted grain since they first got the idea for their operation and, by all accounts, they have no intention of changing their ways now.

The story of the little brewery located deep in the British Columbia interior begins at England's Oxford University where the wives of the two men established a friendship. What seemed at the time like an incidental relationship soon blossomed into a business partnership that saw the resurrection of brewing in the little town that Columbia Brewing forgot.

The impetus for the formation of the business occurred when Feist hurt his back and could not continue in his forestry career in Canada. A longtime home brewer, he felt that the interior was fertile ground for a micro, and soon convinced Glenny to sell his brewery in Witney, England, and join him in the tough British Columbia beer game.

The two men bought a small Welsh brewery and shipped it overseas to the location they had chosen for their home: the little city of Nelson in the Kootenay region of the province.

The choice of locale was not made arbitrarily: Nelson has a history of brewing which dates back to the original Nelson Brewing of 1893 and up to when Columbia Brewing (now owned by Labatt) abandoned the city in 1962. Armed with a sense of history to go with their business sense, the two partners located themselves in the building that originally housed Nelson Brewing in the nineteenth century.

Having found their site in April 1991 and overcome their sole problem of having to clear their name with the proprietor of the Nelson Home Brewing brewery supply store, the two men began producing draught beer later that same year.

By July of the following year, Feist and Glenny were bottling their ale and lager in one-litre plastic bottles in order to meet demand and, by March 1993, the two had raised enough capital to buy the building that housed their brewery.

The unconventional part of the Nelson story arises when one ponders the means of their success. The two men have steadfastly refused to enlarge their delivery area beyond an 80-kilometre radius, forcing pub owners outside of that range to pick up their beer from the brewery. Nelson Brewing has no interest in growth beyond very modest means and Feist and Glenny both abhor the thought of entering the Vancouver market.

It just goes to show that the experts who write the guides to successful operations are not always right.

SCOREBOARD

Old Brewery Ale (5% vol.)
Medium gold in colour with a mildly spicy, caramel malt aroma holding sour grapefruit and sweet apricot notes. The soft, creamy malt start with peach notes leads to a full, caramelly body with flowery hops, more peach and apricot notes. Woody hopping rises through the finish to dry out the taste. ★★¹/₂

Silverking Premium Lager (5% vol.)
Of light to medium gold colour, it has a perfumey caramel and floral aroma. The mildly carbonic start with citric grain notes heads to a full, sweet and malty body with strong caramel flavour touched by woody and rooty hop. It bitters somewhat in the finish with rooty hop but retains enough sweetness to be a bit cloying. ★¹/₂

Okanagan Spring Brewery Ltd.

LOCATION:	*(Brewery) 2801–27A Avenue, Vernon, British Columbia V1T 1T5 (Offices) 3535 Foster Avenue, Vancouver, British Columbia V5R 4X3*
PHONE:	*(Brewery) 604-542-2337, (fax) 604-542-7780 (Offices) 604-443-0088, (fax) 604-433-4401*
OWNERS:	*Jakob Tobler, Buko Von Krosigk, 5 silent partners*
PRESIDENT:	*Jakob Tobler*
SECRETARY-TREASURER:	*Buko Von Krosigk*
BREWER:	*Stefan Tobler*
CONSULTING BREWER:	*Raimond Klinowski*
BREWING CAPACITY:	*100,000 hl*
TOURS:	*On request*
BRANDS:	*Extra Special Pale Ale, Okanagan Spring Premium Lager, Old English Porter, Old Munich Wheat, St. Patrick Stout, Spring Pilsener*

There are many stories about businesses that fail due to tough financial times, but the story of the Okanagan Spring Brewery is one of a business that began due to a tight economy.

According to brewery owner Buko Von Krosigk, the economy of the Okanagan region in the interior of British Columbia died in 1982. It was shortly after that time that Von Krosigk and co-owner Jacob Tobler, both residents of the area, began to investigate the possibility of moving into a new business.

A brew master friend of Tobler's happened to be visiting from Germany at about the same time and the three men got to talking about what would be involved in starting up a brewery. Tobler and Von Krosigk were each suitably impressed at the prospects before them and, by the summer of 1984, the duo were seriously planning their new micro-brewery.

The building the two men chose was an old packing house located in downtown Vernon, and the construction of the brewery began in February 1985. The location was selected based upon the belief that all of their beer would be sold within a radius of about 25 to 30 miles or, at the most, within the confines of the Okanagan Valley. While this scenario is appropriate in certain European settings, the forces at work in Canada are quite different and, in hindsight, Von Krosigk now allows that, were he to do it again, he would choose a more urban setting for his brewery, closer to the coast.

By December 1985, the Spring Premium Lager and 3% alcohol Light were in full production at the brewery. They were joined in the summer of 1986 by the Old English Porter, an 8.5% alcohol beer that, Von Krosigk says, was designed to lay claim to the distinction of brewing both the lightest and the strongest beers on the Canadian market at the time.

In the fall of 1986, the two partners were faced with a most dramatic realization: the Okanagan Valley virtually empties of people after Labour Day.

This discovery stunned Von Krosigk and Tobler; they were forced to scramble to get their brands into the Vancouver area, a feat they accomplished by leasing a small warehouse in the city. They might still have been in trouble, though, except that they happened to receive some very favourable media coverage around the same time.

While their lager was doing well in the market, the Light was not selling as well as the partners expected and they phased the beer out through the winter and spring of 1987, replacing it with the St. Patrick Stout and the bottle-conditioned Old Munich Wheat.

According to Von Krosigk, the stout came about as a result of several publicans requesting a draught porter. Wary about kegging an 8.5% alcohol beer lest it not sell, Von Krosigk and Tobler developed the new stout to satisfy bar owners who were, at the time, legally prevented from having imported beer on tap.

Okanagan's fifth brand, a pale ale brewed with the brewery's lager yeast, joined the family of labels in 1989 and the summer of 1993 saw the introduction of the Spring Pilsener. Along the way, Okanagan has also tapped into the Vancouver Island market through another warehouse, signed an agreement for the Old English Porter to be brewed under licence by the Gambrinus Brewery in Germany and began exporting to Japan.

Apparently, Von Krosigk and Tobler have found that the market for their beer extends much further than their original 25-to-30-mile radius.

SCOREBOARD

Extra Special Pale Ale (5% vol.)
Dark copper in colour with a floral hop and fruity (peach) malt aroma holding hints of fresh tobacco. The sweet, dried apricot front heads to a bitter and lightly sour, rooty hop body touched by mild acidity. The bittersweet finish holds increased acidity, orange notes and leftover bitter hop. ★½

Okanagan Spring Premium Lager (5% vol.)
Medium gold-coloured with extremely floral aroma of hop and caramel malt. The sweetish, creamy and slightly butterscotchy start leads to a rich body of medium bitterness with rooty hopping and some remnants of sweet malt. The finish bitters and becomes distinctly woody ★★

Old English Porter (8.5% vol.)
Very dark burgundy in colour with a strongly alcoholic, sweet licorice aroma having very light chocolate notes. A sweet, plummy start heads into a bittersweet and fruity (cherry) chocolate body. The strong, bitter and alcoholic finish holds touches of brown sugar and a mild astringency ★★★

Old Munich Wheat (5% vol.)
Cloudy rust in colour with a full, spicy clove nose. The very estery body begins spicy with clove and coriander notes before leading to a body of banana and light, lemony grain. The finish is dry and citric with more clover and some leftover banana notes. ★★½

St. Patrick Stout (5.5% vol.)
Very dark, almost black, plum-coloured with a strong coffee nose. A sweet and sugary start with very faint cherry notes previews a mocha body with strong notes of baker's chocolate and a touch of raisin. Bitter and acidic coffee finish the taste. ★★

Pacific Western Brewing Company

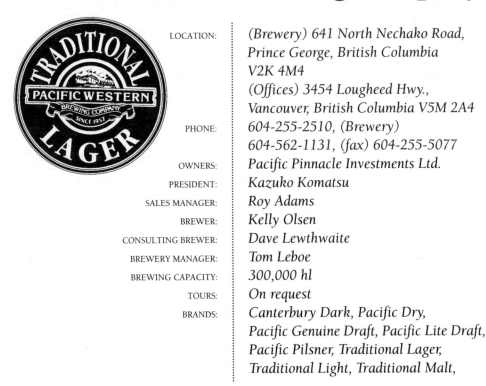

LOCATION:	(Brewery) 641 North Nechako Road, Prince George, British Columbia V2K 4M4 (Offices) 3454 Lougheed Hwy., Vancouver, British Columbia V5M 2A4
PHONE:	604-255-2510, (Brewery) 604-562-1131, (fax) 604-255-5077
OWNERS:	Pacific Pinnacle Investments Ltd.
PRESIDENT:	Kazuko Komatsu
SALES MANAGER:	Roy Adams
BREWER:	Kelly Olsen
CONSULTING BREWER:	Dave Lewthwaite
BREWERY MANAGER:	Tom Leboe
BREWING CAPACITY:	300,000 hl
TOURS:	On request
BRANDS:	Canterbury Dark, Pacific Dry, Pacific Genuine Draft, Pacific Lite Draft, Pacific Pilsner, Traditional Lager, Traditional Light, Traditional Malt,

For a brewery that has only been around since 1957, there is a whole lot of history wrapped up in the Prince George brewery of Pacific Western.

Then again, one could hardly expect anything less from a brewery that has been, at various times, run by the notorious "Uncle" Ben Ginter, advertised by Jim Varnie's Ernest "Hey Vern" P. Warhole character (now immortalized in a series of movies) and promoted by an imitation Mountie running a dog sled on wheels down the coast of California.

The road to the present began in 1957 when the Caribou Brewing Company was established in Prince George under the brewing guidance of an Austrian named Eugene Zarek. Yet Caribou Brewing would become but a footnote in the colourful history of the facility when in 1962, Ben Ginter bought the brewery out of bankruptcy and began applying his particular brand of salesmanship to the operation.

To say that Ginter was colourful is a severe understatement. A powerful, heavyset man, Ginter was responsible for the introduction of canned beer to the British Columbia market in the mid-1960s. He was also responsible for incurring the animosity of the big breweries as he tried to challenge their stronghold on the brewing industry through a series of price- and media-based confrontations.

Ginter lost his war with the majors and ended up losing his brewery to the receiver in 1976. This allowed Bob Naismith to move into the driver's seat with the backing of financier Nelson Skalbania shortly thereafter.

Current Pacific Western distribution manager Murray Miller, who came to Prince George with Naismith, says now that he got the feeling that Naismith was never truly comfortable with the business of beer. Regardless of his comfort level, however, Naismith must have been happy when the brewery workers' union went on strike in 1981 and allowed his non-union brewery to dominate the market for a time.

Unfortunately for Naismith, the impressive sales of what was then called the Prince George Brewery ended at about the same time as the strike did and it was not long before the brewery was once again changing hands. The new owner of the renamed Fort Brewing was Ron Hodgson and his president and right-hand man was Bill Sharpe, the latter of Lakeport Brewing (see separate entry under Ontario).

Although the last thing the old Prince George brewery needed was further notoriety, it received just that during the Fort days. The man responsible for the California dog sled run, Sharpe would do virtually anything to promote the sales of his beers, including undercutting the big breweries in price.

As Ginter had discovered before him, Sharpe soon found out that the majors do not take kindly to price wars and, after losing a brief price war, the brewery was turned over yet again. In 1985, it went to the Ledi brothers, a duo who had made their money in the construction trade and had purchased a limited stake in the operation in 1983.

The brothers, says Miller, put a good deal of money into the brewery and brought in some professional marketing people. It was at that point that several current brands including the Pacific Pilsner and the Pacific Real Draft were developed, their first generic beer brand was launched and the "Hey Vern" campaign was put into play.

Compared to their predecessors, the Ledis' ownership lasted for quite a time and, according to Miller, the brothers used the brewery to effect a reverse takeover of the Potter Distilling Group, which in 1988 became International Potter Distilling.

Toward the end of the 1980s, says Miller, the Potter Group grew to double its size and consequently began to drop its active support of Pacific Western. By 1991, the brewery was poised for yet another sale and, on March 1 of that year, Pacific Pinnacle took over the operations.

Talking to Miller and sales manager Roy Adams, one gets the distinct feeling that they honestly believe that Pacific Pinnacle head Kazuko Komatsu's ownership is the best thing that has ever happened to the

Prince George brewery. Despite its long and checkered past, they say, the direction of the company is now clear and its sights are set for the future.

SCOREBOARD

Canterbury Dark (5% vol.)

Deep rust-coloured with a light, earthy aroma with woody hop and slightly chocolatey, caramel malt cut by a grainy acidity. The light, grainy and carbonic start holds some citric notes and leads to a sweetish malt body with some earthy hopping, bitter chocolate notes and astringency toward the tart, dry and woody finish. ★¹/₂

Pacific Dry (5.5% vol.)

Light to medium gold in colour with a soft aroma of fresh-cut hay with a touch of sour grain. The heavily carbonic front with sweet, candied grain notes precedes a light licorice flavour that rises in the body along with some acidity, rooty hop and a very faint alcoholic taste. The sweet-and-sour finish holds some notes of sweet citrus and grain. ★

Pacific Genuine Draft (5% vol.)

Light to medium gold in colour with a sweet, candied fruit and grain nose. The light and sweet start with buttery notes leads into a sweet-and-sour grain body with citric (lemon and faint grapefruit) flavours. A strong cereal grain character rises through the second half to a sour, grassy finish. ★

Pacific Pilsner (5% vol.)

Light gold-coloured with a fresh and lightly sweet grain aroma. The sweet, lemony start heads to a creamy, confectionery grain body with a thin second half holding some mild astringency and a short, sour hay finish. ★

Traditional Lager (5% vol.)

Light gold-coloured with very light aromatics of fresh hay and kelp notes. A lightly citric, sweet-and-sour grain start leads to a very lemony, sour body that holds into the finish with some rising acidity to dry it out. ★

Traditional Malt (5.5% vol.)

Light to medium gold in colour and light in its largely neutral, wet hay aroma. A sweet, grainy start precedes a full body of creamy caramel malt cut by acidity and citric grain with some rooty hop leading into a quick, bittersweet and grassy finish. ★¹/₂

Shaftebury Brewing Company Ltd.

LOCATION:	*1973 Pandora St., Vancouver, British Columbia V5L 5B2*
PHONE:	*604-255-4550*
OWNERS:	*Paul Beaton, Tim Wittig*
PRESIDENT:	*Paul Beaton*
VICE-PRESIDENT:	*Tim Wittig*
BREWER:	*4 brewery staff*
CONSULTING BREWERS:	*Brad McQuhae, John Mitchell*
BREWING CAPACITY:	*12,000 hl*
TOURS:	*On request*
BRANDS:	*Christmas Ale (seasonal), Cream Ale, Extra Special Bitter (E.S.B.), London Porter (seasonal), Traditional Ale, Wheat Ale (seasonal)*

They say that British Columbia is lager country and that it is pointless to try to sell ale out west. If that is true, it somehow has managed to elude Paul Beaton and Tim Wittig, and the Vancouverites who love their English-style ales.

Like so many of their peers in 1986, Beaton and Wittig were out investigating the job market following their graduation from university that year. When the duo saw a story on television about the Hart brewery in Washington state, it set their minds to wandering; although the two men had no chemistry, microbiology or brewing background between them, they were fascinated by the idea of founding their own brewery, and proceeded to investigate the possibilities.

According to Wittig, they travelled to all sorts of small breweries—both successful and bankrupt—to determine what had made the operations work and what had caused them to fail. The one spot at which they ended up time and again was Victoria's Spinnakers (see separate entry).

Wittig and Beaton both found a lot to be praised in the Spinnakers ales and questioned why such beers were not commercially available. Apparently, John Mitchell was wondering the same thing because, following a great deal of convincing on the part of the two grads, he agreed to assist them in their endeavours.

After Mitchell and the then brewer at Spinnakers, Brad McQuhae (now of Newlands Services Inc., a brewing consultancy) signed a short-term contract with the two men, the next step for the fledgling brewery was to find a home. This the partners discovered in a new industrial building in the east end of Vancouver.

In order to save money on their shoestring budget, Wittig says that they convinced their new landlord to give them little more than the four walls of the building, and constructed the interior themselves. Mitchell and McQuhae had everything down on paper, says Wittig, and the two partners put it all into place.

One interesting note about the Shaftebury start-up is that, in many ways, it was a collection of firsts. Obviously, it was the first brewery for Wittig and Beaton, but it was also the first consultant job for McQuhae as well as the first complete brewery installation for the British Columbia firm Specific Mechanical.

Everything was finally put into place in August 1986 and the brewery began producing draught ales according to recipes developed by McQuhae. As Wittig recalls, the pair of consultants stayed for the first two months of the brewery's existence and then he and Beaton were left on their own.

For the first year and a half, the duo divided all of the work associated with Shaftebury between them, with Beaton brewing and taking care of the inside work while Wittig handled the outside chores. While Wittig admits that people were slow to come around to their brands of ale, word of mouth slowly began to work in their favour and, before long, the Cream and Bitter (now Traditional) ales began to move more quickly.

One Canadian West Coast tendency that did not work in Shaftebury's favour was the British Columbian aversion to heavily hopped beer. Having based many of their perceptions of the ale market on what they saw in the hop-headed northwestern United States, the partners were surprised by the resistance they found to the hoppiness of some of their ales. Perhaps for this reason, their mild Cream Ale has always accounted for the majority of their sales and, as recently as the spring of 1993, was still responsible for 70 percent of their total market, says Wittig.

Beginning in 1988, Shaftebury began offering an annual specialty Christmas Ale and, in September 1989, the two men launched their Extra Special Bitter (E.S.B.). By 1991, Wittig and Beaton felt that the time was right for a new brand, so they released a Wheat Ale for the summer and now alternate it with a 7% alcohol London Porter in the winter. Like all of Shaftebury's ales, these are only available on tap.

The draught-only scheme, says Wittig, came as the result of simple economics. The duo knew that the tap ruled in the licensed establishments of British Columbia and they could not afford a bottling line anyway, so it was decided that keg beer alone would be the future of Shaftebury. Even seven years after their debut, Wittig says that they still have no interest in bottling their ales.

Besides, the Shaftebury slogan of "local beers for local people" wouldn't work well with nationwide bottle distribution.

SCOREBOARD

(Note: All Shaftebury's ales are draught-only.)

Cream Ale (5% vol.)

Deep rust-coloured with a sweet coffee nose holding flowery hop and caramel notes. The start is slightly orangey with a touch of acidity and leads to a lightly bitter body with woody hopping, coffee notes and hints of honey. The mildly bitter finish holds tobacco notes and light acidity ★★½

E.S.B. (5.5% vol.)

Bright rust-coloured with a lightly roasted toffee aroma holding green plum notes. The soft start has light, fruity flavours before an earthy, semisweet body with the sweetness controlled by some bitter hopping. The slightly creamy middle holds sweet apple notes, light florals and some earthy hop. The finish is characterized by a woody bitterness. ★★

Traditional Ale (5% vol.)

Light gold-coloured with a sweet, malty nose of light caramel aromas with a touch of graininess. The slightly thin, sweetish front with evident sugar leads to a malted grain body with some faint florals and woody hop. The finish is bitter with hints of sugary root. ★½

Wheat Ale (5.2% vol.)

Cloudy and lightly copper in colour with a light aroma mixing sour grain and citrus. A tangy and yeasty start precedes a grainy body with citric and very light clove notes. The slightly estery finish has a bit of banana touched with lemon. ★½

Vancouver Island Brewing Co.

LOCATION:	*24–6809 Kirkpatrick Crescent, R.R.#3, Victoria, British Columbia V8X 3X1*
PHONE:	*604-652-4722, (fax) 604-652-5238*
OWNERS:	*Barry Fisher (18%), 39 partners*
PRESIDENT:	*Barry Fisher*
BREWER:	*Ross Elliot*
CONSULTING BREWER:	*Burt Grant*
BREWING CAPACITY:	*18,000 hl*
TOURS:	*On request, scheduled during the summer*
BRANDS:	*Hermann's Bavarian Dark Lager, Piper's Pale Ale, Vancouver Island Premium Lager, Victoria Weizen*

"**T**his is not a new industry, (but) a reborn one."
These were the words Vancouver Island Brewing's Ross Elliot used to describe the micro-brewing business in his province. He might just as easily have used them to describe his brewery.

Conceived by John Hellemond in 1983, Vancouver Island Brewing is, in a sense, the forgotten player in Canada's short, modern micro-brewing history. For whatever reason—its location off of the mainland or the brewery's initially confused identity and low-key nature—Vancouver Island Brewing is rarely thought of as one of this nation's pioneering breweries. It is a mantle the brewery would do well to reclaim.

With financing provided by 16 of Hellemond's friends and business associates, construction began in the early months of 1984 on the Island's third brewery (behind both the Prairie Inn and Spinnakers—see separate entries). The location, in an industrial mall well off of the highway that runs between Victoria and the Swartz Bay ferry docks, was chosen mainly because of the relatively low cost of the area, and may be one of the main factors contributing to the brewery's early anonymity.

When the first keg of Gold Stream Lager rolled out in February 1985, the brewery was called Island Pacific and its purpose was to sell only draught beer. In retrospect, this can be viewed as a fairly odd commitment since, at the time, restaurants in British Columbia were not allowed to sell keg beer at all, thus confining Island Pacific's sales solely to pubs. The brewery was successful in its push to change that law, though, and that first year saw sales of 3,500 hectolitres of lager.

In 1985, Island Pacific hired German brewer Hermann Hoerterer, a man who has left his stamp on several breweries across North America, including the British Columbian company Whistler Brewing (see separate entry). From that move came their second brand, Hermann's Bavarian Dark Lager; Piper's Pale Ale followed some twelve months later.

Island Pacific went merrily along through the rest of the 1980s, effecting expansions to their brewery in 1987 and 1989 and developing a since-discontinued lager to join their other brands. The presidency of the operation also changed in the 1980s when, in 1988, Hellemond left his post to pursue other concerns and brought in Barry Fisher. By the 1990s, Island Pacific was poised for a significant change in direction.

That change peaked at the brewery in early 1991 when a third expansion brought a name change to the company. The rechristening of the operation to the Vancouver Island Brewing Company renewed the brewery's purpose and readied it to tackle the tough bottled-beer market that same year. To help in the new drive, the flagship Gold Stream Lager was reformulated and renamed Vancouver Island Premium Lager in an effort to increase its marketability.

Under the new brewing stewardship of Ross Elliot, who had apprenticed under Hoerterer, Vancouver Island Brewing has finally become a significant presence in the British Columbia micro-beer game. According to Elliot, the company's focus has recently moved back to their home island and the brewery is working to redevelop its community identity. While Elliot says that, as of 1993, a full 65 percent of their beer is sold on the Island, he would prefer to see the figure up around 80 percent.

To make a greater impact on Vancouver Island, the brewery is planning to move to a more central location in the near future, although they have plenty of underutilized space in its current location. There is also hope, says Elliot, that the 1994 Commonwealth Games will permanently establish the brewery's brands as the beers to drink on the Island. And then, perhaps, the rebirth will be complete.

SCOREBOARD

Hermann's Dark Lager (5.5% vol.)
Deep black cherry-coloured with a strong mocha aroma holding gentle raisin notes. A lightly chocolatey start with hints of sugar precedes an earthy, bitter body that mixes sweet licorice with coffee and chocolate flavours and hints of fruit (plum, grape). The finish is bittersweet with black licorice notes. ★★½

Piper's Pale Ale (5% vol.)

Medium to dark copper-coloured with a fairly light, earthy hop aroma containing a few citric notes. The caramelly start quickly succumbs to a fairly assertive leafy and rooty hop body with apple notes and faint hints of fruity brandy. The lightish finish has bitter caramel and hop flavours with just a touch of sugar. ★★

Vancouver Island Premium Lager (5% vol.)

Medium gold in colour with a light, grainy nose holding notes of flowery and woody hop. The very fresh start of moderately sweet grain with buttery notes leads to a leafy hop rising in the body along with touches of sugar and a dry, almost astringent woodiness. The finish is bittersweet with woody hop alongside some sweet grain notes. ★¹/₂

Whistler Brewing Company Ltd.

LOCATION:	*1209 Alpha Lake Road, Whistler, British Columbia V0N 1B1*
PHONE:	*604-932-6185, (fax) 604-932-7293*
OWNERS:	*10 silent shareholders, no single controlling interest*
PRESIDENT:	*Don Konantz*
CONSULTING BREWER:	*Doug Babcook*
BREWERS:	*Brad Wheeler & Richard Johnson*
BREWING CAPACITY:	*9,000 hl*
TOURS:	*4:00 p.m., 7 days; or on request*
BRANDS:	*Black Tusk Ale, Whistler Pale Ale, Whistler Premium Lager*

While resort-based micro-breweries and brewpubs have become increasingly popular with our neighbours to the south, Canadian brewers have shied away from vacation-site locations. All, that is, except Whistler Brewing.

Nestled in the picturesque mountains of British Columbia, Whistler is the brainchild of Gerry Hieter, an entrepreneur who had visions of a brewery in one of the most popular ski resort towns in North America. To realize his goal, Hieter recognized that he would need the assistance of someone with the connections necessary to raise significant amounts of capital. That person was Rob Mingay.

Mingay, the former Ed Broadbent campaign chief (1984 and 1988) and Creemore Springs Brewery investor (see separate entry under Ontario), liked the idea of involving himself more directly in another brewing venture and signed on to secure the necessary investment. After getting the backing of financial heavyweights like Albert Gnat and David Levi, the chairmen of Ikea and VanCity Savings respectively, Mingay and Hieter had their funding and proceeded to purchase a site for the brewery in April 1988.

The location chosen was a small industrial park situated just outside the Whistler resort. As there was no appropriate building in the area, a 17,000-square-foot warehouse was built for the brewery on an empty lot and the sourcing of equipment began.

Most of the brewing necessities were found at a German brewery by the name of Mossinger: these included the dominant copper kettles on view through the brewery's large, front windows. Within a year, the Whistler brewery was taking shape.

During the time of construction, some training had to be done and, by way of Mingay and consultant Doug Babcook's involvement with the two breweries, much of that training took place at the Creemore facility in Ontario. Considering the success of Creemore Springs Lager, it is not terribly surprising that when Whistler did open, they opened with a lager.

The first beer came out of the new brewery on the Thanksgiving weekend of 1989. Response was positive and, as president Don Konantz reports, the Whistler Premium Lager even won a *Vancouver Magazine* taste test within months of its debut.

By the second year of operation, Whistler had more than doubled its initial year's production to a level of 5,000 hectolitres and introduced a new, bottom-fermented ale, Black Tusk, named after the nearby mountain. A short time later, the British Columbia contract to brew Albino Rhino Ale for the Earl's chain of restaurants followed, and Whistler seemed to be well on its way to success.

The first and, to date, largest stumbling block the brewery faced was the falling out of Mingay and Hieter in early 1991. The result of the dispute was that Hieter left the company and Mingay recruited two local businessmen to help him run the business.

A short time later, there was another falling out, this one between Mingay and the two recruits. The outcome of that difference of opinion was that Mingay said goodbye to the two men and the investors, in turn, bade adieu to Mingay.

At this point, the investors met with Don Konantz, a young entrepreneur who was one of the original forces behind the phenomenal success of College Pro Painters. Impressed with his enthusiasm and marketing background, they hired him to take charge of the brewery on December 5, 1992.

As of the spring of 1993, Konantz was still getting his feet wet with the company and admitted that he was amazed by the way that the brewing business worked in contrast to so many other industries. Nonetheless, he was still confident in his products and sure that, despite what he referred to as Whistler's "colourful history," he would be able to make the brewery into a winning enterprise.

Skiers everywhere no doubt wish him the best of luck.

SCOREBOARD

Black Tusk Ale (5.5% vol.)
Dark and port-like in colour with a sweet coffee and caramel aroma holding very light florals. The light, sugary start has some roasted grain notes and heads to a bittersweet coffee body with hints of chocolate and raw sugar. The finish is bitter and espresso-like. ★½

Pale Ale (5.5%)
Medium gold-coloured with a big perfumey and floral aroma. The very soft front with light caramel maltiness leads to a rounded, hoppy middle with predominantly rooty flavours wrapped around a very full, bittersweet malt body holding traces of orange and apricot. A slight acidity creeps in toward the bitter rooty finish. ★★

Premium Lager (5% vol.)
Medium gold in colour with a slightly spicy, nutmeg and hop aroma holding caramel and floral notes. The soft, rather milky start with subtle hints of spice leads to a well-hopped body having flowery and rooty flavours in combination with a slightly candied, butterscotchy malt. There is a touch of sweet malt and acidity in the woody hop finish. ★★½

The Prairies and the Territories

Arctic Brewing Company

LOCATION:	*3502 Wiley Road, Yellowknife,*
	Northwest Territories X1A 2L5
PHONE:	*403-920-BREW, (fax) 403-920-BEER*
OWNERS:	*Victor MacIntosh, Doug Strader &*
	silent partners
PRESIDENT:	*Victor MacIntosh*
BREWER:	*Victor MacIntosh*
VICE-PRESIDENT:	*Doug Strader*
CONSULTING BREWER:	*Brad McQuhae*
BREWING CAPACITY:	*2,000 hl*
TOURS:	*On request*
BRANDS:	*Arctic Diamond Traditional Ale,*
	Arctic Gold Pale Ale

Opening the country's only territorial micro-brewery, and the north-ernmost one in North America, is no mean feat. It is especially tough if you do not have the patience to deal with obstacles like the freezing of your steam pipes in –40°C weather!

Fortunately for the beer-drinking residents of Yellowknife, Victor MacIntosh is a man imbued with great endurance and the patience of a saint. Or at least those are the qualities he has now, after suffering through more than two years of barriers and setbacks on his way to the founding of the Arctic Brewing Company and the Bush Pilot Brewpub.

A home brewer and former naval officer who was stationed in the Northwest Territories, MacIntosh was anxious to return to the Arctic after he had finished his tour of duty, hoping to settle in Yellowknife and bring quality beer to the residents of that city. Had he known what kind of a practical and legislative mess he was going to be facing, he might have reconsidered.

Although there was no law that expressly forbid the establishment of a brewery in the Northwest Territories, neither was there any legislation that openly permitted it. So the first step for MacIntosh and his partner, Doug Strader, was to get a bill into the legislature that would allow them to proceed with their plans.

After two years of lobbying, letter writing and petition gathering, a Private Member's Bill was finally passed to allow for Arctic Brewing's creation. Although the length of the procedure caused MacIntosh to begin bandying the name "Political Monument Brewery" as a substitute title for his enterprise, he was understandably thrilled when the bill became law.

But Arctic Brewing was not out of the woods yet. The last hurdle came as quite a shock and surprise to the partners; the brewery had to receive permission from the local Yellowknives Dene Band council, which had jurisdiction over the Yellowknife area. This gave the entrepreneurs a few sleepless nights as they had already begun test brewing and knew that their plans could be scuttled by a negative vote at council. In the end, however, the Dene leaders voted to neither approve nor disapprove of the brewery, thus permitting it to go ahead by default.

Given that Arctic Brewing is the first commercial brewery in the Northwest Territories, it seems appropriate that it is housed in a historic building: the original floatplane base for Canadian Pacific. It is the aviation connection that gives the attached brewpub, The Bush Pilot, its name.

Having a bottling micro-brewery and a brewpub on the same site is by no means a commonplace occurrence in Canada. However, as MacIntosh explains, when the legislature passed a bill allowing Arctic Brewing the chance to run both establishments out of one operation—a situation not seen anywhere else in the country—he was not about to turn around and refuse the opportunity.

The first commercial beer in Canada brewed north of the 62nd parallel came up for sale March 12, 1993, and the brewpub opened its doors on the Victoria Day weekend of that year. According to MacIntosh, the initial response has been very positive, although he quickly discovered that he had to increase the hop and malt flavours of his brews in order to appeal to his customers.

After all that he had gone through to that point, making some minor changes to the taste profiles of his ales was no problem at all.

SCOREBOARD

Diamond Traditional Ale (5% vol.)

Hazy and deep burgundy in colour with a slightly yeasty, cherry, plum and red apple aroma on a sweet-and-sour molasses base. The tangy start holds some apple skin notes and leads to a slightly sour and medicinal, cherry and licorice body with light woody hopping and a bitter-sweet, red apple finish. ★½

Gold Pale Ale (5% vol.)

Hazy, medium to deep gold in colour with a yeasty, spicy nose holding light orange and butterscotch notes. The soft and nutty (walnut) start leads to a mildly bitter and earthy body with increased nuttiness, faint fruit (canned peaches) and a touch of caramelly sweetness. A little yeasty acidity rises in the finish alongside cereal grains and peanut flavours. ★★

Big Rock Brewery Ltd.

LOCATION:	*6403—35th Street SE, Calgary, Alberta T2E 1N2*
PHONE:	*403-279-2917, (fax) 403-236-7523*
OWNERS:	*Publicly traded; Edward McNally is the largest shareholder*
PRESIDENT:	*Edward McNally*
BREWER:	*Beirnd Pieper*
CONSULTING BREWER:	*Charlie McElevey*
BREWING CAPACITY:	*120,000 hl*
TOURS:	*Groups on request*
BRANDS:	*Buzzard Breath Ale (contract-brew for Buzzard Café and United States only), Classical Ale, Cock O' The Rock Porter (seasonal), Cold Cock Winter Porter (seasonal), McNally's Extra Ale, Pale Ale, Royal Coachman Dry Ale, Springbok Ale, Traditional Ale, Warthog Ale (for United States only), XO Lager*

As a director of the Western Barley Growers Association in the early 1980s, it was perhaps only logical that Ed McNally's next step would be to start up a micro-brewery. In the legislative world of the Canadian beer business, his background as a lawyer probably did not hurt, either.

McNally first became interested in the malting of barley when, in his director's position, he was addressing some of the legal problems the association was having with the sale of select barley grains, the ones used in brewing beer. His interest was further piqued when he read about the American craft-brewing pioneer Fritz Maytag and that man's experiences with San Francisco's Anchor Brewing.

Recognizing that in Calgary he was surrounded by some of the finest malting barley in the world, McNally saw no reason that those grains should continue to be exported to the States rather than used in Canada, and began the process that would result in the building of Canada's largest ale micro-brewery.

After gathering his investors from the farmers and ranchers he knew in the area, McNally proceeded to purchase a former aluminum fabrication plant, gut it and build his brewery. Much of the equipment he needed for the project arrived with his new brewer, Beirnd Pieper.

Given the relative drought of good brewers in North America at the time, McNally had one of his company's directors who lived in Zurich scout for brewing talent in Europe. Out of the 52 applicants they interviewed, Pieper, a German brewer with 14 years' experience in Liberia, Africa, was the man chosen.

The way McNally tells it, the early days of planning Big Rock were not easy. Provincial government officials, who had not issued a new brewing licence in over a decade, were baffled at what McNally wanted to do and, he says, acted as if they thought he was crazy. Nonetheless, even without confirmation from the government, McNally pushed ahead with his brewery construction, theorizing that the licensing process would move much more swiftly if he had a standing brewery waiting to go into production.

Despite, or perhaps because of the fact that the Alberta beer market is predominantly populated by lagers, McNally's first brews in September 1984 consisted of two ales and a porter. The ales were the Traditional and Bitter (since renamed Classical) and the porter, described by McNally as almost a stout, drew on Pieper's background of brewing Guinness in Africa.

The reason for his top-fermenting direction, says McNally, was that he did not want to immediately start into the crowded lager market and, instead, chose imported English ales as his target.

The going was slow at first for Big Rock. Beer drinkers loyal to imports were very set in their ways, says McNally, and there was significant distrust of locally brewed beers. Especially tough were the pub owners who were loathe to discard their British taps in favour of an unproven, upstart micro.

Big Rock beers persisted, however, and were selling well enough by 1987 that they were able to enter the highly competitive northwestern United States market. The exports began with Seattle, Washington, a city McNally felt was significant because it was on the cutting edge of the micro-brewing market. Six years later, Big Rock brands are available in six western states and the brewery is unique among Canadian micros due to the large volumes of beer it sends southward.

While Big Rock's bestselling brand is their Traditional Ale, perhaps their most well known is the McNally's Extra Irish style ale, a beer originally developed with the American market in mind. Its 7% alcohol make it amongst the strongest beers brewed in this country and it is perhaps the most popular Canadian brand in the United States outside of those of Molson, Labatt and Moosehead.

Big Rock's one building has since expanded to four structures. With nowhere to go on either side of them, the brewery began adding on to the backs of their buildings in the summer of 1993.

Needless to say, nobody thinks Ed McNally is crazy anymore.

SCOREBOARD

Classical Ale (5% vol.)

Medium gold in colour with a full, perfumey butterscotch and floral aroma. A soft, mildly sweet front with honey notes leads to a full, bitter body of woody hop, toffee and apple. The strongly bitter finish holds leaf and nutshell notes. ★★★

Cock O' the Rock Porter (5.5% vol.)

The deep and dark colour approximates that of a port wine and the soft aroma is reminiscent of sweetened coffee. The sweet and sugary start leads into a coffee body with a moderate roastiness, very light, earthy hop and hints of nuts. The bitter finish tastes of burnt coffee beans. ★★

McNally's Extra Ale (7% vol.)

Bright copper-coloured with a very full aroma of toffee, apricot and honey. The soft and fruity start with definite apricot notes precedes a strong, bittersweet body with sour orange, woody hop and toffee flavours. The moderately alcoholic finish holds brandy characteristics and is relatively bitter. ★★★¹/₂

Pale Ale (5% vol.)

Medium gold to light copper in colour and very soft and tobaccoey in aroma. The bitter start holds faint honey notes leading to a lightish, walnutty body with very soft caramel notes. The ale bitters moderately in the finish with some woody hop. ★★

Royal Coachman Light Dry Ale (3.9% vol.)

Light to medium gold in colour with a sweet and flowery brown sugar aroma. A lightly sweet and buttery start draws to a full, bitter and very dry body holding woody hop notes and very faint florals. The finish is bitter and nutty. ★★¹/₂

Traditional Ale (5% vol.)

Deep copper-coloured with a very nutty aroma holding green apple notes. The sweet and fruity start with light cherry and melon notes leads to a mildly bitter body with flowery hopping, more pronounced cherry flavours and notes of demerara sugar. The finish is still fruity though moderately bitter and caramelly as well. ★★¹/₂

XO Lager (5% vol.)

Medium gold in colour with a bitter, woody hop aroma holding soft, floral notes and touches of sweet grain. A very soft, flowery start precedes a bittersweet body that mixes toasted grain with nutty (walnut) hop. The bitter, leafy finish has some fruit and caramel notes. ★★

Drummond Brewing Company Ltd.

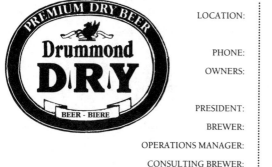

LOCATION:	*2210 Gaetz Avenue, Red Deer, Alberta T4R 1W5*
PHONE:	*403-347-6633, (fax) 403-347-7235*
OWNERS:	*Alberta Wheat Pool, employees & Red Deer investors*
PRESIDENT:	*Charlie Clark*
BREWER:	*Wolfgang Hoess*
OPERATIONS MANAGER:	*Tom Hazlett*
CONSULTING BREWER:	*N/A*
BREWING CAPACITY:	*190,000 hl*
TOURS:	*On request*
BRANDS:	*Beer Beer, Drummond Draft, Drummond Dry, Drummond Light, Drummond Dry Light, Premium Lager, Summit Lager, Wolfsbrau Amber Lager*

Red Deer, Alberta, lies at the midpoint between Calgary and Edmonton, a location that makes it the ideal site for a brewery wishing to serve both markets easily and efficiently. At least, that was the thinking of Ben Ginter when he built what is now the Drummond Brewing Company in Red Deer in the early 1970s.

The man who was, in his day, *the* rogue of the Canadian brewing industry left more than just a building for Drummond; he also left a legacy of inventive and aggressive marketing ideas which, consciously or unconsciously, Drummond has followed throughout its existence. It is a legacy that current Drummond president Charlie Clark shrugs off as a non-issue, but does so with a smile on his face.

Ginter built Drummond at his personal peak which, unfortunately, occurred not long before his final downfall and exit from the industry. That meant that there was a virtually new brewery for sale at a very good price around the same time as Alberta was basking in an oil-induced economic boom. Given that construction companies were thriving by feeding on the fruits of that boom, it comes as no surprise that one such company purchased the Red Deer brewery.

The buyer was the Fort McMurray-based Steeplejack and, according to Clark, they used the brewery as a method of investing some of their excess profits. There was not a lot of surplus capital left in the early 1980s, however, and Steeplejack lost the brewery to its mortgage company, Matrix Investments.

Matrix ran the brewery until 1989 when a movement to divest the company of Drummond led Matrix investment manager Terry Myers to bring together a group of local businesspeople interested in the purchase of the brewery. The sale was successful and Drummond became entirely owned and operated by Red Deer citizens.

That situation changed in 1991 when Drummond negotiated a deal with the Alberta Wheat Pool that gave the Pool a 50 percent stake in the operation. As of the summer of 1993, Drummond remained the only brewery in Canada, and likely the only one in North America, to have a farming cooperative involved in its ownership.

Over the years and through its transitions in ownership, Drummond has been responsible for several unique and occasionally questionable marketing strategies.

The early 1980s saw Drummond, under the name of the Heritage Brewery Inc., introduce the country's first generic beer brand named, appropriately, Beer Beer. Priced below any other brand in Alberta, it was an immediate hit in that province and remains the number-one seller in the Drummond line.

A decade later, Drummond launched another, not so successful marketing strategy, this time in Saskatchewan. Frustrated by the Saskatchewan government's continued reluctance to allow Drummond to sell their Beer Beer at a reduced price, the brewery took to sticking a $2.00 bill in each twelve-pack of beer it sold in that province. The practice did not last long —the Saskatchewan Liquor Licensing Commission saw to that—but it garnered Drummond national press coverage and, according to Clark, made the company's point.

Other Drummond "firsts," says Clark, were the introduction of Alberta's first packaged draft beer, the establishment of a toll-free phone number for customer service queries and the sale of a 19.5-litre, plastic sphere of draught lager known as the Drumball. They also, adds Clark proudly, take draught account service very seriously and receive and fill keg orders literally up to the point that the truck is leaving the lot.

Clark feels that beer sales in Canada are going to revolve much more strongly around specialty brands in the future and plans to make sure that Drummond keeps up with the times. To that end, he sees room for growth in the market for their premium Wolfsbrau Amber Lager and the possible introduction of further specialty brands in the future.

But, no doubt, there will always be room for a little Beer Beer, as well.

SCOREBOARD

Beer Beer (5% vol.)
Light gold in colour with a sour, lightly toasted grain aroma carrying sugar notes. The sweet and buttery, light caramel start heads into a sweet-and-sour grain body with soft, rooty hop notes and a quick, off-dry roasted cereal finish. ★

Drummond Draft (5% vol.)
Light gold in colour with a very sweet, perfumey aroma that smells strongly of icing sugar. A light and carbonic start with cereal notes precedes a sweet and grainy body with light, sour grass notes and caramel malt flavours. The finish bitters while retaining cereal notes. ★

Drummond Dry (5.5% vol.)
Light to medium gold in colour with a sour and rooty aroma holding notes of plastic and petrol. The sweet, sugary and carbonic start leads into a sweet-and-sour body of grassy and sour root flavours with light hints of candied lemon peel and a touch of woody hop before a short, sugary finish. ★

Premium Lager (5% vol.)
Light gold-coloured with an off-dry aroma blending lightly toasted grain with sweet, buttery notes. A mildly sugary start precedes a sweetly sour, grassy body and a dry, bitter and chalky finish. ★

Summit Lager (5% vol.)
Light gold in colour and very sweet in aroma with the caramel malt holding a touch of fresh grain. A dry and slightly sour grain start precedes a bittersweet body of mildly sweet malt and medium-strength, woody hop. The finish is bitter and rooty. ★¹/₂

Wolfsbrau Amber Lager (5% vol.)
Medium copper-coloured with a hop and malt aroma mixing caramel and floral notes with faint nuttiness. A soft and mildly sweet caramel start with chocolate notes leads to a more mocha body with bitter, woody hopping and a faintly sweet, nutty finish. ★★¹/₂

Great Western Brewing Company

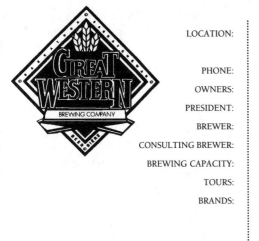

LOCATION:	*519—2nd Avenue North, Saskatoon, Saskatchewan S7K 2C6*
PHONE:	*306-653-4653, (fax) 306-653-2166*
OWNERS:	*Brewery workers*
PRESIDENT:	*Peter McCann*
BREWER:	*Gib Henderson*
CONSULTING BREWER:	*N/A*
BREWING CAPACITY:	*250,000 hl*
TOURS:	*10:30 a.m. daily, or on request*
BRANDS:	*Christmas Goose (seasonal), Gibbs Ale, Great Western Gold, GW Lager, GW Light, GW Natural Draft, Prairie 3.2, Saskatchewan Beer, Western Dry*

After start-up capital, perhaps the most important asset a fledgling brewery can have is brewing experience. It is also something that Great Western Brewing has in spades.

Between the 16 original shareholders in Great Western, there are more than 400 years of background in the Canadian brewing game, says president Peter McCann, and each man brings his own piece of expertise to the business. Fourteen of the owners are brewery workers and two were retirees who chose to invest their money in the venture rather than risk seeing the plant in which they had worked for so many years close down. With that kind of basis for ownership, it is no surprise that Molson was initially reluctant to sell the operation to the employees group at first.

The genesis of GW, as it is known in Saskatchewan, lies largely with McCann, a veteran of the brewing industry who managed the plant under Carling O'Keefe for eight years before transferring to Calgary to run a much larger brewery. After three years in Alberta, McCann moved back to Saskatchewan in order to assume the presidency of Prairie Malt. Following the privatization of the crown company, however, McCann found himself without a job. Coincidentally, this occurred at the same time as the Molson-Carling O'Keefe merger was in its final stages and the closure clock was beginning to tick at the Saskatoon plant.

While McCann himself is perhaps too modest to offer the complete details of his role in the employee purchase plan, senior brewer and shareholder Greg Kitz is not so tentative. He says that the worker purchase scheme would never have come together but for McCann. The employee group that had been formed to investigate the purchase option, says Kitz, was formed entirely of workers from the technical side of the brewing business. With the addition of McCann, he continues, they added an industry veteran with important administrative experience, thus giving their group added legitimacy in the eyes of Molson.

The hesitation of Molson to approve the sale was, according to McCann, motivated by what must have seemed to them a no-win proposition. If they sold and the brewery was a success, they lost important market share points, and if it was a failure, they would be maligned by the community for letting such a thing happen. Furthermore, if they did not sell, they would be accused of sacrificing jobs to feed their greed. It was a situation that must have caused some uneasy times for Molson's western operations.

In the long run, the perceived community benefits of keeping the brewery open were the decisive factors and Molson agreed to the sale in January 1991. The first GW beer came out of the facility in March of that same year and the Lager and the Light were, to say the least, instant successes. While it is normal for a new brand of Canadian beer to soar in sales immediately following its launch, the GW case was an extreme example of that "introduction curve." Within one weekend, says McCann, what the brewery thought would be a three-week supply of beer sold out completely and, by the end of the week, there was virtually no GW beer left in the province.

While the popularity of the Great Western brands has settled down since then, the brewery owners easily passed their goal of a six to seven percent market share within two years and, according to McCann, were holding between ten and 12 percent of the total Saskatchewan beer sales by the spring of 1993. And all this occurred prior to their entry into the draught beer market.

The key to the GW success, says McCann, has been innovation and local focus. The former factor has resulted in moves like the GW technicians assembling a million-dollar canning line from assorted parts for $300,000, while the latter, evident in their proud use of the words "Saskatchewan's Own" on their labels, has delivered them tremendous support from longtime residents of the province.

The pride of ownership is almost tangible in the Great Western brewery as workers who have toiled for others all of their lives now have a stake in the entire operation. Admitting that he is still not completely used to the idea of owning the brewery, Kitz says that it is a thrill when he sees the GW television spots that were launched in the spring of 1993 and realizes that it is his own advertising that he is watching.

And that is one experience of which he will likely never get enough.

SCOREBOARD

Gibbs Ale (5% vol.)

Medium gold in colour with a sweet caramel malt aroma cut by bitter
and oaky hopping. The full, sweet and peachy start precedes a slightly
sugary body of canned peach, caramel malt and floral hop. The bittersweet candied finish carries sour, rooty hop notes. ★½

Great Western Gold (6.5% vol.)

Medium gold-coloured with a bittersweet malt and fresh hay aroma.
The sharply sweet and caramelly start leads to a full body of candied
malt, grassy hop and touches of orange brandy before a strongly
alcoholic finish. ★★

Great Western Light (4% vol.)

Light gold in colour with a sweet and sugary grain nose. A heavily carbonic and lightly sweet start with citric notes heads in to a light body
of off-dry graininess and candied lemon peel. The cereal finish is quick
and dry. ★

GW Lager (5% vol.)

Light to medium gold in colour with a sweetish grainy nose carrying
light, woody hopping and a hint of root. The somewhat sugary start
precedes a toasted grain body with a light, grassy sweetness, cereal
notes and a hint of sour orange. The taste bitters through the finish
with a heavier roasted grain taste and woody hop notes. ★½

Natural Draft (5% vol.)

Medium gold-coloured with a sweet and peachy nose holding
caramelized sugar and floral notes. A sweet and sugary start with
strong butterscotch notes leads to a sweet and fruity body with canned
apricot and sour grass notes and a slightly drier, cereal finish. ★

Prairie 3.2 (3.2% vol.)

Light gold-coloured and slightly sweet in the fruity aroma holding perfumey
grain notes. A very light, sour grain start leads to a light, lemony grain body
where some slightly bitter hop appears before a strong cereal finish. ★

Saskatchewan Beer (5% vol.)

Light to medium gold-coloured with a very soft, sweet and perfumey malted grain aroma. A very carbonic, sweet-and-sour cereal start leads into a sugary grain body holding strong, sour citric notes and a bittersweet, grassy finish. ★

Western Dry (5.5% vol.)

Light to medium gold in colour with a sugary aroma carrying candied fruit notes. A bittersweet cereal start leads to a strongly sugary, malted grain body with light bitter and rooty hop notes. The sugary finish has cereal notes. ★

Ontario

Algonquin Brewing Company

LOCATION:	*(Brewery) One Old Brewery Lane, Formosa, Ontario N0G 1W0 (Offices) 1270 Central Parkway West, Mississauga, Ontario L5C 4P4*
PHONE:	*(Brewery) 519-367-2995, (Offices) 905-949-0790, (fax) 905-949-1076*
OWNERS:	*Kaneff Holdings (50%), Drew Knox, Rob Knox, Allan Sneath & Evan Hayter (50%)*
PRESIDENT:	*Evan Hayter*
VP MARKETING:	*Drew Knox*
BREWER:	*Jack Massey*
BREWING CAPACITY:	*80,000 hl*
TOURS:	*To begin in the spring of 1994; call for details*
BRANDS:	*Algonquin Light, Bank's Lager, Bruce County Lager (regional), Country Lager, Formosa Bavarian Bock (seasonal), Formosa Draft, Formosa Draft Light, Marconi's European Lager, Royal Amber Lager, Special Reserve Ale*

"If you don't have problems, you go out and buy yourself one." With that tongue-in-cheek attitude, Ignaf "Iggy" Kaneff, the man whose Kaneff Properties is responsible for the building of much of Toronto's suburbs, took the plunge into brewery ownership by becoming a partner in one of Canada's largest small brewers.

The time was the spring of 1988 and the catalyst for the move was an old, dilapidated building in the small, rural town of Formosa south of the Bruce Peninsula and northwest of Toronto. That building was the historic Formosa brewery, a site for Ontario brewing from 1876 until it was closed, apparently for good, at the end of 1971.

The purchase of the brewery was not an anticipated event for the principals of the Algonquin Brewing Company, but it was nonetheless a welcome one. One, indeed, that transformed a small marketing company with two contract-brewed beers into a force in provincial brewing.

The original company was The Pinetree Group, a vehicle designed for the selling of two contract-brewed Canadian beers in the United States. Evan Hayter, a former in-house marketer for Carling O'Keefe, got the idea when he investigated the lucrative American imported beer market and concluded that two properly positioned brews that played on the "great outdoors" theme would likely fare well south of the border.

For his project, Hayter enlisted the help of Allan Sneath and Rob Knox, as well as the interest, but not the active assistance of Drew Knox —at the time still employed by Carling.

With two brands—Algonquin Special Reserve Ale and Canadian Light —brewed for them by Carling, Pinetree entered the U.S. market at a New York City food show in November 1987. By early 1988, however, word reached them about the availability of the Formosa brewery, and the small marketers became the small brewers.

As historic and quaint as the Formosa brewery was, it was also a mess after years of neglect, and capital was desperately needed if it was ever to be made into a proper brewery again. As it happened, the group shared an accountant with Kaneff Properties and, after two meetings, hands were shaken with Iggy Kaneff and his associate Eric McKnight, bringing them both into the company.

Renovation and construction of the old building took, to say the least, longer than any of the men expected, but by October 1989, brewing had begun once again in the sleepy town of Formosa.

After launching the ale, lager and light in the fall of that year, the thinkers at Algonquin took a mind to resurrecting the old Formosa Brewing labels. The only problem was that Molson, which had bought out Formosa Brewing in 1973, owned the rights to all the Formosa brand names. Algonquin, however, had an ace in the hole: the copyright to the name "Canadian Light," a moniker Molson was quite anxious to get a hold of because without it, they were unable to introduce a light version of their flagship lager, Canadian.

A swap was arranged and, by late 1990, Formosa Draft was released, a move that, according to Drew Knox, tripled the company's sales almost immediately.

Since then, Algonquin has more than doubled their product line with a light, a seasonal bock, a couple of licensing deals and a couple of new and original brands. And, in the spring of 1993, they beat all of Ontario's brewers to the punch with the release of their five-litre, take-home draught keg.

Next on the slate for the busy brewers? According to Iggy Kaneff, the time is right to build a brewery in Bulgaria. It looks as if, once again, Iggy is looking for a new problem.

SCOREBOARD

Algonquin Light (4% vol.)

Pale to light gold in colour with a citric grain and wet hay nose. The slightly sweet and corny start leads to a bittersweet body of pronounced grain and soft sugar coupled with mild acidity and a light, grassy hop. The taste turns slightly drier in a still-grainy finish. ★½

Banks Lager (5% vol.)

Light gold in colour with a lightly vegetal, sweet-and-sour aroma holding mild hints of citrus. The carbonic and brown sugary start leads to a sweet and rather chewy body with strong grain notes and notes of faintly woody hop. There is distinct grassiness in an otherwise sweet and quick finish. ★

Bruce County Lager (5% vol.)

Light gold-coloured with a light aroma of fresh grass and sweet grain. A sweet, light grain start leads into a very creamy and sweet body moderated by a touch of citrus. The finish sours to an acidic and biting end. ★

Country Lager (5% vol.)

Light gold in colour with some light hop leaf notes in the otherwise grainy and sweet aroma. The creamy body has a light, slightly lactic start leading into a generally sweet malted grain flavour with a bit of leafy hop and some grassy notes before a slightly bitter and rooty finish. ★½

Formosa Springs Bavarian Bock (6% vol.)

Rust-coloured with a caramel and candied orange aroma. The sweet start has sour cherry and molasses notes rising through the taste to a sour, medicinal second half and an acidic, cherry pit finish. ★½

Formosa Springs Draft (5% vol.)

Light gold in colour with a faintly hopped nose carrying grassy notes mixed with the sweet grain. The sweet-and-sour grain body begins grassy and sweet but is buoyed by some lightly woody hop in the middle leading into an acidic finish that has some hop providing a slight bitterness. ★½

Formosa Springs Light (4% vol.)

Pale gold in colour with a mildly sweet and slightly lemony grain nose. It is light-bodied with an acidic, citric grain start heading into a body strongly dominated by cereal and a lightly sour, still very grainy finish. ★

Marconi's European Lager (5% vol.)
Pale to light gold-coloured with a full, fresh-cut grass and grain nose.
The sweet, sugary start heads to a creamed corn body balanced by sour
hop notes and a lightly acidic, grassy and confectionery finish. ★

Royal Amber Lager (5% vol.)
Light copper in colour with a sweet-and-sour aroma carrying fragrant
hop and faint maraschino cherry notes. A creamy, off-dry front leads to
a malty, caramel body with grass and spicy grain notes. The bittersweet
and rooty finish carries some spice notes through to the end. ★★

Special Reserve Ale (5% vol.)
Amber-coloured and sweet and fruity in the nose with notes of cherry,
passion fruit and caramel. The sweet-and-sour body carries a lightly
oaky start into a body with some fruitiness (apricot, bitter orange)
tempered by a light, woody hopping. The taste dries out somewhat in
the bitter and slightly alcoholic finish. ★★

Brick Brewing Company

LOCATION:	*(Brewery) 181 King Street South, Waterloo, Ontario N2J 1P7 (Offices) 219 Dufferin Street, Suite 100, Toronto, Ontario M6K 1Y9*
PHONE:	*519-576-9100, (Toronto) 416-532-5949, (fax) 416-532-0280*
OWNERS:	*Publicly traded, majority control by Jim Brickman*
PRESIDENT:	*Jim Brickman*
BREWING HEAD:	*Steve Smith*
START-UP BREWER:	*Harald Sowade*
SALES MANAGER:	*Fred Gallagher*
BREWING CAPACITY:	*73,500 hl*
TOURS:	*Call to schedule*
BRANDS:	*Amber Dry, Anniversary Bock (seasonal), Henninger Kaiser Pils, Pacific Real Draft, Premium Lager, Red Baron Lager, Waterloo Dark*

Jim Brickman attributes his formation of Ontario's first modern micro-brewery to what he terms a "drinking problem." Not that Brickman got bombed one night and decided to invest all his cash in the venture, but, rather, he had a problem finding a beer he enjoyed drinking in the province.

It was the early 1980s and the powers that be (Molson, Carling and Labatt) had decided that the market wanted increasingly light-tasting and homogeneous brews. In marked contrast to that attitude, Brickman felt that there was a definite segment of the same market, himself included, that longed for a full-flavoured, all-barley malt beer.

Brickman's background was in the packaged goods side of marketing, an ironic twist considering that Canadian major brewery beer sales—the exact area Brickman felt was failing him and other beer drinkers—were, and are, so heavily marketing-driven. Even with no practical brewing experience, Brickman could see a gap in the beer supply lines, a hole in the market that he felt could be filled by his beer.

So the first four years of the 1980s were spent in research as Brickman toured some 60 breweries around the globe and discussed beer with some of the top people in the small-brewery business, including numerous conversations with American craft-brewing pioneer Fritz Maytag of Anchor Brewing. One of his biggest surprises, however, occurred right at home in Ontario.

Brickman had assumed that there existed rolls upon rolls of bureaucratic red tape designed to prevent the establishment of new Ontario breweries. It was with a shock, therefore, that he discovered a distinct absence of legal impediments. It appeared that the only reason no one had established a micro-brewery in the province was that no one had thought to do so.

Of course, at the time, both Upper Canada and Wellington County were also in the works but there was no contact between the groups. In fact, Brickman says that he found out about Upper Canada the same way the rest of the province did—through the newspaper.

Deciding that the community-minded, ethnic German base of the Kitchener-Waterloo region would be well suited to his European lager brewing plans, Brickman purchased a historic, yellow-brick building in the shadow of Labatt's huge Waterloo brewery in February 1984 and began renovations to turn it into a brewery in May of that same year.

On December 18, 1984, Brickman's birthday, the first Brick Premium Lager, and the first of a new wave of Ontario beer, rolled out of the brewery and onto the palates of thirsty beer drinkers. Like all of Brick's subsequent products, that first brew was bottom-fermented because that is the way Brickman likes it. Not a lover of ales, Brickman has said in the past that he only brews the styles he likes, and that necessarily excludes all top-fermented brews.

On the first anniversary of the brewery, Brick came out with their first seasonal Anniversary Bock and followed it up a half a year later with Red Baron, a beer brewed in more of a national style and with a mind to serving the tastes of a greater portion of the local community.

With an awareness of popular beer market trends, Brick launched their Amber Dry, a beer that was originally intended to serve the draught market alone, in March 1991. Only the subsequent success of Amber, according to Brickman, forced the brewery to bottle it.

In the wake of Heineken's closure of Hamilton's Amstel brewery, Brick took over the licence to brew the brands of Germany's Henninger Brewing, choosing to brew only the Kaiser Pilsner label, and after the West Coast Potter Distilling (owners of Granville Island Brewing—see separate entry under British Columbia) decided to close their St. Catharines operations, Brick began selling their version of Pacific Real Draft, as well.

Brick's Toronto operations head, Bill May, likes to answer the phone with "the little Brick Brewing Company" and, when they began production at 4,200 hectolitres in 1984, that was actually true. If the brewery's tremendous rate of growth and expansion continues, however, May might soon have to change his tune.

SCOREBOARD

Amber Dry (5.5% vol.)
Cognac-coloured with a sweet, malty nose that contains notes of caramel, woody hop and even faint grape. The start is slightly bitter and hoppy before moving to a sweet-and-sour, lightly fruity body and a quick finish with some rooty flavours and a trace of licorice. ★½

Anniversary Bock '92-'93 (6.6% vol.)
Coloured deep amber with hints of ruby port tones and a complex, grapey malt nose with molasses and berry notes. The full and round body has pronounced cherry malt with anise and rich tobacco notes and is sweet and slightly syrupy without being heavy. The finish bitters slightly with some fruit pit. ★★½

Henninger Kaiser Pilsner Lager (5% vol.)
Light gold colour with a sweet, hoppy grain nose holding herbal notes. The grassy start with sucrose notes leads to a hoppy and floral body that bitters gradually through the taste and becomes rooty toward the finish, which is largely sour and vegetal. ★★

Pacific Real Draft (5% vol.)

Pale to light gold in colour with a sweet, canned corn aroma. The sweet and carbonic start contains raw grain flavours and notes of bitter lime prior to a bittersweet body of grass and sugar with more bitter citrus notes. The finish is sour and rooty. ★

Premium Lager (5% vol.)

The brewery's flagship brand with a light to medium gold colour and a delicate, perfumey and hoppy aroma. The start is lightly sweet with a soft grain character leading to a dominant, grassy and bitter hop body. A little too creamy for its style, it finishes with a not-too-rooty bitterness and light acidity. ★★

Red Baron (5% vol.)

Light gold-coloured and sweet and grainy in the aroma with some floral hop notes. The taste starts softly with sweet grain and faint hop notes before becoming sugary in the middle with some elements of rooty hop and sour grain holding forth. The bittering hop shows in the finish, which holds a slight rootiness along with the residual sweetness. ★

Waterloo Dark (draught only, 5.4% vol.)

Dark brown-coloured with a lightly sweet aroma of molasses, soft notes of coffee and some faint hints of burnt toast. The sweet and sugary start has some light, roasted grain notes before it moves into a roasted and slightly burnt grain body with notes of demerara sugar and light, sweet coffee. The sweet and sugary finish continues the coffee notes with a touch of anise. ★½

Conners Brewery

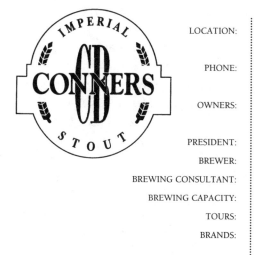

LOCATION:	*227 Bunting Road, Unit J,*
	St. Catharines, Ontario L2M 3Y2
PHONE:	*905-988-9363, (Toronto)*
	416-488-1406, (fax) 905-682-4430
OWNERS:	*Glen Dalzell, Marc Bedard,*
	silent partners
PRESIDENT:	*Glen Dalzell*
BREWER:	*Liam McKenna*
BREWING CONSULTANT:	*Doug Morrow*
BREWING CAPACITY:	*15,000 hl*
TOURS:	*Sunday, 3:00 p.m.; on request for groups*
BRANDS:	*Ale, Best Bitter, Premium Lager,*
	Special Draft, Stout

Conners is one of two breweries in Ontario (Great Lakes being the other —see separate entry) that have pulled Lazarus acts by folding and resurfacing later on under new ownership. If resurrecting a failed brewery in tough economic times appears to be an idea of questionable value, it will come as quite a surprise to Marc Bedard and Glen Dalzell.

The original Conners sprang up in a tiny Mississauga brewery just west of Toronto shortly after the Ontario micro-brewery frontier had been broken in 1985. It produced draught and one-litre bottle versions of Best Bitter, Ale and, later, Pale Ale and Stout. Buoyed by an excellent reception in the marketplace, the brewery expanded its operations into Toronto and Thunder Bay within a couple of years.

The honeymoon was not to last, however, and soon the Thunder Bay brewery broke from the parent company to become an independent named Renegade (since closed), the original Mississauga operation was moth-balled and Conners was in deep trouble. In a final attempt to stay solvent, Conners revamped their image and changed to 341 ml glass bottles before finally giving in to the irresistible forces of bankruptcy in mid-1990.

As the original Conners was floundering, Bedard was working as a financial analyst and Dalzell was employed in the petroleum industry. Neither had any brewing experience but they did share one very impor-tant characteristic: a desire to change careers.

When Bedard came across the auction notice for Conners in *The Globe and Mail*, he phoned his friend Dalzell and the two decided to bid for the business. Shortly thereafter, the partners had their own brewing company, if not an actual brewery.

The reason they lacked this essential component was that, having seen the former Toronto brewing operations of Conners, the pair had enough business savvy to know that the brewery was far too large for what they required and therefore chose not to bid on the building or equipment. Insofar as a brewing company without a brewery is akin to a cheese shop *sans* cheese, Dalzell and Bedard went after the bones of another micro-brewery to complete their business venture.

This time, the two men headed southwest of the big city to St. Catharines where production at Sculler Brewing had ground to a halt some time earlier. On reaching a purchase agreement with the disenchanted president of Sculler, Mike Driscoll, Conners Brewing was officially reborn in late November 1990.

The first goal of the newest faces in Ontario brewing was to protect the integrity of their beer and, to this end, they enlisted the services of the original Conners brewer, Doug Morrow. Obviously enthusiastic about the prospect of seeing his recipes in use once again, Morrow took to the small brewery right away and, by the last week of January, had his first test brew in the tank.

Conners's most popular brand had always been their bitter, so it was only logical that the new Conners released Best Bitter as their first brand in March 1991. Dalzell and Bedard were half expecting a negative or, at least, tentative reaction from Toronto-area bars and restaurant owners due to the questionable practices of the old sales force toward the end of the brewery's existence; the partners were pleasantly surprised when they received very good feedback upon their first foray into the market.

With a positive reaction to the Bitter under their belts, Dalzell and Bedard quickly followed it up with the launch of their Ale later that same month. As summer is not exactly the best season for stout sales, the introduction of their Imperial Stout was delayed until the fall of that year and the most commercially oriented of their brews, Special Draft, completed the quartet of original Conners brands in the summer of 1992. In early 1993, the brewery entered the bottom-fermented beer market with their Premium Lager.

Since the brewery opened, they have expanded their operations three times for a full tripling of their brewing capacity, changed their labels from the virtually unreadable script bequeathed to them by the old Conners and radically altered their packaging. Their young, energetic and enthusiastic brewer completed the transformation from the old to the new.

If nothing else, at least the story of Conners proves that, in brewing at least, there can be life after death.

SCOREBOARD

Ale (5% vol.)

Earthy copper colour with a fragrant nose combining caramel notes with both floral and fruity aromas. Sweet-and-sour start with some light cherry notes mixing with molasses and hop. The hop rises in the middle making for a full-bodied character with notes of fruit, caramel, and bitter hop with nutty notes. Bitter, earthy and slightly alcoholic finish. ★★½

Best Bitter (5% vol.)

Caramel-coloured with golden tones. The full nose is ripe with the sweet-and-sour aromas of the Cascade hop and a sweet hint of grain. Its body is characterized by a sweet, fruity taste with apple and hop notes and a pleasantly bitter finish with lingering caramel flavours. ★★½

Premium Lager (5% vol.)

Medium gold in colour with an aroma that is a mix of fresh hay and light bittering hop. It is medium-bodied with a slightly sweet and creamy start leading to a sweeter, malt middle, which then eases to rooty, bitter hop. The finish, while significantly grainy, carries a grassy bitterness and a lingering sweetness at the very end. ★★

Special Draft (5% vol.)

Medium gold colour with a sweet, slightly woody and hoppy nose. Its somewhat woody start leads to a sweet, leafy and slightly grainy body with faint apple notes. Typically Conners in flavour but lighter and drier. Some hop and slight maltiness in the finish. ★½

Stout (5% vol.)

An ebony brew with a strong coffee nose holding bittersweet chocolate notes. The sweet, dark chocolate start leads to a creamy, bittersweet body dominated by mocha flavours. Espresso bitterness characterizes the finish. Complex and forceful despite some toning down of the character from the previous year. ★★★

Creemore Springs Brewery Ltd.

LOCATION:	*139 Mill Street, Creemore, Ontario*
	L0M 1G0
PHONE:	*705-466-2531, (fax) 705-466-3306*
OWNERS:	*John Wiggins, Sylvia Wiggins, Russ*
	Thornton, Kurtis Zeng & Don Mingay
PRESIDENT:	*John Wiggins*
BREWER:	*Kurtis Zeng*
CONSULTING BREWER:	*Doug Babcook*
BREWING CAPACITY:	*18,000 hl*
TOURS:	*On request*
BRANDS:	*Creemore Springs Lager*

The story of the Creemore Springs Brewery is the story of one man and one beer. That man is John Wiggins; the beer is his Creemore Springs Lager.

With a background in advertising and design, Wiggins would appear more suited to the big business of the major breweries than the peculiar world of Ontario micro-brewing but, for him, the move to small brewery ownership was a logical one proceeding from his enchantment with rural life.

Prior to the brewing phase of his life, Wiggins ran an advertising consultancy business from the back door of his farmhouse in the Collingwood area, located roughly two hours north of Toronto. Tired of making that long drive on an all-too-regular basis, he began to investigate the possibilities of micro-brewing in the summer of 1986, after Ontario's pioneer brewers had begun to garner some well-deserved press.

According to Wiggins, the first decision he made was to pursue the production of a superior-quality beer and, to realize that end, he recognized a need for superior-quality people. Mindful that he would not be able to afford the permanent services of a top brewer, Wiggins then opted for the next best thing, a top brewing consultant.

Doug Babcook was, at one time, the vice-president of brewing for Stroh Brewing in the United States and, upon his retirement, had formed a consultancy. Babcook had just finished work with a now-defunct brewery on Prince Edward Island when he managed to hook up with Wiggins. As fate would have it, according to Wiggins, they had similar ideas on the best way to establish a small brewery, with Babcook especially excited by the fledgling company's commitment to quality in all regards.

Ever mindful of appearances, Wiggins chose an old hardware store located on the main drag of the sleepy rural town of Creemore as the future home of his brewery. If it was going to be a cottage brewery, apparently it was also going to have a cottagey appearance.

The quaint small-town feel of the brewery was important, but Wiggins was more interested in making as perfectly functional a brewery as possible and, therefore, put Babcook in charge of the engineers designing the project. The result was a small operation "shoehorned" into an even smaller space with a maximum expansion potential of 18,000 hectolitres, not even enough to dent one percent of the provincial market.

Of course, the most important aspect was the beer and, for that, Wiggins chose the famous flavour of the original pilsner, Pilsner Urquell, as his goal.

Once Babcook had developed the recipe and the brewery, with its 7,500 hectolitre capacity, was under way, the next step was to sell the beer. This was where Wiggins, with his diverse marketing skills, really hit his stride.

As he could not afford a sales staff, Wiggins made the decision to limit his market for the 12 to 18 months to the local Collingwood area and, for the licensees, exclusively draught beer. The theory, he says, was that draught sales meant the bar or restaurant owner was making a commitment to the brand.

Within a short time and, as Wiggins says, "partly by design," a waiting list for Creemore taps was born that stretched all the way into the city of Toronto. Before too long, it was time to hit the big city with his beer.

Using the Danforth Avenue beer bar Allen's as his first account and city base, Wiggins continued to foster the myth of Creemore in Toronto, picking and choosing his sales sites carefully so as to draw the most interest from the smallest number of accounts.

Creemore's famous and almost mythic waiting list continues to this day, but Wiggins downplays its role in the brewery's success. The real key, he says, is the family feeling the company creates through its personalized sales calls, brewery-fresh deliveries and commitment to the licensee.

As for Wiggins himself, he has intentionally structured his business plan to make himself redundant and leave the operations of the Creemore Springs Brewery to his three-man management team of brewer Kurtis Zeng, sales manager Howard Thompson and Gordon Fuller.

Not that he's contemplating slowing down at all. Having made his impact on the local brewing trade, John Wiggins has now partnered with another John, John Denbock, in the Brother John's Cellars cidery. As Wiggins puts it, he's simply too young to stop now.

SCOREBOARD

Creemore Springs Lager (5% vol.)

Golden-brown in colour with a dry, leafy and fruity nose holding green apple and faint orange notes. The soft start is lightly sweet with tangerine notes and leads into a very flowery body with a round and fruity (peach, orange) sweetness cut in the second half by a leafy hop bitterness. The bitter hopping continues in the faintly woody finish, which also carries some remaining notes of canned peaches. ★★★

Great Lakes Brewing Co. Inc.

LOCATION:	*30 Queen Elizabeth Boulevard, Etobicoke, Ontario, M8Z 1L8*
PHONE:	*416-255-4510, (fax) 416-255-4907*
OWNER:	*Peter Bulut*
PRESIDENT:	*Peter Bulut*
BREWER:	*Bruce Cornish*
CONSULTING BREWER:	*Viv Jones*
BREWING CAPACITY:	*22,000 hl*
TOURS:	*Group tours for 15 or more; call ahead for scheduling*
BRANDS:	*Great Lakes Lager*

To say that the story of Great Lakes Brewing is an unusual one is to miss half the point; this is one brewery that, through both of its incarnations, has done things in a dramatically and decidedly different fashion. In its original form, Great Lakes was the only brewery in the province to work purely from malt extract, something they did surprisingly well. In its second coming, the brewery has placed a very high level of importance on draught accounts outside of the normal purview of micro-breweries, concentrating on, to paraphrase one employee, everything from strip clubs to fine dining restaurants.

The latter approach appears to be working much better than the former.

The original Great Lakes was the brainchild of current brewer Bruce Cornish and four other partners, none of whom are still involved with the company in any way. Much smaller than today's version, it was, however, every bit as enigmatic.

Established in Brampton, Ontario, in late 1986, Great Lakes I brewed two brands, Great Lakes Lager and Unicorn Ale, bottling both of them in the one-litre plastic bottle and concentrating on the home consumer market. The brands were characterful and well-bodied to the point that they almost belied their extract origins. Unfortunately, they were not also self-sustaining and the brewery was forced to close its doors when the owners ran out of money in December 1990.

Resigned to the sale of the brewery but still holding a glimmer of hope for a renaissance, Cornish met Peter Bulut through their respective real estate agents in the early months of 1991 and, through persistence and salesmanship, convinced the construction trade magnate to try his hand at the brewing game.

The first move for the new Great Lakes was to reformulate the lager for a full-mash brewing system and a more commercial appeal. This was accomplished with the help of former Upper Canada brewer and now consultant Viv Jones, who has reportedly had less success developing a recipe for an ale that would suit the new company's corporate tastes.

The next step was to locate a larger space in which to brew, as this revived company had much loftier goals than its predecessor. The new brewery was located on the north side of the Queen Elizabeth Way, the main commuter highway for downtown Toronto traffic, and the move was complete by the beginning of 1992.

In its first year, Great Lakes claims to have sold over 10,000 hectolitres of their lager, all on draught and with little in the way of public exposure. Sales manager Annetta Bulut estimates that up to 40 percent of their accounts are "house" taps, either billed as the establishment's own brew or sold as generic draught, and says that success has been in attracting establishments that are not traditionally micro-oriented.

While Cornish admits that it sometimes bothers him to be an employee of the company he founded, he is nonetheless happy to see his "baby" still on the go and hopes that he may be able to buy shares in the business in the future.

Either way, Great Lakes appears ready and able to quietly and unconventionally continue brewing and selling their beer, just the way they have all along.

SCOREBOARD

Great Lakes Lager (draught only, 5% vol.)

Light gold in colour with a sweet and grainy aroma holding light hay notes. The very carbonic and mildly sugary start holds sweet grass and very light lemon notes before moving into a sweet-and-sour grain body with notes of candied lemon peel in the front and grassy sourness in the back. The finish is acidic, rooty and grassy with lingering notes of refined sugar. ★

Hart Breweries Limited

LOCATION:	*175 Industrial Avenue, Carleton Place, Ontario K7C 3V7*
PHONE:	*613-253-4278, (fax) 613-253-3705*
OWNERS:	*Lorne Hart, Gary Lawton, Frits Bosman, Leo Richer*
PRESIDENT:	*Lorne Hart*
BREWER:	*Keith Hart*
CONSULTING BREWER:	*Alan Pugsley*
BREWING CAPACITY:	*10,000 hl*
TOURS:	*Sundays, noon–5:00 p.m.; or on request for groups*
BRANDS:	*Amber Ale, Cream Ale, Dragon's Breath Pale Ale*

The romance of the micro-brewing industry has drawn many a good man and woman into the fray. Unfortunately, even with the best market research, brewing experts and facilities, that romance can often lose its appeal, at least temporarily, in the face of twelve-hour days and frustrating weeks.

Just ask Lorne Hart.

When Hart was offered the choice of relocation or early retirement from his position as an engineer, he chose the latter and began to contemplate his future in the folksy Ottawa Valley region. With his extensive background in home brewing and wine making, it was quite natural that Hart would think of the micro-brewing industry as a potential second career. After a brainstorming session with old friends Leo Richer and Gary Lawton on July 20, 1989, the concept for Hart Breweries was born.

In this business, however, the road between concept and realization is a long and winding one indeed and the new partners soon recognized that there were many stages to go through before they would drink the first bottles of their own ale.

After researching the viability of their operations and consulting a number of veterans of the brewing industry like Peter McAuslan and John Wiggins (of Brasserie McAuslan and Creemore Brewing respectively), they took the first concrete step in setting up their brewery. They obtained the services of a professional brewing consultant. For this job, Hart, Lawton and Richer got one of the most recognized and prolific beer professionals in eastern North America, Alan Pugsley of Peter Austin & Partners (Contracts) Ltd.

The story of Pugsley is itself one of great interest for Canadian beer aficionados, since the man's name pops up in connection with no fewer than six breweries and brewpubs in this country.

A brewing *wunderkind* of sorts, Pugsley's progress from his apprenticeship with Peter Austin at England's Ringwood Brewery to his present status as company chair and majority owner has been impressive to say the least. At the tender age of 34, he can now claim direct or indirect involvement in over 60 breweries on four continents and has earned the respect of the industry for his tireless devotion to his work and expert recipe compositions.

Pugsley originally became involved with the project in October 1989, when the brewery was still very much in its infancy. As the development grew, so did Pugsley's involvement until, in June 1991, he contracted to formulate Hart Amber Ale and serve as brew master for the first year of operation.

The next progression, seeing as they hadn't a physical structure in which to brew yet, was to find a builder and a site. For the former, the partners got lucky; in October 1990, they met Frits Bosman who not only signed on to build their brewery, but was so enthusiastic about the project that he became the fourth shareholder, as well.

By late 1990, the brewery was definitely on track and the group purchased most of the assets of the defunct Ottawa Valley Brewing Company. Then, on June 10, 1991, with tanks in hand, they broke ground for their new brewery in an industrial centre in Carleton Place.

The first official beer flowed out of Hart on September 27, 1991, and the mood of the partners was jubilant. Unfortunately, as with so many new-product launches, the glee was quick to pass.

The original intent of Hart's owners was, as their market research told them, to concentrate on the Ottawa Valley region and leave the Metro Toronto and surrounding areas alone. But while marketing pundits can easily assure you of one thing, the reality is often the exact opposite, and this was what Hart faced. For despite good reviews and press all around, the small size of the Ottawa market and the pathetically slow start of the summer of 1992 soon had the partners scrambling to stay above water.

In mid-August, Hart was forced to blitz the Toronto market at both the bar and Brewers Retail levels and, a couple of months later, the contract-brewing of Dragon's Breath Pale Ale for the Kingston Brewing Company had begun. Soon after followed the introduction of Hart Cream Ale, an all-ale cream developed while the Dragon's Breath was in its testing stages.

By all reports, the two new brands have met with relative enthusiasm in the southern Ontario market and Hart's recently appointed general manager, Jonathan Hatchell, has been enjoying a certain amount of success in his promotion of the company's brews.

Why, it's almost enough to make even Lorne Hart believe again in the romance of his adopted industry.

SCOREBOARD

Amber Ale (5% vol.)

Orangey-amber in colour with a sweet, hoppy nose carrying hints of fruit (apricot, plum), wood and honey. The faintly sweet start holds woody hop and traces of fruitiness leading to an explosion of woody hop in the bitter centre and fruit (berry, grape, banana) in the second half with a bitter and hoppy fruit pit finish. ★★½

Cream Ale (4.5% vol.)

Deep gold-coloured with a rich, thick aroma full of fruit (apricot, orange, peach), caramel and floral notes. The moderately sweet start with notes of confectioners' sugar and orange peel leads to a body with candied orange and green plum flavours in the front and earthy and bitter hop in the back. The finish is bitter, woody and lasting. ★★

Dragon's Breath Pale Ale (4.5% vol.)

Medium gold in colour with a perfumey hop nose holding notes of candied apple. The very full body blends rooty and bitter hopping with caramel malt and some fruitiness (peach, apricot). Bitter, earthy finish. ★★½

Lakeport Brewing Corporation

LOCATION:	*201 Burlington Street East, Hamilton, Ontario L8L 4H2*
PHONE:	*905-523-4200, (fax) 905-523-6564*
OWNERS:	*Bill Sharpe, Cott Beverages*
PRESIDENT:	*Bill Sharpe*
VICE-PRESIDENT:	*Vince Lubertino*
BREWER:	*Adam Foye*
BREWING CAPACITY:	*420,000 hl*
TOURS:	*Sundays on request; booked in advance otherwise*
BRANDS:	*Around Ontario Lager, Around Ontario Light, Laker, Laker Light, Lone Star, Lone Star Light, Pabst Blue Ribbon, President's Choice Draft, President's Choice Light Draft, President's Choice Strong Draft*

When the famous Dutch brewer Heineken made the decision to shut down their Hamilton-based Amstel operation, there was a great deal of speculation over who would buy the brewery as well as a court challenge over who had the rights to Amstel's brands in Canada. When the dust finally did settle, Molson had the Amstel and Amstel Light labels and Lakeport had the brewery. And Bill Sharpe had been at the centre of both deals.

A veteran of the brewing industry, Sharpe had been with Molson's imported and specialty brands wing, Santa Fé Beverages, when the Hamilton brewery closed its doors. Sharpe says that he saw the closure as an ideal opportunity to grab two well-known brands for his employers and orchestrated the licensing arrangement for the Amstel brands with Heineken. Not too much later, when Sharpe found himself a victim of Molson's own downsizing plans and was asked to leave Santa Fé, his mind drifted back to the Hamilton brewery.

According to Sharpe, he had the deal to buy the plant sealed within days in early 1992 and then went out to raise capital interest in the place. He must have knocked on the right doors because, before long, he had the prominent soft drink company Cott Beverages investing in his plans.

Those plans were largely based on Sharpe's history in the West Coast beer business when he was president of the Fort Brewing Company in Prince George, British Columbia (now Pacific Western—see separate entry under British Columbia). In those days, Sharpe had set the industry on its ear when he introduced a competitive pricing policy that undercut the major breweries. Even though Sharpe says that particular episode eventually resulted in the big brewers ganging up on him, he thought that the time was right to try that strategy again, this time in Ontario.

Sharpe's first challenge at Lakeport was to use up a large float of old Amstel glass bottles so that he could launch his main brands in the industry's new, standardized bottle. For this purpose, his first brand was a mainstream lager in a non-returnable bottle that was priced at the lowest possible cost allowed in the province. The beer, called Around Ontario, was packaged to capitalize on the 125th birthday celebrations of Canada and Sharpe hoped to sell much of his stock at the Canada-U.S. border to returning tourists. When the beer did not sell as well as he had anticipated, Sharpe sold his surplus off to Russia and introduced the former Amstel brands Laker and Laker Light.

Just before Christmas, 1992, Sharpe unveiled what must be considered his biggest coup: President's Choice (PC) Premium Draft Beer. Priced at the Ontario minimum, the bottled draft is a spin-off of Loblaws president Dave Nichol's phenomenally successful line of low-priced, "premium" goods that runs the gamut from cookies to laundry detergent.

With the solid reputation of the other President's Choice products behind his beer, Sharpe was virtually assured of receiving a huge response to the brand and receive it he did. In the spring of 1993, the PC Draft was joined by PC Strong Draft and PC Light Draft, both derivatives of the same beer that is the original President's Choice brand.

Along the way, Sharpe took enough time out from his dealings with Dave Nichol to organize licensing deals with Pabst (for their Blue Ribbon brand) and Heileman (Lone Star), both from the States and both also priced at the minimum. In the wake of the restructuring of Ontario's retail beer prices in the fall of 1993, Sharpe resurrected the Around Ontario brand, and added a light version.

What Sharpe's next move will be is anyone's guess, but with a still unused brewing capacity available through a summer of 1993 expansion, it is a safe bet that it will not be to rest on his laurels.

SCOREBOARD

Around Ontario Lager (4.8% vol.)

Light gold in colour with a very sweet, grainy aroma carrying bubble gum notes. Sour green grass and refined sugar flavours blend together in the very carbonic start prior to a fairly thin and sweet body that carries more fresh grass with some lightly toasted grain notes. The finish tastes strongly of cereal and adds a significant acidity. ★

Laker (5% vol.)

Light gold-coloured with a sweet grain aroma holding a hint of orange peel. The creamy, sweet and grainy body is offset by a touch of perfumey hop before moving to a sour, grapefruity finish. ★

Lone Star (5% vol.)

Light gold in colour with a sweet and sugary nose holding light licorice aromas. The creamy and mildly sugary start leads to a lightly fruity body (orange and peach) with a sweet grassiness and hints of icing sugar. The finish remains sweet but adds a touch of bittersweet nuttiness. ★

Pabst Blue Ribbon (5% vol.)

Light gold with a sweet, grainy nose having toffee and confectioners' sugar notes. The light body starts with a sugary cereal taste before a few sour and vegetal notes creep into the otherwise very sweet and creamy body. The very short finish carries icing sugar notes along with a light rooty sourness. ★

President's Choice Premium Draft (5% vol.)

Light gold in colour with sweet grain and leafy hop aromas in equal proportion. The sweet and very creamy body mixes perfumey hop with grain for a faintly lactic taste that bitters to a reasonably dry finish. ★½

Niagara Falls Brewing Company

LOCATION:	*6863 Lundy's Lane, Niagara Falls, Ontario L2G 1V7*
PHONE:	*905-356-BREW, 905-374-1166, (fax) 905-374-2930*
OWNERS:	*Mario & Bruno Criveller, Claude Corriveau, Wally Moroz*
PRESIDENT:	*Mario Criveller*
GENERAL MANAGER:	*Claude Corriveau*
BREWER:	*Wally Moroz*
CONSULTING BREWER:	*Harvey Hurlbutt*
BREWING CAPACITY:	*11,000 hl*
TOURS:	*2:00 p.m., 7 days a week; groups on request*
BRANDS:	*Brock Extra Stout, Eisbock (seasonal), Gritstone Ale, Niagara Falls Light, Niagara Falls Maple Wheat, Olde Jack Bitter Strong Ale, Trapper Lager*

Eisbock

For decades, tourists have descended on the southern Ontario community of Niagara Falls for the natural wonderment of the Falls and the man-made amusements surrounding the area. Lately, however, a relatively new spot has been attracting sightseers in the region—the Niagara Falls Brewing Company.

The brewery is the creation of Mario and Bruno Criveller, two brothers who came to Canada in 1977 after their brewery in the Ethiopian capital of Addis Ababa was nationalized. Following some involvement with other projects, including a deluxe chocolate shop, Niagara Falls Brewing was finally conceived in the fall of 1988.

The final project involved the two Crivellers, two active partners and five silent partners including a prominent Niagara region wine maker. Within a year and a half, however, this had been trimmed to six partners, Mario Criveller controlling the lion's share of the company with 60 percent of the holdings.

The other two active partners, Claude Corriveau and Wally Moroz, each came from the wine business and had a keen interest in making the move to brewing. However, since both were primarily wine makers and not brewers, the decision was made to hire retired brew master Harvey Hurlbutt as a consultant.

The first beer that the new brewery came up with was Trapper Premium Canadian Lager, a commercially styled brew intended to establish a place for the brewery amidst the light lager tastes that dominated the area. Even today, despite a growing portfolio of six brands and a general lack of enthusiasm for Trapper among many of the company's upper echelon, it remains the top seller for the brewery.

It was the brewery's second beer launch, however, that made the local beer community stand up and take notice. Having established themselves with a beer of pedestrian taste, the Crivellers, Corriveau and Moroz were anxious to brew something that would make them unique among Canadian brewers. They accomplished this in spades when Hurlbutt handed over the recipe for Eisbock, the first and, to that time, only beer of that style brewed outside of Germany.

The brewing method of cooling the beer until ice forms and then extracting the frozen water was both complicated and costly but, in the eyes of numerous beer connoisseurs, well worth the effort and expense. News of this sweet and strong (8% alcohol by volume) beer spread like wildfire and soon, despite the then $5.95 per 750 ml champagne bottle price tag, the brewery had a certified hit on its hands.

But good brewers never relax for too long and the decision was made to brew Eisbock as a seasonal specialty for winter only and proceed with plans to produce an ale or, as it turned out, two.

Now working in concert with Corriveau, Hurlbutt concocted a sweet, strong ale reminiscent of those brewed for Belgian tastes. The working name for the ale was Griststone and the idea was to brew something stronger than conventional Ontarian ales with a full body and identifiable character. What resulted, though, was a formidable beer with 7.2% alcohol by volume and some serious sweetness. Thus was born Olde Jack Bitter Strong Ale.

The search for Griststone, however, had not been abandoned, and the next try produced an ale a little closer to the original expectations. The problem this time resulted from the name which, it appeared, no one could pronounce! So the first "s" was dropped from the moniker and Gritstone Ale hit the market.

The next two labels to join the Niagara portfolio remain the least well known. Niagara Falls Light came on the scene in the summer of 1991; it is a 3.5% alcohol by volume draught-only derivative of Trapper that appears sporadically in the southern Ontario licensee market. Brock Extra Stout, a draught and bottled brew, came as part of the stout explosion of the winter of 1991 when the Ontario market suddenly grew from one stout (Labatt-produced Guinness) to five (Upper Canada, Wellington County and Conners in addition to Labatt and Niagara).

The latest move in Niagara's esoteric business strategy was the introduction of modern Ontario's first bottled maple beer: Maple Wheat. Originally conceived as one of three flavoured brews, Maple Wheat was to pave the way for strawberry and blueberry brews in the summer of 1992. Instead, labelling, listing and brewing capacity problems intervened and the Maple ended up as the sole member of the triad to make it to market.

It is hard to predict what will come next from what is arguably the most innovative and experimental brewery in Canada, but it is a good bet that, whatever it is, it won't be what you expect.

SCOREBOARD

Brock Extra Stout (5.6% vol.)
Jet-black in colour with a sweet chocolate and burnt grain nose. It has a soft and mildly sweet roasted grain start leading to a bittersweet dark chocolate and coffee body holding hazelnut notes. The finish has a prominent coffee flavour with a hint of black licorice. ★★★

Eisbock '92–'93 (8% vol.)
Very orangey-copper colour, bright and clear. The aroma is of bittersweet fruit (apricot, peach and perhaps even cherry) with evident but not notable hopping. The sweetish, fruity malt front holds hints of the full mouth-feel to come and the body holds a pronounced alcohol presence almost in the style of a barley wine. The bittering hop second half has rising alcohol to an almost liquorish finish. This beer has been better in past years (★★★★ in 1990) and the '90–'91 version was outstanding after having aged for two years. ★★★

Gritstone Ale (5.8% vol.)
Rust in colour with a malty, orange toffee nose holding the faintest hint of alcohol. The full, malt-generated body has a slightly confectionery sweetness and a good mouth-feel. A caramel start evolves to a fruity body faintly reminiscent of canned apricots. Alcohol and some bittering hop rise in the finish. ★★★

Maple Wheat (8.5% vol.)
Surprisingly complex for a flavoured beer, it has an understandably maple character that changes dramatically with its temperature. Cold, it has a light, sweet malt nose and a highly maple syrup body. Chilled, the aroma turns to a robust maple and the character becomes a mix of maple, malt and hop. At room temperature, the nose begins to resemble

that of a fruity brandy and the body develops to a burnt maple wood with the alcohol showing in the second half and finish. ★★★

Olde Jack Bitter Strong Ale (7.2% vol.)

Copper-coloured with a full, caramelly malt nose holding orange notes and traces of alcohol. The sweet, almost candied orange start precedes a fruity (orange, apricot) and bittersweet body with strong notes of brandy alongside some hints of toffee. The alcohol, which is evident throughout, rises sharply in the finish along with a mild bittering and some lingering fruit. ★★★

Trapper (5% vol.)

Light gold in colour with a somewhat sour grain nose bordering on grapefruit. It has a light, slightly creamy and predominantly grainy body with a mild, sweet corn start and a souring, rooty second half with a still-sour and leafy tang in the finish. ★$^{1}/_{2}$

Northern Breweries Ltd.

LOCATION:	*503 Bay Street, Sault Ste. Marie, Ontario P6A 5L9 (Site of offices and brewery, other breweries located in Sudbury and Thunder Bay)*
PHONE:	*705-254-7373, (fax) 705-254-4482*
OWNERS:	*Employee-owned*
PRESIDENT:	*Ross Eaket*
VICE-PRESIDENT:	*Barry Didier*
BREWER:	*Robert Shami*
CONSULTING BREWER:	*N/A*
BREWING CAPACITY:	*305,000 hl for all three breweries*
TOURS:	*Scheduled throughout the summer (check retail store or call for times) on request at other times.*
BRANDS:	*Edelbrau Lager, Encore Light Lager (draught only), 55 Lager, Northern Ale, Northern Extra Light Lager Superior Lager, Thunder Bay Lager*

Walking through Northern Breweries's Sault Ste. Marie operation, one gets the definite impression that this brewery has a lot of history behind it and still in it! Apparently, the brewing equipment in the Northern plant is replaced only when it can no longer be mended or revived. This homage to history does not necessarily have a negative effect on the taste of the beer, but it does make for what is perhaps the most interesting brewery tour in Canada.

Northern Breweries is made up of three separate brewing operations, each dating back to at least the early 1900s. Built in 1876, the oldest of the triad is the Thunder Bay brewery. While it is no longer in operation, it is still owned by the company and, according to vice-president Barry Didier, could be activated at any time.

The origins of Northern date to the 1907 construction of the Sudbury Brewing and Malting Company by the Doran, Mackay and Fee group, later to become simply the Doran Company. Led by J. J. Doran, the organization later acquired Sault Ste. Marie's Soo Falls Brewing Company in 1911, the Kakabeka Falls Company just outside of Thunder Bay in 1913 and Thunder Bay's Port Arthur Beverage Company in 1948. In addition, the Doran group built Doran's Brewery Ltd. in Timmins in 1919.

In 1960, the five breweries were consolidated under the name of Doran's Northern Ontario Breweries, thus separating the brewing operations from Doran's soft drink plants. The quintet became a quartet when, in 1962, Doran's closed the Kakabeka Falls plant for good.

As befell so many independent Canadian brewing operations, Doran's was taken over by the acquisition-happy Canadian Breweries in 1971, although all four plants continued to operate under the Doran's name. What is less known about the time, however, is that that year also marked the first attempt by the employees to gain control of the breweries themselves. With the large Canadian Breweries as their competition, however, their bid was destined for failure.

Success finally did come to the employees in 1977 when Carling O'Keefe, the successor to Canadian Breweries, sold the entire Doran's operation to them. With that deal, Northern became the only worker-owned brewery in North America at the time.

Since the sale of the breweries to the employees, Northern has gone through surprisingly few changes. The year 1987 saw the sale of the soft drink business—a Pepsi franchise—at the behest of the cola giant that was, at the time, seeking to consolidate its operations. The plus side of that deal was the elimination of all Northern's outstanding debts through the financial return, but the down side was the necessary closure of the Timmins brewery, a plant that was run in conjunction with the pop business.

One move that Northern made but did not wish to make was the switch out of the compact, or "stubby," beer bottle that was for years the industry standard. With a wry grin, Didier noted in the summer of 1993 that, after having had the cost of new bottles forced on them when the stubby went by the wayside, the Ontario industry was moving back to a standard bottle again. He further offered that Northern would likely head in to the new standard bottle eventually, but that, once more, they would not be happy about it.

However, bottles would seem to be the least of their worries when, after having had the northern Ontario draught market to themselves for years due to an agreement that dated back to the 1940s, Northern had to face the prospect of Molson and Labatt invading their turf in 1993 when that deal was scrapped. According to Didier, that was not going to be a problem given Northern's customer base in the north country and he was ready to welcome the competition.

If Didier proves to be correct, that old equipment will keep creaking along for a while longer.

SCOREBOARD

Edelbrau (5% vol.)
Light gold-coloured with a thick, off-dry aroma of grass and faint sugar. A very sweet and sugary start begins a candied malt body with banana and icing sugar notes. The sweet and slightly grassy finish contains a hint of root at the end. ★

55 Lager (5% vol.)
Light gold in colour and dry and woody in aroma with a hint of hazelnut and a touch of leafy hop in the nose. The sweet and appley start leads into a bittersweet body with rooty hopping, caramel malt and banana peel notes. The sour, grassy finish has a moderating touch of sugar. ★$^{1}/_{2}$

Northern Ale (5% vol.)
Light to medium gold in colour with a woody and slightly sweet nose holding green apple notes. The banana notes in the sweet and appley start lead to a slightly metallic, sour grain body with very light caramel and pear notes alongside some woody hopping. The slightly astringent finish is of dried grass with apple skin notes. ★$^{1}/_{2}$

Northern Extra Light (2.4% vol.)

Pale gold in colour with a light, sweet and mildly acidic creamed corn aroma. The mildly sweet and highly carbonic grain start leads into a thin, bittersweet cereal body and a dry, citric finish. ★

Superior Lager (5% vol.)

Light gold-coloured with a sweet, wet hay aroma having light notes of banana. The sweet and flowery start leads into a very grassy, sweet-and-sour body holding a few rooty notes. The grainy finish turns dry and astringent. ★

Thunder Bay Lager (5% vol.)

Light gold-coloured with a dry, woody aroma holding hay and fruity notes. The sweet and fruity, candied apple start heads to a sweet grass body with evident candy sugar and an underlying rooty sourness. It bitters slightly in the short, sugary finish. ★

Sleeman Brewing & Malting Co. Ltd.

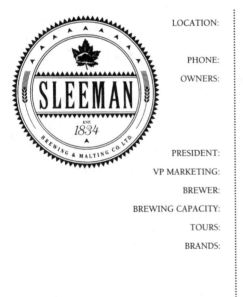

LOCATION:	*551 Clair Road West, Guelph, Ontario N1H 6H9*
PHONE:	*519-822-1834, (fax) 519-822-0430*
OWNERS:	*John Sleeman (22%), silent partners (33%), employees (6%), Manulife Financial (10%), Stroh Breweries (19%), Michael Woods (10%)*
PRESIDENT:	*John Sleeman*
VP MARKETING:	*Kevin Means*
BREWER:	*Al Brash*
BREWING CAPACITY:	*250,000 hl*
TOURS:	*Request group tours by mail*
BRANDS:	*Schlitz, Silver Creek Lager Sleeman Cream Ale, Sleeman Light, Sleeman Original Dark Ale (due in late 1993), Stroh's Lager, Stroh's Light Lager*

When your family has two generations of brewing history behind it, it is easy to be lured into the "family business," even if you didn't know it ever existed.

This is the story of two John Sleemans, the elder and the younger.

John Sleeman the elder, the family history says, was born in England in 1805 and emigrated to Canada in time to establish himself as a brewer and maltster, opening his first brewery in the St. Catharines area in 1836. By 1867, Sleeman's son George had become a partner in the business, now located in what was to become Guelph, and the patriarch of the family had retired.

It wasn't long before the next generation of Sleemans got involved in the brewing business and took on a bit of trouble, as well. It seems that there was a little matter of shipping beer to the States during Prohibition, an action that not only bought the family no small amount of grief, but also cost them the family business. By the mid-1930s, no Sleeman remained in the Canadian brewing industry.

Fast forward to the late 1970s and John Sleeman the younger, great-grandson of the original Sleeman family brewer, was returning to Canada after a year of living in England with his British wife. With no knowledge of his family's beer-related history—it appears that the Prohibition fiasco had shamed the family into silence—Sleeman set about founding an Oakville pub in which he could serve imported British ale, something he sorely missed from across the pond.

It wasn't long before the idea of British beer caught on with other local publicans and Sleeman found himself acting as a full-time beer importer and bar owner. When business got too brisk, the Liquor Licensing Board of Ontario made him choose between the two trades. He chose importing, and the Imported Beer Company was born.

With no micro-brewery beer available at the time and an ever-increasing trend toward the homogenization of the major brewery brands, Imported Beer took off and was soon distributing European brands across the country. John Sleeman the younger still did not know about his family's heritage of the hop.

All that changed in 1984 when Sleeman claims that an aunt gave him his great-grandfather's original beer recipe book and he decided to pursue the reestablishment of the Sleeman Brewing & Malting Company in Guelph.

The first step for Sleeman was to reclaim the trademarks for the name and insignia of the old brewery, a job that turned out to be quite simple as the owners of the marks, Standard Brands and Canadian Pacific, gladly gave them up without a fuss. It would be the simplest step of this brewery's new life.

Anxious for a cross-border brewing relationship with a major American player, Sleeman approached Stroh Brewing of Detroit and pitched his micro-brewery concept. While they expressed an interest in the idea, Stroh offered the opinion that Sleeman was thinking too small and insisted that, if they were going to get involved, the brewery would have to be of a significant size. Sleeman agreed to a 100,000-hectolitre starting capacity with expansion potential, and the number-four brewer in the United States signed on for 19 percent.

Now all Sleeman had to do was find the rest of his financing, buy the brewing and bottling equipment and build the brewery—that's all.

After the Ontario Development Corporation came on for $500,000, further backing came about more easily and Sleeman even found a Guelph businessman who was willing to build the brewery and lease it back to the company. Furthermore, Sleeman and partners were fortunate enough to find a brewhouse for sale in Germany that suited their specifications to a tee, and the idle bottling line at the Molson airport brewery became available for a fraction of its original price. Things were indeed looking up.

By August 1988, the first draught Sleeman Cream Ale was sold in Guelph and, by November of the same year, the now-familiar clear-glass Sleeman bottles were dotting the southern Ontario beerscape.

By virtue of the American interest in the company, Stroh and Stroh Light soon joined the company's portfolio along with the clear-bottled Silver Creek Lager, named after the original Sleeman brewery. The latest additions are a Sleeman Light, also in the trademark clear-glass bottle, and the economically priced Schlitz, a Stroh brand.

The brewery has now more than doubled its original capacity to 250,000 hectolitres and Sleeman says that the company is contemplating a stock issue for public trading in order to finance further expansion.

And a member of the Sleeman family is even selling beer south of the border again, albeit legally this time.

SCOREBOARD

Schlitz (5% vol.)
Pale gold colour and very sweet and sugary in the grain nose. A soft, watery start leads to a sour-bitter body with notes of wood and sour herbs. The finish is very sour and acidic; like chewing on a sour root. ★

Silver Creek Lager (5% vol.)
Light gold colour with a soft, fresh hay aroma. A sweetish and confectionery start changes to a medium body that is a blend of sweet grain (faint creamed corn) and grassy hop without too much bitterness. The finish is grassy and slightly rooty. ★½

Sleeman Cream Ale (5% vol.)

Medium gold in colour, it has an earthy but floral hop nose with soft metallic notes. The body is appropriately creamy after a lightly bitter, perfumey start and is characterized by sweet caramel in the first half and bitter, woody hop in the second with a finish that is more sour than bitter despite the lingering hop. ★★

Sleeman Premium Light (4% vol.)

Pale to light gold in colour with a sweet cereal nose cut by hop and wood notes. A brief, slightly sweet grain start precedes a thin body that is dominated by an earthy hop flavour with a touch of sour grain toward a bitter and acidic hop finish. ★★

Stroh's (4.4% vol.)

Pale gold in colour with a light, leafy aroma punctuated by sweet, malted grain notes. The sweet body has a strongly creamy mouth-feel and some faint hop over a sugary and caramelly character. The finish is sour and rooty. ★

Thames Valley Brewing Co.

LOCATION:	*1764 Oxford Street East, Unit D12, London, Ontario N5V 3R6*
PHONE:	*519-457-2023*
OWNERS:	*18 shareholders*
PRESIDENT:	*Don Hayden*
PRODUCTION MANAGER:	*Steve Hannon*
BREWER:	*Steve Hannon*
CONSULTING BREWERS:	*Glen Fobes & Keith Armstrong*
CAPACITY:	*6,000 hl*
TOURS:	*On request; call first*
BRANDS:	*Thames Valley Lager*

The London Community Small Business Centre, sandwiched between Fanshaw College and the London 3M plant, is not the type of place you would go into looking for a brewery. Driving over the potholed driveway to the rear of this slightly decaying warehouse, one gets the impression that this is a place much more suited to the welding or carpentry trades than the art of brewing. Then again, no one ever said that breweries had to be pretty.

Stuck in a small space at the very back of the Centre is the Thames Valley Brewing Company, Ontario's smallest micro-brewery. Although it does not approach the small scale of, say British Columbia's Nelson or Horseshoe Bay breweries (see separate entries under British Columbia), Thames Valley is nonetheless an operation of extremely modest proportions.

The inspiration behind Thames Valley lies at the feet of Don Hayden and Norm Stoneburgh, the former a doctor specializing in biochemistry and the latter a man whose family owns interests in a pair of Ontario brewpubs. The two men were interested in entering the brewing industry and, through their research, decided that a regionalized, small-volume micro-brewery was the best way for them to accomplish their goal.

After the pair assembled a group of interested investors from among their friends and business associates—many of them London residents—they arranged a home for the brewery-to-be at the Small Business Centre in October 1991.

The Business Centre location, says Hayden, was chosen because of its attractive rent and workable area. With the decision already made that the brewery would not enter the bottled beer market, there was no need to present an attractive face for walk-in business, making the tumble-down atmosphere of the building irrelevant.

Ironically, it was while they were pricing brewing equipment in Hungary and Germany that the principals in Thames Valley heard of a brewery for sale in Canada through a close contact. And so, equipment from the defunct Hanshaus brewery in New Brunswick came to be housed in London at Thames Valley.

While doing their research, Hayden and Stoneburgh discovered that many failed breweries had relied too heavily on the bottled beer market. Determined not to make the same mistake, they left the Hanshaus bottling line in New Brunswick and chose instead to concentrate their resources on the direct delivery of kegged lager.

Now prepared to begin the brewery setup, the fledgling company needed a brewer and they found an experienced one in Steve Hannon. Hannon had been with Amstel brewery in Hamilton since the 1970s, when it was owned by Henninger. Out of work for seven months since the closure of that brewery, Hannon was reluctant to work in the small London brewery, but eventually agreed to a contract with Thames Valley.

Brewing at the Small Business Centre began in August 1992 and the first keg was in a London licensee by mid-September. Since then, Hannon reports that business has been growing steadily through word of mouth and minimal advertising. The word of mouth aspect must be working particularly well, as Hayden reports that, by the summer of 1993, a full quarter of their business was being done through special-occasion permits for private functions.

Expansion, says Hayden, is a non-issue for the brewery. The partners are already agreed that instead of increasing the size of the existing plant, they would rather establish a whole new facility in a different community. Hayden even hints that the partners are already looking at possible new locations.

All of which spells good news for the residents of some small Ontario cities and towns who thought that they would never rate a brewery of their own.

SCOREBOARD

Thames Valley Lager (draught only, 5% vol.)

Light to medium gold in colour with a sweet and grainy aroma holding floral notes and light, leafy hopping. A sweet and slightly sugary start precedes a moderately sweet body of fresh grass with notes of sour grain and bittering hop rising through the second half alongside rooty and lightly floral notes. The bittersweet finish carries with it some low acidity. ★½

Upper Canada Brewing Company

LOCATION:	*2 Atlantic Avenue, Toronto, Ontario, M6K 1X8*
PHONE:	*416-534-9281, (fax) 416-534-6998*
OWNERS:	*Frank Heaps, Corby's Distillers (40%), employees*
PRESIDENT:	*Frank Heaps*
VP MARKETING:	*Greg Cromwell*
BREWER:	*Richard Rench*
ORIGINAL BREWER:	*Klaus Antz*
BREWING CAPACITY:	*35,000 hl*
TOURS:	*M–F 2:00 p.m.; Sat 11:00 a.m., 1:00, & 3:00 p.m.; Sunday 1:00 & 3:00 p.m.*
BRANDS:	*Colonial Stout, Dark Ale, Lager, Natural Light, Pale Ale, Point Nine (.9% alc.), Publican's Bitter, Rebellion Malt Liquor, True Bock (seasonal), Tsingchuen Silver Springs Lager (contract-brew for Tsingchuen Brewing Co., China), Wheat Beer (seasonal)*

Frank Heaps has often said that he would not wish brewery ownership on his worst enemy.

For Heaps, the founder and president of one of Ontario's first breweries, the road to success in micro-brewing has not been a smooth one.

A born-and-bred Torontonian, Heaps moved to Vancouver in 1980, shortly before the first stirrings were heard from Granville Island Brewing. Three years later, the banking company for which he was working was contracted to raise the financing for Granville, and Heaps was so taken with the concept that he himself became an investor. A few months later, he began to plan the founding of his own brewery.

Although he was confident in the market for premium quality beer, Heaps was not comfortable with the idea of competing for that market with Granville and decided instead to base his brewery in the much larger metropolitan area of Toronto.

Heaps spent much of 1984 scouting for a site. What he wanted was a locale similar to that of Granville Island with its centrality and high tourism appeal. After much time spent in negotiation and research, including some serious discussions with the city's Harbourfront area, he ended up with the only site that met his planning and financing requirements, an empty building facing the Queen Elizabeth Way highway in a warehouse district west of downtown.

Capital was raised through a limited partnership. Heaps, along with four others, formed the management team and 23 other partners were also brought in.

The fact that the pre-expansion Upper Canada did, and still does to a certain degree, resemble the Granville Island brewery is no accident. Heaps had two planners assisting him—Dr. Robert McKechnie and Larry Sherwood —both of whom had worked on the Vancouver project, as well.

The plan for Upper Canada Brewing was completed in June 1984, and one year later, brewing had begun. The first two brands brought out of the brewery in early August were the Dark Ale and the Lager.

According to Heaps, the first four years were "horrible." He says that he is stunned by the amount of naiveté he brought to the business. He admits that he was not at all prepared for how tough it was going to be and recollects how, in the early years, they were chronically short of money.

By the end of 1987, Upper Canada had a portfolio that included a seasonal bock beer, a light lager and a 6.5% alcohol lager. Experimentation had been done with a cask-conditioned ale known as Olde York, but Heaps says that the lack of understanding of the product on the part of bar and restaurant staff signalled the end of that brand.

In late 1989, Frank Heaps was finally breathing a little more easily and the brewery, as he puts it, was out of the woods financially.

A significant infusion of cash came to the brewery in the spring of 1991 when Corby Distilling purchased 40 percent of the company with an option to buy the rest four years later. While initial fears that the deal would affect the quality of the brands proved to be unfounded, Heaps admits that, while the agreement's financial aspect has been welcomed, the impact he was expecting in terms of exposure and sales has not materialized. Whether Corby will wish to exercise their option now remains to be seen.

Many other brands have come and, occasionally, gone from the house that Heaps built. Two licensed brews—Sichuan Snow Waves and Banks Lager—didn't work out for the brewery, and a contract brew called Beaver Valley Amber last year metamorphosed into Upper Canada Pale Ale in 1993.

The winter of 1992–1993 saw Upper Canada put a new, uniform face on their labels and rework their then badly hurting ales. As a result, the following spring and summer reportedly brought such brisk sales that the brewery was unable to find the tank space to make more than one brew of their seasonal Wheat Beer.

As well, Upper Canada launched a major radio-and-print advertising campaign in 1993 that emphasized the purity of their ingredients and immediately vaulted Heaps into hot water with the Brewers Association of Canada, an industry organization which claimed that Upper Canada was not acting responsibly by running the ads.

For Frank Heaps, it was all in a day's work at the job he wouldn't force upon anyone.

SCOREBOARD

Colonial Stout (4.8% vol.)

Deep plum colour with a charred oak nose. Fairly light-bodied with some acidity, burnt and roasted grain tastes and a touch of carob. Bittering hop notes in the finish. ★★

Dark Ale (5% vol.)

Cherrywood colour with a light, burnt toffee nose holding sweet cherry notes. The faintly acidic start settles down to a walnutty and slightly caramel body with soft berry notes. Bitter hopping rises through the second half to an off-dry, faintly burnt, woody finish. ★★½

Lager (5% vol.)

Medium to deep gold in colour. The aroma is soft, lightly floral and contains notes of metallic hop and the faintest touch of kelp. The body begins slowly with a malted grain start leading to a strong hop character holding metallic and grassy notes along with a faint grain sweetness. The finish is decidedly bitter and rooty. ★★

Light Lager (4.0% vol.)

Light to medium gold with a flowery nose mixing sweet hop aromas with a touch of grain and evident acidity. Soft, sweetish creamy grain start turns to a hoppy, nearly tinny body with some barley notes developing in the middle. Tart finish, with the hop returning strongly to the palate. ★★

Pale Ale (5% vol.)

Deep and rich orange colour. The full Cascade hop nose has notes of pecan, nut shell and faint florals. The body starts soft and quickly develops a bitter Cascade character alongside subtle fruitiness and caramel flavours. The finish is very earthy and bitter bordering on sour. ★★½

Publican's Special Bitter (4.8% vol.)

Copper-coloured with a doughy aroma holding floral and woody hop and caramel notes. Very woody in character, the taste begins malty with strong molasses notes before entering a woody, rooty and bitter body, strongly but not gently hopped. Bitter, earthy and slightly sour finish with some acidity. ★$^{1}/_{2}$

Rebellion (6.5% vol.)

Medium gold colour bordering on light copper. The roasty malt nose has traces of fireplace embers, sausage and even stewed tomatoes. The body begins full and sweet with apricot and raisin notes before turning bittersweet in the middle and picking up an orange brandy flavour along with hints of caramel and very light cocoa. A bitter, woody and alcoholic finish complete the profile. ★★★

True Bock '92–'93 (6.5% vol.)

Deep amber colour with defined brown tones. Faintly toffee nose with notes of licorice and fruit in low aromatics. Dryish body (though still sweet) with licorice and molasses blending with light cherry and hop notes. Bitters strongly in the dry finish with alcohol and sour hop taking hold. ★★$^{1}/_{2}$

Wheat Beer 1993 (draught only, 4.3% vol.)

Medium gold bordering on coppery in colour with a light, fresh and very mildly citric aroma carrying a mix of wheat and barley grain notes. The taste begins lightly sweet and spicy (clove) before it moves to a wheat and lime body containing a distinctive and dry graininess, mild earthy bitterness and a bit of astringecy in the second half before a very dry, bitter and sour finish. ★$^{1}/_{2}$

Wellington County Brewery Ltd.

LOCATION:	*950 Woodlawn Road, Guelph, Ontario N1K 1B8*
PHONE:	*519-837-2337, (fax) 519-837-3142*
OWNER:	*Philip Gosling*
PRESIDENT:	*Philip Gosling*
BREWER:	*Michael Stirrup*
ORIGINAL BREWER:	*Charles MacLean*
BREWING CAPACITY:	*8,000 hl*
TOURS:	*By appointment only*
BRANDS:	*Arkell Best Bitter, County Ale, Imperial Stout, Iron Duke, Lager, Special Pale Ale, Special Reserve Iron Duke*

It is quite common to hear arguments among beer aficionados as to what constitutes a true "real ale." Some maintain that any natural ale is worthy of the title while other puritans insist that only cask-conditioned, hand-pumped, British-style ale or bitter rates the moniker.

Whatever the "proper" definition, there can be little doubt that the ales of Wellington County fit the bill. One of the three original Ontario micros, Wellington did, after all, originate in one man's need for authentic British-style ale in what was then a virtual top-fermenting wasteland.

The man was Charles MacLean, now a contract brewer to Ontario brewpubs, and his dream was to found a brewery that would supply others like him with the style of beer they couldn't find on this side of the Atlantic. Fittingly perhaps, MacLean's dream likely never would have come to fruition were it not for a chance meeting in a local Guelph pub.

At the time, MacLean had organized a small group of investors who shared his vision, among them Dr. David Moorsom, a Newmarket, Ontario, internist. What the group lacked was a building for their brewery and it was in this regard that the chance meeting shaped the future of Guelph brewing.

The man MacLean met was Philip Gosling, a local real estate developer and fellow lover of British ale. Shortly after their shared pints, Gosling joined the group, found an appropriate site for the brewery, got its construction under way and set off with MacLean and Moorsom for England to source out a brewery.

The three settled on a duplicate of the John Hickey Brewery in London and made arrangements to have it built in England and shipped to

Guelph. After a few unfortunate delays, including the appropriation of the ship for the purposes of assisting in the search for survivors of the Air India disaster, the brewery finally arrived and was installed in the freshly completed building.

It was not smooth sailing yet, as there were numerous problems associated with the mechanics of setting up a new brewery so far from its point of origin. Perseverance prevailed, however, and Wellington County Ale and Bitter were, by the fall of 1985, being found on tap at a dozen or so British pubs throughout the Toronto and Guelph areas.

Looking back, Gosling remarks on the "wild optimism" shown by the investor group in the early days. They were so sure, he says, that the world would beat a path to their door for cask-conditioned ale that they had not put any contingency plans in place and therefore had to scramble quite a bit when this turned out not to be the case. The original, one-litre real ale pack of plastic containers in a cardboard box, for example, had to be changed almost immediately, and it quickly became evident that Canadian publicans were not going to embrace the extra work that accompanied the serving of cask-conditioned ale.

The immediate problem of sales was solved by the introduction of a one-litre plastic bottle and filtered draught kegs. The answers to the technical problems that continued to plague the operation over a year after opening were not so easily arrived at and, over time, all the investors, save Gosling, dropped out.

Faced with the dilemma of whether to jump wholeheartedly into the operation or give up the ghost, Gosling chose the former path and soon Wellington County, then under the brewing leadership of Brad Veitch, was back on its feet.

Over time, the original two-ale product line was expanded to include a Special Pale Ale, a strong ale (Iron Duke), a top-fermented Lager and an Imperial Stout. While the brewery, says Gosling, is now profitable, he has no plans to expand it beyond its current size.

To Gosling, quality and tradition, not size, are of paramount importance.

SCOREBOARD

Arkell Best Bitter (4% vol.)
Deep honey colour with a fragrant, leafy hop nose, sweet but not heavy. Complex character that starts slightly sweet and fruity but quickly develops a strong, earthy hop body. The bitterness is tempered by a perfumey malt to a soft, bittersweet and floral finish. ★★★

County Ale (5% vol.)

Amber-coloured with a sweet but tart fruit (apricot and mango) nose. Sweet, caramel and cherry start turns to a still-fruity body bittered by full, woody hopping. The finish stays bittersweet with a touch of confectionery sweetness. ★★¹/₂

Imperial Stout (8% vol.)

Very deep black, almost opaque with a rich, winy aroma carrying notes of fruit (plum, prune), sweetened Turkish coffee, chocolate and caramel. The start is dry with a bitter coffee character and hints of burnt raisins while the body sweetens somewhat with notes of licorice, sweeter coffee, baker's chocolate and faint black currant. The finish marks a return to dryness with more and stronger coffee flavours and a brandy-like bite of alcohol. ★★★

Iron Duke (6.5% vol.)

Deep rust colour and fragrant with sweet, toffeeish malt and evident alcohol. An almost syrupy start with subtle cherry flavours in the malt leads to a bittersweet, fruity and complex body containing molasses, sour cherry and rooty hop notes with some "heat" from the alcoholic strength. The strong finish is bitter, bordering on sour and strongly alcoholic. ★★¹/₂

Premium Lager (4.5% vol.)

Medium gold-coloured, this top-fermented lager has a malty aroma mixing very light apricot notes with a slightly sour grain and hints of petrol. The body is full to the point of almost being syrupy and begins caramelly and sweet before bittering with a faintly floral hopping and a roasted malt holding some plastic notes. The finish is of moderate bitterness and dominated by a woody hop. ★¹/₂

Special Pale Ale (4.5% vol.)

Deep copper-coloured with a full, perfumey hop and caramel malt aroma. Soft and slightly sweet, almost honeyish start turns decidedly bitter in the body with oak and other woody flavours wrapped around a faint, chocolatey malt. Bitter, leafy and, in the end, somewhat sour finish. ★★

Special Reserve Iron Duke (6.5% vol.)

A longer-aged version of the strong ale unavailable at the time of writing.

Quebec and
the Maritimes

Brasal—Brasserie Allemande Inc.

LOCATION:	*8477 Rue Cordner, Lasalle (Montreal), Quebec H8N 2X2*
PHONE:	*514-365-5050, 1-800-463-2728, (fax) 514-365-2954*
OWNERS:	*Marcel & Etan Jagermann*
PRESIDENT:	*Marcel Jagermann*
BREWER:	*Harald Sowade*
CONSULTING BREWER:	*N/A*
CAPACITY:	*20,000 hl*
TOURS:	*Mondays 5:30–8:30 p.m., call to reserve*
BRANDS:	*Bock (seasonal), Hopps Bräu Lager, Spécial, Vrai Légère*

Father and son Marcel and Etan Jagermann are Montreal's self-described "immigrant brewers." They are also the purveyors of what may be Quebec's most foreign beer styles.

Foreign because Quebeckers are notorious for choosing ales over lagers when they reach for their brews. This tradition, if it can be called that, even has the lagers sold in *la belle province* tending toward a bit of a fruity, ale-like character. So what are two displaced Austrians doing brewing Germanic lagers in French Canada?

According to Etan Jagermann, it was simply a matter of his father's spying a niche in the local micro-brewery market that was not, at the time, being filled. An entrepreneur, Marcel Jagermann thought that it would be a sound business move to address that gap in the beer supply.

Marcel Jagermann came to Montreal in the early 1980s from his native Vienna. By the middle of that decade, he had identified the need for German-style lagers in Quebec, largely through his own need for a decent beer of that type. Seeing that the provincial liquor board, the Société d'Alcools de Québec (SAQ), had only a limited selection of frequently stale, imported brands, he enlisted the assistance of his son, and together they made plans to deliver the lagers they so loved to the Quebec market.

Being purists of the highest order, the Jagermanns decided that, if they were to obtain the flavour they desired, they would need equipment designed specifically for their type of brewing. So while Marcel scouted for a site and organized the construction of the building that would soon house their brewery, Etan remained in Europe and sourced the equipment they would need.

The Lasalle site in the southeast part of the city, says Etan, fit the requirements the two men had established for their brewery's location in that it was well-placed for ease of distribution and also near a residential neighbourhood. Thus the Jagermanns felt entirely justified in building a new structure rather than simply renting and remodelling an existing one as so many other micros had done before them.

Although the similarity of the names Brasal and Lasalle might understandably lead one to conclude that the brewery is named in honour of its location, the name the Jagermanns invented for their company has nothing to do with the Lasalle area. Rather, it is a combination of the two words BRASserie (brewery) and ALlemande (German) or, as Etan explains it, the purpose and the inspiration of the business.

Etan finally joined his father for good in October 1989, at the same time as the first bottles and kegs of Hopps Bräu were ready to leave the brewery. Unlike some of their micro-brewing competitors, the new brewery owners were determined to hit both the bottle and draught markets straight off the mark.

The positive reception to the beer known simply as Hopps led to the creation of a second brand a little over a year later. Like the Hopps, the Spécial also tapped into an empty part of the Quebec micro-beer market, this time with higher alcohol to back up its bottom-fermentation. The following spring, the Jagermanns reversed themselves and, having already presented Quebeckers with a stronger beer, followed with the 3.1% alcohol Vrai Légère (True Light).

The Légère was and is the second lightest beer in the Canadian market, exclusive of the non-alcoholic category of beers with 1% or less alcohol by volume and behind the 2.4% alcohol Northern Extra Light. This is a position of which Etan is visibly proud and one that he was only too pleased to point out to Molson after that brewery launched their Special as the lightest brew in the nation in February 1992.

The fourth brand released by Brasal reversed their course yet again with a powerful 7.8% alcohol in their Bock. Brewed first as a draught-only winter specialty in October 1991, the Brasal Bock was bottled in 1992 but remains available only from October through March each year.

The summer of 1993 saw Brasal become one of the first two Quebec micros (McAuslan being the other—see separate entry) to ship their beer across the border into Ontario and, if Ontarians prove as thirsty for Germanic lager as Quebeckers, the "immigrant brewers" may have a lot more brewing ahead of them.

SCOREBOARD

Bock (7.8% vol.)

Dark burgundy-coloured with a sweet cherry malt nose. The sweet and fruity start precedes a slightly sucrose body (lighter than the start or finish) with lots of malt character, berry notes and a trace of coffee. The round, sweet and alcoholic finish carries a light tartness and acidity. ★★★

Hopps Bräu Lager (5% vol.)

The colour is that of dark straw and the aroma is of fresh hay with notes of toasted grain. The taste starts light, grainy and slightly sweet before moving to a hoppy body with the moderate bitterness balanced by faintly fruity (peach and pear) malt and a hint of petrol. The finish combines a rooty bitterness with the light remaining sugars. ★★

Spécial (6.1% vol.)

Reddish, nut-brown in colour with a sweet, spicy (allspice) and alcoholic nose. A sweet and fruity (canned peaches) start with nutmeg notes leads to a full and malty body with a distinct, cognac-like alcoholic heat and a touch of nuttiness toward the finish. The finish is bitter with some sour orange notes and more alcoholic than the content would indicate. ★★½

Vrai Légère (3.1% vol.)

Light gold in colour with a slightly metallic hopping and sweet cereal and caramel notes in the aroma. A semisweet grain start with some tinny hop showing forth leads to an off-dry, cereal body with woody and metallic hop notes. The finish has a strong remainder of bitter and mostly woody hop flavour along with a lingering note of grain. ★★

Les Brasseurs du Nord Inc.

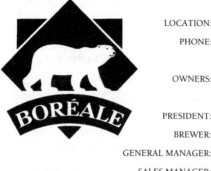

LOCATION:	*18 Kennedy, St. Jérôme, Quebec J7Y 4B4*
PHONE:	*514-438-9060; (Montreal)*
	514-434-2392; (fax) 514-438-3179
OWNERS:	*Laura Urtnowski, Bernard Morin,*
	Jean Morin
PRESIDENT:	*Laura Urtnowski*
BREWER:	*Laura Urtnowski*
GENERAL MANAGER:	*Bernard Morin*
SALES MANAGER:	*Jean Morin*
CONSULTING BREWER:	*N/A*
BREWING CAPACITY:	*23,400 hl*
TOURS:	*On request*
BRANDS:	*Boréale Blonde, Boréale Noire,*
	Boréale Rousse

It could very well be that several, or even numerous, Canadian micro-brewers got their starts bootlegging home brew out of their garages, apartments or basements. But it is only Bernard Morin and Laura Urtnowski who will admit to it.

Urtnowski says that, following her graduation from university in 1984 and during her subsequent dabbling in post-grad work, Morin got interested in brewing in their Montreal apartment in order to save on beer money. Urtnowski herself was conscripted into the endeavour very shortly thereafter because, unlike Morin at the time, she could read English and had a chemistry background.

The proposal to save money soon turned into an opportunity to make some cash as their friends began to inquire about buying some of their increasingly popular home brews. It was that phase of the experience that taught Morin and Urtnowski the potential the brewing business had as a full-time occupation.

One trend the couple had noticed to be the rule rather than the exception with their home brew customers was the general preference toward darker over lighter beers. Thus it was determined that, if they were to open a brewery, their focus would be on the dark ale market.

Through connections she had gradually developed in the micro-brewing industry, Urtnowski was able to unofficially apprentice at a few breweries in Ontario and the northeastern United States. Like her apartment-brewing roots, the apprenticeships were less than completely above board, so Urtnowski hesitates to be too specific about the details of her training.

The next step for the trio—for they had now added Morin's brother Jean—was to obtain financing, not an easy task for three young and broke home brewers. A 180-page business plan was enough to secure them a government loan through an entrepreneurial program, however, and they were soon on their way to becoming micro-brewers.

Although they were extremely undercapitalized at first, Urtnowski says that finances were not the main reason for locating north of the city in St. Jérôme. Instead, she says that it was Montreal's water that kept them away. While she had been home brewing with city water in their apartment, she says that she was quite simply not comfortable with the idea of brewing commercially with the same, hard water and preferred the softer H_2O available farther north.

The first keg of Boréale Rousse was delivered in June 1988, making Les Brasseurs du Nord the third micro-brewery in the late-starting province. Because they could not afford a bottling line with their available funds, the initial two years of production was entirely in draught ale and, proving the beer business is not always romantic, their first deliveries were made in a Subaru station wagon.

Like most other aspects of the brewery's origins, their preliminary sales technique was certainly unique. At the time, the micro GMT (see separate entry under Les Brasseurs GMT) was publishing current lists of their bar accounts in their advertising, so the Brasseurs du Nord plan was to take those lists and visit all of their competitor's customers. Not that they were looking to replace GMT's Belle Gueulle in those bars, says Urtnowski; rather, they would suggest that Boréale would complement the lager quite well on *another* tap.

By reinvesting their profits in the business, Les Brasseurs were able to grow to the point that, in September 1990, they began to bottle their beer and were also able to introduce two new brands to their portfolio a year later. By 1993, that little apartment brewery had grown to 8,000 square feet and 16 full-time employees.

One of the reasons for their success, says Urtnowski, is that she believes Montrealers are very open to new and inventive beverages and cuisines. This ability to be comfortable in trying new things, she suggests, has really been a boon to all of the Quebec micros.

One mystery that remains with Les Brasseurs is the true identity of the beer styles they are brewing. While it is clear that the Noire is a stout, the other two brews are not as obvious and Urtnowski is intentionally vague when she speaks of style. The Rousse, which roughly translates to rust, is not what one would easily call a red ale and Urtnowski bristles when the Blonde is described as a Pale Ale. To her, they are simply what they are called.

SCOREBOARD

Blonde (4.5% vol.)
Medium gold in colour with fragrant, floral and leafy notes resting on a sweet, caramel malt nose. The full and off-dry malty start carries slight lactose and floral notes while the body blends a fruit (apricot, pineapple) and caramel malt with a soft, leafy hop bitterness. The taste then dries out to a pleasantly bitter, rooty and leafy hop finish. ★★★

Noire (5.5% vol.)
Very dark, almost opaque purple in colour with a sweet and rich mocha nose holding light toffee notes. The thin and slightly sugary front has a few licorice notes and leads to a mildly acidic body that is sweet, chocolatey and creamy with apparent sugar notes and a faintly bitter coffee taste. The bittering hop dries the finish slightly, the coffee and acidity remaining. ★$^{1}/_{2}$

Rousse (5% vol.)
Cherrywood-coloured with a very fruity (cherry and currant) nose with notable spiciness (clove?). A slightly sweet and faintly chocolatey start changes quickly to a bitter plum and cherry body marked by leafy and floral hopping and a light brandy character. The bitter, woody and still-leafy finish also has a remnant of fruit. ★★$^{1}/_{2}$

Les Brasseurs GMT

LOCATION:	*5710 Garnier Street, Montreal, Quebec H2G 2Z7*
PHONE:	*514-274-4941*
OWNERS:	*André Martineau, Gilbert Gravel, Yves Thibault, Daniel Trepanier, Richard Tremblay*
PRESIDENT:	*André Martineau*
OPERATIONS MANAGER:	*Normand Guerin*
BREWER:	*André Lafremiere*
CONSULTING BREWER:	*Georges Van Ghuluwe*
BREWING CAPACITY:	*11,000 hl*
TOURS:	*On request*
BRANDS:	*Belle Gueule, Tremblay*

When, in his heavily accented English, brewery manager Normand Guerin explains that Les Brasseurs GMT were intent from the outset on establishing their brewery as a thoroughly French enterprise, you believe him. Not that anglophones are unwelcome at the brewery located halfway between Mount Royal and the Olympic Park, just that there is a, well, "Frenchness" to the operation.

It is a difficult thing to put one's finger on, this difference between francophone, anglophone and bilingual enterprises in Quebec and per-haps it is best that way. It is, after all, that unique blending of cultures and language that makes Montreal such a fascinating city and, if that blending shows up in the brewing culture of the province, as well, then it is something that should be welcomed by the beer drinkers of Quebec.

The name GMT was taken from the initials of the three men who founded the company—Gilbert Gravel, André Martineau and Yves Thibault—and the idea for the brewery was taken from a European trip the three partners-to-be went on in 1987. According to Guerin, the men were captivated by the small, craft breweries they saw on the continent and became determined to see if the same thing could be done in Quebec.

Upon returning from their trip, Gravel, Martineau and Thibault imme-diately set out to shape the face of their brewery and, by the winter of 1987, were in construction at their new site in an industrial park on the edge of the city's core. The location, says Guerin, was selected to ensure reasonable proximity to the downtown market and, by way of helping along the aforementioned French image, happened to be smack-dab in the centre of a very French area of the city.

Ironically, the two major players in the successful operation of GMT from start-up to present became involved almost by accident. The first key person, brewing consultant Georges Van Ghuluwe, dropped by the half-finished brewery to see if he could help after hearing about the pro-ject from friends in Belgium. Pleased to have a professional along, the partners signed him on quickly and Ghuluwe helped to guide GMT along the bumpy road of emergence in a new market.

The second key person was Guerin, who was living in Quebec City when he was asked to come down and handle Thibault's bar operations while his friend was getting the brewery up and running. Guerin agreed and subsequently found himself switching places with Thibault shortly after beer production had begun, a move Guerin says he has never regretted.

Quebec's first complete micro-brewery (the others to that point had been built for direct service to pubs), GMT was kegging beer by March 1988 and, according to Guerin, had no trouble getting word out that they were on the market. The originality of the business, he says, along with the free publicity that came as a result, enabled the new micro to become recognizable without the need for a great deal of advertising.

It also did not hurt that the three partners were all in the hospitality trade and had many friends in the bar business, friends who would happily try out the new brew as a favour. Favours only last so long in the face of a recession, though, and Belle Gueule soon had to, and did, make it in the market on its own merits.

It is in speaking of Belle Gueule—the name means a beautiful mouth —that Guerin again resurrects the idea of a French identity. The beer was intended, he says, to belong to the French community and become a new part of their culture, right down to its name, which is virtually unpronounceable to an anglophone.

Two and a half years after opening, the first Quebec micro-brewery became the last to venture into the bottle market and, a year after that, the minds behind the brewery—including new partners Daniel Trepanier and Richard Tremblay, who joined in 1990—began to consider the possibilities offered by a more commercial lager. As it happened, GMT was approached a short time later with the opportunity to contract-brew a house beer for a large licensee, so the experiment to brew a more mainstream beer was begun at that bar.

In April 1993, the new brand—Tremblay—was launched as the second beer in the five-year history of GMT. Christened with the most popular surname in Quebec (also the name of one of the partners), Tremblay continued the GMT tradition of being a predominantly French brewery, a tradition that is as unlikely to change as the province itself.

SCOREBOARD

Belle Gueule (5.2% vol.)

Medium gold to copper in colour with a thick aroma combining mandarin orange with light hopping, some spiciness (clove, nutmeg) and a trace of alcohol. The fruity (orange) start holds some tobacco-leaf notes and moves into a hoppier body that has bitterness blending with orange brandy flavours and light, sugary notes. Some orange peel and root flavours make up the bittering finish. ★★¹⁄₂

Tremblay (5% vol.)

Light gold in colour with a full, sweet and caramelly aroma holding light florals and toasted brown sugar notes. The sweet and mildly fruity (peach) start leads to a sweeter, caramel and butterscotch body with more fruit (peach, apricot, trace of banana). The finish bitters with woody and rooty hop. ★

Brasserie McAuslan Brewing Inc.

LOCATION:	*4850 St. Ambroise, Suite 100, Montreal, Quebec H4C 3N8*
PHONE:	*514-939-3060, (fax) 514-939-6136*
OWNERS:	*Peter McAuslan, Ellen Bounsall, Fred Harris & a 40-member holding company*
PRESIDENT:	*Peter McAuslan*
BREWER:	*Ellen Bounsall*
CONSULTING BREWER:	*Alan Pugsley*
BREWING CAPACITY:	*20,000 hl*
TOURS:	*Wednesday evenings by appointment; out-of-town guests can be accommodated by advance arrangement*
BRANDS:	*Croco Pale Ale (contract-brew for the Crocodile chain), Griffon Brown Ale, Griffon Extra Pale Ale, St. Ambroise Oatmeal Stout, St. Ambroise Pale Ale*

Two white Scottish terriers—Daisy and Maestro—guard the doors to Peter McAuslan's brewery in the low-income St. Henri district of Montreal. This is your first indication that you are not stepping into an average brewery.

Brewery president and owner, Peter McAuslan, says that he has long been fascinated by breweries, both for their products and their role in the sociological and cultural makeup of a community. As such, his decision to enter the micro-brewing industry was, he says, motivated as much by the finances of the opportunity as by the strength of the brewing history of Quebec.

McAuslan spent his teenage years in the Montreal suburb of Lachine and he fondly recalls some of the more characterful Quebec ales he drank in those days. He also remembers being drawn to home brewing in Lachine, an affair that lasted off and on for over 20 years before he got himself involved with the commercial side of the business.

Even back then, McAuslan says that he was fascinated by commercial breweries and the impact they had on the culture that surrounded him. In fact, he was so interested in the breweries of the day that he began to collect bits and pieces of brewery artifacts and lore in the hopes of somehow sharing in that culture. Little did he know how involved he would eventually become.

When micro-brewing began to rise in popularity in Canada in the mid-1980s, McAuslan found that his slight obsession with the industry became a more major one and he began to ponder the opportunity to, as he puts it, plug into both the past and the future through craft brewing. In 1987, that whim took him to a micro-brewing conference in Boston where he met Alan Pugsley.

Pugsley, now so much a feature name in the eastern North American micro market, was just establishing himself on this side of the Atlantic and was consulting at the D.L. Geary Brewing Company in Portland, Maine. As fate would have it, Geary Brewing had been chosen to brew a special ale for the conference that year and, upon tasting it, McAuslan decided that he wanted to know more about the man who was responsible for it.

Following his initial contact with Pugsley, McAuslan threw his dream into high gear. While formulating his business plan, he managed a trip to England in order to view the ale scene in general and the Pugsley-influenced breweries in particular and came back convinced that he should indeed be brewing ales in his home province and that Pugsley was the man to help him. With completed business plan in hand, McAuslan then went searching for financing in February 1988, a chore which, he says, did not take long to complete.

Capital funding in place, McAuslan, his wife, Ellen Bounsall, and Pugsley set about to construct a brewery in the fall and winter of 1988 and 1989. While the project was coming together, Pugsley formulated the recipes for the future ales (with input from McAuslan and Bounsall) and instructed Bounsall on the intricacies of brewing. By the time February 1989 came around, the new brewery was ready to brew some ale.

The style of ale McAuslan and Bounsall chose is one that can be called, without fear of exaggeration, extremely hoppy. The reason for that particular taste, says McAuslan, goes back once again to his sense of history. With Quebec's tradition of hoppy ales, McAuslan felt that enough people would respond to the tastes of the past to make his brewery successful.

Hitting the draught and bottled beer market at the same time, McAuslan's first ale was the St. Ambroise Pale Ale which, says McAuslan, was named after the street on which the brewery is located in order to endow the brew with local character. The pale ale was followed a year later by the Croco Pale Ale for the Crocodile chain of clubs, bars and restaurants (see separate entry) and the Oatmeal Stout just less than a year after that.

The stout, says McAuslan, was a special surprise because it was intended to be only a seasonal specialty. The response proved to be so great, however, that they could not discontinue its production. The newly matched pair of St. Ambroises were then joined by the Griffons scant months after the stout's introduction.

In the spring of 1993, McAuslan was still floating on the success of his five-litre mini-kegs of the pale ale introduced the Christmas before, and was investigating ways of improving the package to make it reusable. For the former teenage home brewer from Lachine, it was just another way of bringing more beer history to Quebec in the 1990s.

SCOREBOARD

Griffon Brown Ale (5% vol.)

Chocolate brown with a touch of red in the colour and a roasted nose with notes of coffee, cigar and berry. The body begins with a berry sweetness before leading to an oaky hoppiness laid over a smoky malt base with cherry and chocolate notes. The bittersweet chocolatey finish carries a receding hop character. ★★¹/₂

Griffon Extra Pale Ale (5% vol.)

Light to medium gold in colour with a sweet aroma blending caramel malt with floral hopping and soft orange brandy notes. A sweet and somewhat sugary start leads to a hop body with a bitter, woody taste offset by a light, sweet and fruity (apricot, plum) malt. The finish begins with a slight candied taste but holds a lingering, woody bitterness. ★★

St. Ambroise Oatmeal Stout (5.5% vol.)

Black in colour with a coffee aroma holding strong black licorice notes and just a hint of brown sugar. A faintly sweet and sugary start leads to a dry body of coffee with notes of bitter chocolate, anise and traces of porridge and plum. Notes of alcohol rise in the bitter espresso finish. ★★★¹/₂

St. Ambroise Pale Ale (5% vol.)

Orange-rust colour with a white head and a nose mixing nutshell hop with butterscotch malt and a touch of peach. The body starts soft with a distinct nuttiness joined by some lightly orange malt. The body is very full and tremendously hoppy with dominant flavours of slightly smoky wood and filberts on a mandarin orange malt. The finish is bitter and distinctly earthy. ★★★

Moosehead Breweries Limited

LOCATION:	*(Offices & Brewery) 89 Main Street, Saint John, New Brunswick E2M 3H2 (Offices & Distribution) 656 Windmill Road, Dartmouth, Nova Scotia B3B 1B8*
PHONE:	*(Offices & Brewery) 506-635-7000, (fax) 506-635-7029 (Offices & Distribution) 902-468-7040, (fax) 902-468-0502*
OWNERS:	*Oland family*
CHAIRMAN:	*Philip W. Oland*
PRESIDENT:	*Derek Oland*
VP MARKETING:	*Rick Knudson*
VP BREWING:	*Lawrence Barry*
CONSULTING BREWER:	*N/A*
CAPACITY:	*1,000,000 hl*
TOURS:	*June 14–Aug. 31, 9:30 a.m. & 2:00 p.m.; call for reservations*
BRANDS:	*Alpine, Alpine Genuine Cold Filtered Alpine Light , Clancy's Amber Ale, Molson Canadian (under license), Moosehead Beer, Moosehead Dry, Moosehead Light, Moosehead Pale Ale, Ten Penny Ale*

Writing a short history of Moosehead Breweries is akin to trying to run a mile in a closet; one quickly runs out of space. Then again, that is not so surprising when dealing with a family business that is as old as the country.

For years, Moosehead Lager was the beer that central and western Canadians all knew about but had rarely if ever tasted. That strange turn of events came about because of this nation's odd but now, fortunately, antique laws that required a brewery to have a facility in each province in which it wished to sell. As a result, Moosehead Lager spent years as one of the top-selling imported brands in the United States while it remained unavailable in most of its native country.

According to the company's records, John and Susannah Oland first began the commercial brewing of beer in 1867, the year of Confederation.

It was reportedly at the behest of the aide to the Nova Scotia Governor General that the Olands turned their backyard home-brewing setup into the Army and Navy Brewery in Dartmouth. The couple's efforts hit the first of many tragic bumps after a mere three years of operation, however, and Susannah renamed the brewery S. Oland & Sons & Co. in 1870 following the death of her husband.

After Susannah's death in 1886 and the complete destruction of the brewery in the Halifax explosion of 1917, some of the family chose to leave Nova Scotia and begin afresh in New Brunswick with the purchase of a brewery they renamed the Red Ball Brewery.

Eventually, there was a split in the family business and the Halifax branch of the family created the Oland Brewery (sold to Labatt in 1971) while Susannah's son and grandson purchased the James Ready operation in New Brunswick in 1928. New Brunswick Breweries became Moosehead Breweries in order to keep from alienating the residents of Nova Scotia when the attraction of that province's beer market prompted the company to expand there in 1947.

The post-war years were kind to Moosehead as the brewery continued to grow and increase its market, largely under the leadership of Philip W. Oland who invested in the construction of a new Nova Scotia brewery in 1963 and oversaw the introduction of his beer to the States in 1978. By the mid-1980s, Moosehead was a common sight in all fifty states and was on its way to the United Kingdom.

Moosehead's growth since its name change has been largely based on its export market, a logical course of events when one considers that it was easier to sell beer from the Maritimes to the United States than to the rest of Canada. By 1993, Moosehead was sold either directly or as a licensed beer in Canada, the United States, the United Kingdom and Australia.

But Moosehead is not just the giver of licensed brewing opportunities, it is also the recipient of what is perhaps the oddest licensing contract in Canadian brewing. This agreement—which resulted from the same curious brewing laws that barred Moosehead from other provinces—has Moosehead brewing Molson Canadian under licence in the Maritimes, a situation one suspects Molson is reviewing carefully, now that the inter-provincial restrictions have been dropped.

While Moosehead may not necessarily have changed its direction, it certainly reoriented it a bit when, in the spring of 1992, the company launched its beer in Ontario, Alberta, British Columbia and Newfoundland. That country-wide introduction was facilitated by Moosehead's earlier acquisition of the Imported Beer Company (now the Premium Beer Co.) whose network of distribution it used to storm the central and western provinces.

The almost continuous blur of Moosehead expansion in the second half of the century hit a snag in the spring of 1992 when company president, Derek Oland, made the announcement of their intention to close down the Dartmouth, Nova Scotia, brewery. This, he said, was being done in the interests of rationalizing their production and making the brewery more competitive in the national market.

Competitiveness notwithstanding, Moosehead Lager is still among the most recognized Canadian beer brands around the globe and, considering its size relative to the national breweries, that should be enough to raise a few eyebrows, if not pint glasses. Safe to say, John and Susannah likely would have wanted it that way.

SCOREBOARD

Alpine Genuine Cold-Filtered (5% vol.)

Light gold-coloured with a soft and sweet, fresh hay nose. The sweet and grainy start holds some faint notes of leaf and leads into a thin body of fairly sweet and grainy malt with a leafy hop taste lingering lightly throughout toward a sour, rooty finish. ★

Alpine Lager (5% vol.)

Light gold in colour with a sweet nose of fresh-mown grass and sugar. The sweet and leafy start carries a significant but not dominant amount of hop. A definite metallic edge hangs over a predominantly sweet and sugary body with some earthy hop drying it slightly in the finish. ★

Clancy's Amber Ale (5% vol.)

Medium to dark amber in colour with a smoky aroma of grain, tobacco leaf and light licorice. The slightly sweet and rye bready start leads to a full, sweet body of roasted grain, sweetened coffee, smoke and light, nutty hop. The finish has a pronounced peanutty flavour with some sugary and caramel notes. ★★

Moosehead Beer (5% vol.)

Light gold-coloured with a bittersweet, grassy nose holding light sugar notes. The mildly creamy, sweet cereal start leads into a sugary body containing strong grass and root notes along with a light, woody hop. The finish is very sugary with a hint of drying hop and light alcohol notes. ★

Moosehead Pale Ale (5% vol.)

Light gold in colour with a sweetish, wet straw nose holding very mild, woody hopping. The lightly sweet and flowery start with buttery notes leads to sugary body-holding fruity (orange, peach) notes along with a sour, rooty hop and a sweet-and-sour, creamed corn finish. ★¹/₂

Moosehead Premium Dry (5.5% vol.)

Light gold in colour with a sweet cereal nose holding fresh hay and very faint hop notes. The creamy and very lightly grainy start precedes a sweet and sugary body with a sour, grassy edge. The finish turns very bitter with vegetal notes ★

Ten Penny Old Stock Ale (5.3% vol.)

Light gold-coloured with a woody and hoppy nose containing hay notes and a faint malty sweetness. The tart and carbonic body begins and ends with notes of sweet grain and is dry and somewhat acidic with woody hop and creamy grain notes. The bitter and metallic finish carries more hints of sweet grain. ★½

Unibroue Inc.

LOCATION:	*80 Des Carrieres, Chambly, Quebec G3L 2H6*
PHONE:	*514-954-9009, (fax) 514-658-9195*
OWNERS:	*André Dion, Riva Brewery (10%), Robert Charlebois (20%)*
PRESIDENT:	*André Dion*
BREWER:	*Gino Vantiegen*
CONSULTING BREWER:	*Pierre Celis*
BREWING CAPACITY:	*28,000 hl*
TOURS:	*On request*
BRANDS:	*Abbey-style blond double ale (due in late 1993), Blanche de Chambly, Massawippi Pale Ale (draught only), Maudite*

It is a long way from hammers, saws and screwdrivers to brew kettles, fermenters and draught taps, but André Dion has successfully negotiated himself through the transition. In the process, he also managed to build one of the larger micro-breweries in Quebec.

In his former life as a hardware magnate, Dion had no intention of becoming involved with the business of brewing. In fact, he had only a marginal interest in the industry even after he was out of the hardware business, but the beer industry can sometimes be terribly enticing and, if you let it, it will get you in its clutches. Dion let it.

Formerly an owner of the successful Rona chain of hardware stores, Dion was looking forward to at least semi-retirement when he sold off his holdings in the hardware business in 1990. Restlessness took its toll, however, and Dion was soon listening to some offers from other businessmen.

One such offer came from a coalition of Quebec micro-brewers with the intention of organizing a distribution network for their brands. Would Dion, they inquired, be interested in getting behind the idea? Intrigued by the challenge, Dion agreed and Unibroue was born.

The domestic beer distribution arrangement didn't pan out, though, and Dion soon found himself travelling through Belgium in search of beer labels there that he could import into his home province through his already established company. It was during one of these trips that he discovered the Riva Brewery in West Flanders.

Conscious of the success that other Belgian white beer brands had enjoyed in Quebec, Dion decided that, rather than acting as a mere importer for Riva, he would better serve his and beer drinkers' interests by purchasing the recipe for the wheat beer (in exchange for a 10 percent stake in Unibroue) and brewing it in the province itself. Now all he needed was a brewery.

Since, Dion says, the government of Quebec was very reluctant at the time to issue new licences to brew, he chose instead to buy the floundering Massawippi Brewing Company of Lennoxville. One of Quebec's two original craft breweries, Massawippi had been struck by hard times and was in danger of closing down completely. So, when Dion bought the brewery, he actually gave it a second life.

When Dion took over the brewery in early 1991, he decided to continue the production of the Massawippi Pale Ale but, at the same time, concentrate on developing his white beer for the Quebec market. To this end, Dion was fortunate enough to secure the services of Pierre Celis, late of the famous white beer brewery Hoegaarden in Belgium and en route to establishing his new brewery in Austin, Texas. With Celis subtly modifying the original Riva recipe, Blanche de Chambly was soon ready for brewing and the first kegs of the wheat beer were ready by March of the same year, thereby becoming the first beer of that style ever to be brewed in North America.

By almost all reports, Quebec beer drinkers immediately took to the new Blanche and Dion was soon planning for his second brand. This, too, it was decided, would be Belgian in character and, notably, Belgian in attitude, as well.

Belgian beers are well known for many reasons, not the least of which is their variety of flavour, but one particularly interesting trait is the morbid or satanic imagery present in many of the beer names. Dion endowed his new, double-fermented and 8% alcohol beer with that latter characteristic when he dubbed it Maudite, a French word meaning "damned" or "cursed." He even went so far as to package the brand in a carton decorated with a picture of a devil and a short prayer to Lucifer.

Since his devilish pursuits began, Dion has charged ahead with his Belgian attack on the Quebec micro market. In early 1993, he moved his brewery from Lennoxville to its namesake Chambly and doubled its size. He also planned, in the fall of 1993, to introduce a third Belgian-style ale which will be, he says, in the tradition of the world classic, Duvel.

For a man who came from a completely different industry, Dion displays none of the hesitancy that normally affects newcomers to the brewing business. Testament to the man's tenacity is his expansion to a size well beyond that of several long-established micros and his inclusion of Quebec singing legend Robert Charlebois in the ownership of the brewery. Then again, perhaps it is just that Dion has decided to shape the industry to his standards rather than the other way around.

SCOREBOARD

Blanche de Chambly (5% vol.)
Cloudy (from bottle-fermentation), sandy colour with a moderately spicy nose with citrus, clove and fresh grain notes. Lightly spiced and zesty front leads into a refreshing body with elements of lemon and lime, noticeable yeast, spice (coriander, clove) and light rye bread flavours. The finish is decidedly lemony with the remaining yeast carrying what is left of the spice. ★★½

Maudite (8% vol.)
Earthy brown colour with cloudiness from the bottle-fermentation. It has a mild nose with yeast, pear and light clove and wood aromas. The lively and spicy front leads to a full and complex body holding notes of cinnamon, yeast, green apple, alcohol and earthy hopping. The finish is slightly fruity, alcoholic and bitter with a touch of yeasty sourness. ★★★

CHAPTER SEVEN
Brewpubs

British Columbia

Prairie Inn Neighbourhood Pub and Cottage Brewery

LOCATION:	*7806 East Saanich Road, Victoria, British Columbia V0S 1M0*
PHONE:	*604-652-1575, (fax) 604-652-4368*
OWNER:	*Ted Anderson*
MANAGER:	*Ted Anderson*
BREWER & PUB MANAGER:	*Brian Mayzes*
CONSULTING BREWER:	*Malcolm McDonald*
CAPACITY:	*1,200 hl*
TOURS:	*On request; phone ahead*
BRANDS:	*Black Bitters Lager, English Gold Lager, Old Tavern Ale*

L ike so many brewpubs in Canada, the Prairie Inn has a great deal of history behind it, more than 100 years in fact.

For it was in 1859 that a businessman by the name of Henry Simpson built the first Prairie Tavern on Vancouver Island. It is doubtful that, at the time, he had any idea what he was starting.

Reading the history of the Prairie Inn, one gets the impression that over its long existence, it has drawn controversy like a moth to a flame. No doubt some neighbours and patrons were distraught when, in 1893, Simpson built the new, larger Prairie adjacent to the old location and tore down the original. Similarly, residents were disturbed over reports that the inn was running illegal booze out of a back room during Prohibition and, no doubt, equally frustrated when a police raid of the building failed to reveal any liquor.

In 1990, the inn found itself back in the thick of things when its application for a cold beer and wine store raised allegations of unscrupulous conduct on the part of opponents. Those charges were later proven to be of no substance and the inn got its store after a long battle.

Despite the controversy that seems to dog the Prairie Inn, it has survived and flourished through the century and into the 1990s. At least part of that success is attributable to the inn's move to cottage brewing in the early 1980s.

The second craft-brewing operation in Canada, the Prairie Inn added a bit more to its history when then-owner Dave Duncan installed the malt extract brewery in 1983. Because the laws had not yet been amended to allow for the brewing and serving of beer in the same building, the brewery is housed outside of the inn itself. However, the use of direct lines from the aging tanks to the tap handles—at the time a unique process in this country—was definitely a factor in the British Columbia government's decision to change said laws.

Two years after establishing his brewery, Duncan sold out to Ted Anderson, himself a veteran of the hotel and restaurant trade.

According to Anderson's pub manager and brewer, Brian Mayzes, the biggest effect Anderson had on the inn was the importation of his personal specialty: home-style cooking. His "down home" tendencies in the kitchen have led to the inn's blackboard menu of pub food, pies, sandwiches and specialty foods.

Anderson's acquisition of the inn also had the effect of introducing Mayzes to the world of brewing. Building on a five-year association with Anderson, Mayzes accompanied him to the pub portion of his new business and soon found himself in charge of brewing. It took a little time, some good advice and a lot of work, but Mayzes thinks that he has the hang of it now.

When you visit the Prairie Inn, you have the choice of dining in the very homey restaurant portion or joining the locals in the pub part with its 18 (!) televisions tuned to various sporting events. Either way, you can expect to be dished up a heaping helping of history with whatever you order.

SCOREBOARD

Black Bitters Lager (5% vol.)

Of dark amber colour with a sweet, bready aroma holding toffee notes. The thin, yeasty start heads into a light, tangy, rye bread body with faint chocolate notes. A thin, coffeeish finish with lingering malty notes completes the profile. $\frac{1}{2}$

English Gold Lager (5% vol.)

Medium gold in colour with a strong and sweet, butterscotchy nose. The sweet, tangy front leads to a very malty, sweet and sour body with candied orange flavours. The very tangy, confectionery finish is almost reminiscent of sweet-and-sour candies. $\frac{1}{2}$

Spinnakers Brew Pub

LOCATION:	*308 Catherine Street, Victoria, British Columbia V9A 3S8*
PHONE:	*604-384-0332, (fax) 604-384-3246*
OWNERS:	*Paul Hadfield, Ian Hadfield*
MANAGER:	*Paul Hadfield*
BREWER:	*Jacob Thomas*
CONSULTING BREWER:	*N/A*
CAPACITY:	*1,500 hl*
TOURS:	*On request*
BRANDS:	*Frequent wheat beers (RotesWeizen, Dunkle Heffeweizen, Weizenbrau), I.P.A., Jameson's Scottish Ale, Mitchell's ESB, Mt. Tolmie Dark, Rotating specialties, Rotating stouts (Imperial, Oatmeal, Empress, Old Knucklehead), Spinnakers Ale*

The opening of Canada's first "in-house" brewpub was, according to owner Paul Hadfield, a bit of a game of chicken played with the government.

As Hadfield recalls, he and the rest of the owners of Spinnakers (including Canadian brewing pioneer John Mitchell) were going ahead with the construction of the brewpub before the legislation allowing its existence was even in place. Fortunately, the change in the law to allow the on-site brewing of beer for pub consumption came just before the partners were finished.

Such are the risks of trailblazing in the Canadian brewing business.

Since its long-anticipated opening in May 1984, Spinnakers has blazed perhaps more than its fair share of trails. From the original problems associated with their location (they had to find a non-residential site for their neighbourhood pub!) to the owners' money-losing foray into the Seattle brewpub market, Spinnakers has faced and overcome many difficulties in its short history and, no doubt, will face a few more as it continues its progress and evolution.

Nothing, however, is likely to rival the exhilaration and excitement of those early days, says Hadfield.

Beginning with the site selection, says Hadfield, the community was fascinated by what the partners were attempting to accomplish. He recalls the days of construction when local residents would drop by to ask how things were progressing and find out when the brewing would commence. And when the beer making finally did start, the curiosity simply became more intense as neighbours from near and far began to thirst for the Spinnakers brews to appear.

Hadfield also remembers the response when they did open their doors as being "phenomenal."

Potential customers, says Hadfield, were running in the door and going directly to the pay phone to call their friends and beckon them to come down. For the partners, it was the fruition of a dream.

That dream cruised along quite nicely until one of the partners (who is no longer with the pub) decided that it would be a good idea to expand their operations to Seattle and, from there, move into the larger American market. That kind of pressure was reportedly not what Mitchell had in mind and, due to the impending move and other issues, he left the group in 1986.

His departure did nothing to slow the expansion plans, though, and Spinnakers hit Seattle in 1988 with two locations, one by the university and another in a shopping mall. Unfortunately for the owners, neither pub was destined to survive and, by the early 1990s the Victoria pub was once again the only Spinnakers.

Following the failed experiment in the United States, Hadfield says that he refocused on Victoria and got back into a hands-on management style. That management resulted in the birth of the Spinnakers Brew Pub dining room in the pub's space on the first floor, moving the pub up to the second level.

While the pub retains its traditional, self-serve approach to food and drinks (customers order and pick up everything at the bar), the restaurant's birth marked the beginning of table service at Spinnakers. Now, says Hadfield, some of his longtime customers who are married with children can come to the pub restaurant for dinner with their kids, something they could not do under provincial law in the pub itself.

Despite all the ups and downs over the years, Hadfield still says that it has been a "great ride" being part of the pub. And one look at the man's grin tells you that he is most definitely sincere on that count.

SCOREBOARD

E.S.B. (5% vol.)

Copper-coloured with chocolate toffee in the nose alongside barnyard notes. The bittersweet, soft malt start with very light cherry notes heads into a very full and rich body of woody, bitter hop and the occasional caramel note creeping in. The finish is of strong and bitter hop. ★★★ As a cask-conditioned ale it has a full leafiness to it with a slight edge of saltiness and a more strongly bitter finish. ★★★

I.P.A. (4.9% vol.)

Light gold colour with a honeyish malt nose holding floral hop notes. The surprisingly sharp start (considering the aroma) has an almost lime-like bitterness leading to a full, very rooty and bitter hop body with touch of a saline. Bitter to the point of nearing sourness in the grassy finish. ★★

Jameson's Scottish Ale (4.7% vol.)

Copper-coloured with a malty aroma holding sweet notes of toffee and pear. A soft, slightly sugary start with mixed fruit heads to a dry body with woody hopping, bitter chocolate malt notes and mild astringency. Very dry, earthy finish. ★½

Mt. Tolmie Dark (4.2% vol.)

Of light mahogany colour, it has a mild, plummy nose with hints of coffee. The soft coffeeish start leads to a lightly bitter, earthy hop body with notes of roasted sugar and coffee. The finish is strong, dry and earthy. ★★

Old Knucklehead Stout (5.7% vol.)

Jet-black in colour with a roasted coffee bean nose holding hints of burnt sugar. It has a malty start with a touch of saline in the coffee character. A rich, mocha body with woody and earthy hop leads to a dry, slightly bigger coffee finish. ★★½

Spinnaker's Ale (4% vol.)

Light to medium gold in colour with a faintly cinnamony, caramel malt nose. A soft, slightly toffeeish start leads to a woody, bitter hop and slightly plummy malt body with a bitter, faintly sour sugar-root finish. ★★

Swan's Brewpub/
Buckerfield's Brewery

LOCATION:	*506 Pandora Street, Victoria,*
	British Columbia V8W 1N6
PHONE:	*604-361-3310, (fax) 604-361-3491*
OWNERS:	*Michael Williams*
MANAGER:	*Janina Ceglarz*
BREWER:	*Chris Johnson*
CONSULTING BREWER:	*Frank Appleton*
CAPACITY:	*2,000 hl*
TOURS:	*On request; phone ahead*
BRANDS:	*Appleton Brown Ale, Arctic Ale,*
	Buckerfield's Bitter, Old Towne Bavarian
	Lager, Pandora Pale Ale, Porter,
	Rotating specialties,
	Swan's Oatmeal Stout

The first thing you notice as you enter the Swan's Brewpub is that this is no ordinary brewpub.

With its intrinsic elegance that speaks of an era long past, Swan's is a place that you might have trouble associating with the word "pub." Then again, it is also the last place you would expect to have had its origins in sheep farming.

Owner Michael Williams came to Canada from the United Kingdom in 1950 determined to become one of the best sheep farmers in the nation. According to him, he pretty much attained that goal, having risen to the rank of manager of one of the country's largest sheep farms by 1958.

Following this success, Williams moved into dog breeding for a time before beginning a career in real estate speculation in 1964 and, by 1977, he had graduated once again, developing his own properties. After a flirtation with bankruptcy through what Williams calls "political pressures," he recovered to become a major landholder in and around the Victoria area.

In 1987, Williams bought and remodelled the building which is now home to Swan's, the very same warehouse he used to visit to buy animal feed many years earlier. The remodelling, however, had little to do with brewing beer. Rather, Williams converted the place into a group of apartments with stores underneath.

Less than a year later, the former sheep farmer saw the bottom dropping out of the economy and thought that he had best effect another change on his building. This one was to turn it into a brewpub and hotel.

The Swan's building is now home to a café, a seafood and chicken restaurant, a 29-suite hotel, a cold beer and wine store and, of course, a brewpub. And the pub is what the owner bashfully refers to as "likely the busiest in the city."

Equally likely is the chance that the Swan's brewery is the largest pub-based facility in the country. Set off from a hallway outside of the pub, the brewery rambles for square metre after square metre, providing a sharp contrast to the cramped quarters that normally define a house-brewing operation. Should demand warrant, there is still plenty of room for expansion.

Williams is a man who prides himself on his appreciation of beauty and, accordingly, everything in the pub is fastidiously maintained. From the fresh flowers that sit on every table to the rotating selections from Williams's own private art collection that adorn the walls, Swan's is an exercise in aesthetics.

The crowds that line up most nights outside of Swan's appear to approve.

SCOREBOARD

Appleton Brown Ale (5% vol.)
Of medium brown, slightly coppery colour, the nose is lightly chocolatey with nutty notes. The full, chocolate and caramel body tastes sweet but not candied. It starts soft with a little leafy hop and carries nutty (walnut) flavours in the body with brown sugar notes rising through the slightly syrupy finish. ★★

Arctic Ale (4.5% vol.)
Coloured light to medium gold with a perfumey and fruity (especially peach) aroma. The creamy malt body is light at the start but turns fruity through the taste with orange and apricot notes. A woody hopping develops in the second half to dry out the finish along with a yeasty tang. ★$^{1}/_{2}$

Buckerfield's Bitter (5% vol.)
Copper-brown in colour with a strong brewhouse aroma of wort and very nutty hop. The start, middle and end are all dominated by nutty notes of Brazil nut and hazelnut with a little light chocolate up front, coffee notes in the middle and an earthy, bitter finish. ★★$^{1}/_{2}$

Old Towne Bavarian Lager (5.4% vol.)

Medium gold in colour with a spicy nose holding fruity, caramel malt and floral hop. The slightly thin, sweet malt front leads to a lightly woody, hopped body with sour orange notes and a yeasty tang that extends to the dry and grainy finish. ★

Pandora Pale Ale (4.5% vol.)

Light amber-coloured with its leafy hop aroma subdued by an evident fruity malt. A light start of faint nutmeg and orange malt leads to a medium-hopped body with a leafy hop blending with fruity malt and notes of caramel. The finish dries somewhat with the hopping but remains notably fruity and sweet. ★½

Porter (5.6% vol.)

Deep black in colour with a roasted, slightly burnt grain nose holding notes of candied sugar. A slightly astringent start carries light coffee notes with the body turning dark chocolate with nutty hop and espresso flavours. Bitter chocolate finishes the taste along with earthy hopping. ★★

Swan's Oatmeal Stout (5.4% vol.)

Deep, rich plum-coloured with a thick, sweet aroma of chocolate-covered cherry and light orange. The taste accelerates from a light, coffee-and-sugar start to a sweetish, roasted mocha body with some woody hop. A strong, bitter coffee finish with acidity and a touch of refined sugar complete the profile. ★★

The Prairies

Barley Mill Brewing Company

LOCATION:	*6807 Rochdale Boulevard NW, Regina, Saskatchewan S4X 2Z2*
PHONE:	*306-949-1500, (fax) 306-949-0006*
OWNERS:	*Dave Dunn, Perry Dunn & Dalbert Dunn*
MANAGER:	*Kevin McCutchon*
BREWERS:	*Perry Dunn & Touy Bonnouvong*
CONSULTING BREWER:	*Cask*
CAPACITY:	*520 hl*
TOURS:	*On request*
BRANDS:	*Classic Lager, Electric Lager, Golden Grain Wheat, Prairie Lager*

If it is true that there is not a whole lot of difference between baking and brewing, then the Dunn brothers are likely more aware of that than anyone else in Canada.

The former owners of the franchise operations for Robin's Donuts in both British Columbia and Saskatchewan, the three Dunns have had their hands in both the dough and the malt through the years. The fact that they have opted for beer over donuts in the long run is probably indicative of which area they preferred. Of course, who could blame them? I cannot recall ever having seen a donut shop owner hang around his store and buy a round of apple fritters for his friends.

The first foray into the brewpub business for the Dunns came in 1988 when the Saskatchewan government accepted tenders for the first four brewpub licences to be granted in that province. With their long background in the hospitality industry, the Dunns felt that making an application would be a wise business move.

The Dunns' history of involvement in the hospitality trade extended beyond the selling of donuts. In the late 1970s, the brothers owned a neighbourhood pub in Vancouver called the Last Straw and, following their return to Regina in the early 1980s, the three had bought and sold several restaurants and nightclubs over the intervening years. It was their neighbourhood pub experience, however, that best prepared them for their entry into the brewpub field.

According to Dave Dunn, the brothers felt that a brewpub was essentially just a neighbourhood pub with brewing facilities and were therefore confident in their bid for a licence. When their proposal was chosen as one of the four, they realized that they had to learn about the brewing of beer and learn it quickly.

Working in concert with The Lanigan Group, the other brewpub licensees, Dunn says that they listened to proposals from both Cask and Continental systems representatives and eventually chose Cask because they felt that the proximity of a western versus an eastern company would better serve their interests. By the late winter and early spring of 1989, the Barley Mill was in construction.

The brothers were lucky, says Dunn, because their landlord had just finished building what would become the home of the Barley Mill, so there were no delays in beginning the interior. Dunn also adds that the location was ideal because it was in a developing residential area with minimal off-sale beer service. Since the first four brewpubs were granted cold beer store licences along with their brewing permits, the latter characteristic was as important as the former, if not more so.

Being new brewpub owners with an eye focused more toward the potential off-sale profits than the brewing of beer, the Dunns opted for malt extract brewing in their new pub. Cask-trained Perry Dunn and he, in turn, showed longtime employee Touy Bonnouvong how to brew. Bonnouvong had formerly been the head baker with Robin's Donuts, so the partners believed that it would be a logical progression for him to turn his hand to brewing.

While Dunn admits that the house beer sales at the Barley Mill are slow because they have a hard time switching the regular customers from their favourite drinks, he adds that they may consider making a conversion to full grain brewing in the future. He and his brothers, says Dunn, are much more aware of the importance of their beer now than they were in their donut years.

SCOREBOARD

Classic Lager (5% vol.)
Light copper-coloured with a soft butterscotchy aroma holding light bitter and woody hop notes. The very malty body begins lightly fruity and sweet before turning caramelly with light fruit (apricot) and flower notes along with a very faint yeastiness. The finish is fairly dry with a touch of leafy hopping. ★

Electric Pilsner (5% vol.)
Pale gold-coloured with a sour toffee and yeast aroma. An acidic, toffee front precedes a very sour and yeasty body containing strong citric notes and a sour and rooty lime finish. ★

Golden Grain Wheat (5% vol.)

Light amber in colour with a banana and caramel aroma carrying a yeasty tang. The sweet and tangy sugar front leads to a slightly fruity (banana) and very lightly spicy malt body with some sharp, bitter hopping showing in the second half toward the sour and grassy finish. ★

Bonzzini's Brewpub

LOCATION:	*4634 Albert Street South, Regina, Saskatchewan S4S 6B4*
PHONE:	*306-586-3553*
OWNERS:	*Barry Armstrong, Gord McCormick, Dave Dunn & Perry Dunn*
MANAGERS:	*Rob Doborowski & Phil Shaw*
BREWER:	*Phil Shaw*
CONSULTING BREWER:	*Cask*
CAPACITY:	*520 hl*
TOURS:	*On request*
BRANDS:	*Bearr Lager, Great Plains Pilsner Nut Brown Ale, Red Tail Ale*

There were numerous Italian restaurants in the developing south end of Regina in 1990, but there was a distinct lack of pubs and, especially, brewpubs. So when longtime restaurateur Barry Armstrong decided that the time had come to renovate and renew his nine-year-old restaurant, the choice of a replacement motif seemed obvious.

The problem Armstrong had, however, was that his partner, Peter Gulf, was in no mood for beginning a new enterprise and wanted nothing to do with the proposal. The Dunn brothers and Gord McCormick, on the other hand, were very much interested in getting involved in a new brewpub and so a deal was made for them to buy out Gulf.

Given that Bonzzini's was an old-style Italian restaurant and the new ambience was to be that of a neighbourhood pub and sports bar, extensive renovations were obviously required. Most important, a craftsman carpenter was necessary for the planned design. To that end, a call was made to Phil Shaw.

Shaw had known and worked with the Dunns for over a dozen years and it was he who crafted the showpiece bar at Bonzzini's. As it happened, Shaw was also interested in another form of craftsmanship, namely brewing. When the renovations were complete, he approached the owners with the offer to brew their beer for them; his services were accepted. By June 1991, Phil Shaw was brewing malt-extract ales and lagers at the brewpub.

The dramatic change at Bonzzini's has, according to Dave Dunn, worked quite well. No doubt keeping the original name has confused a few patrons over the years, but overall, the move appears to have been successful.

Dunn says that once the full-grain brewing is mastered by Shaw at their new Regina brewpub, The Last Straw (see "Coming Soon" chapter), the ownership group will be looking very seriously at converting Bonzzini's to all-grain brewing, as well.

The reason behind this move, says Dunn, is that they have received a very good response to their house beers at the brewpub and feel that the reception to grain brews would be even better. He adds that the provincial government's allowance of the sale of brewpub beer for home consumption has also played a role in the possible move. If the demand for carryout beer is there, he says, they would like to be in a comfortable position to make the most of the opportunity.

If the change is made to Bonzzini's, the effect on the Regina market could be tremendous. With the opening of the all-grain Last Straw, three out of the five brewpubs in the city were full grain by the summer of 1993 and, with Bonzzini's joining the fold, only the Dunns' own Barley Mill would remain an extract brewery. That's the kind of grain-to-extract ratio that could really put Regina on the brewing map.

SCOREBOARD

Bearr Lager (4.5% vol.)
  Light gold-coloured with a very sweet and sugary aroma holding strong butterscotch notes. The soft, carbonic start holds a touch of butteriness before a sour and grassy body containing sweet grain notes and a sour, lemony finish. ★

Great Plains Pilsener (4.5% vol.)
  Light to medium gold in colour with a sweet, maple-butter aroma. the soft and mildly sweet, buttery start leads to a very tart and acidic grain body and a very sour and rooty finish holding yeast notes. $\frac{1}{2}$

Nut Brown Ale (4.5% vol.)

Copper-coloured with a sweet toffee aroma holding yeast notes. A mildly sweet and appley start precedes a very lightly toasted malt body with sweet toffee flavours and a yeasty tang. The finish has woody notes in a bitter and sour character. ★

Red Tail Ale (4.5% vol.)

Deep rust in colour with a sweet candied cherry aroma. A soft and very lightly chocolatey start heads into a sweetish malt body with hints of dark chocolate and weak coffee before a slightly bitter, earthy finish. ★½

Brewsters Brew Pub and Brasserie

LOCATION:	*834—11th Avenue SW, Calgary, Alberta T2R 0E5*
PHONE:	*403-263-2739, (fax) 403-265-2620*
OWNERS:	*The Lanigan Group*
MANAGER:	*Aaron Adams*
BREWER:	*Clifford Aukland*
CONSULTING BREWER:	*N/A*
CAPACITY:	*1,500 hl*
TOURS:	*On request*
BRANDS:	*Big Horn Bitter, Blue Monk Barley Wine, Bow Valley Brown Ale, Continental Light Lager, Ernest Bay Premium Pilsner, Flying Frog Lager, Hammerhead Red Ale, Original Lager, Palliser Pale Ale, Shaughnessy Stout, Specialties, Wild West Wheat*

Looking back on the Lanigan mini-empire of two brewpubs in Alberta and two in Saskatchewan, it is hard to imagine that it all started with a rural, prairie hotel purchased on a second mortgage by Michael Lanigan. One wonders what the Saskatchewan native would have said if, at that time, someone had told him that he would soon be running a pair of brewpubs in Calgary!

The Alberta locations—the second and fourth in the Brewsters chain—are largely the domain of Michael Lanigan and he splits his time between the two brewpubs. It is the downtown site, however, that one suspects takes up most of his attention.

The Lanigans moved to Alberta from Saskatchewan for expansion because they felt that there was limited room for the industry in their home province. Market saturation was no worry at all in Calgary, though, as the only brewpub that had ever opened in the city had closed two or three years earlier. So, when the brothers made the move to Alberta, they made it in a big way.

In fact, big is an understatement when one is talking about the downtown Calgary Brewsters. Seating 375 people, the brewpub definitely qualifies as one of the larger ones in Canada. That kind of business, one suspects, must keep brewer Cliff Aukland very busy.

One of the many former brewers of Victoria's Spinnakers (see separate entry under British Columbia) who dot the landscape of the Canadian brewing industry, Aukland not only has to keep up with the demand for draught that the massive brewpub places upon him, but must also find time to keep the off-sale beer fridge fully stocked with one-litre bottles of Brewsters's 11 regular brands. Add to this count the several specialty brews Aukland insists on dabbling in and you have one very busy brewer.

When questioned about the rather odd southwestern location of the Calgary Brewsters, the Lanigans explain that, in their minds, the site was ideal for the crowds they were seeking to draw. Situated about equal distance from the downtown core and Calgary's infamous Electric Avenue of singles bars and dance clubs, the brewpub draws from the denizens of both areas, says Laurie Lanigan, by appealing to those who are looking for something just a little different.

And, with the only house-brewed beer in Alberta, the Lanigans can certainly lay claim to the status of something different.

SCOREBOARD

(Note: To provide points for comparison but also avoid over-duplication, the Hammerhead Ale, Original Lager and Stout were reviewed at all four locations while the other brands and specialties were tasted in only one location each.)

Ernest Bay Premium Pilsner (5% vol.)

Light gold in colour with fairly soft aromatics of flowers with notes of icing sugar. The light, bittersweet front carries a hint of toffee toward a well-hopped and bitter body with some grassiness and a moderating light, sweet maltiness. The finish is dry and grassy. ★★

Hammerhead Red Ale (5% vol.)

Amber in colour with a full, caramelly aroma holding some floral hopping. The light, slightly appley start leads to a plummy body with some notes of sour fruit pit and a dry vinous finish holding some woody hopping. ★★

Original Lager (5% vol.)

Light gold-coloured with a sweet-and-sour, citric grain aroma. A light, faintly citric start moves to a grainy body with sour, caramelly notes and a dry, cereal finish. ★$^{1}/_{2}$

Shaughnessy Stout (5% vol.)

Dark chocolate-coloured with a bitter chocolate and woody hop aroma. The roasted to burnt malt start leads into a bittersweet mocha body with raw sugar notes and some light acidity before a bitter coffee finish. ★★

Brewsters Brew Pub and Brasserie

LOCATION:	176—755 Lake Bonavista Drive SE, Calgary, Alberta T2J 0N3
PHONE:	403-225-BREW, (fax) 403-225-2742
OWNERS:	The Lanigan Group
MANAGER:	Jim Cassie
BREWER:	Michael Tymchuk
CONSULTING BREWER:	N/A
CAPACITY:	1,500 hl
TOURS:	On request
BRANDS:	Big Horn Bitter, Blue Monk Barley Wine, Bow Valley Brown Ale, Continental Light Lager, Ernest Bay Premium Pilsner, Flying Frog Lager, Hammerhead Red Ale, Original Lager, Palliser Pale Ale, Shaughnessy Stout, Specialties, Wild West Wheat

One popular characteristic of prairie brewpubs is a shopping mall location. Of the ten pubs that are found in Saskatchewan and Alberta, half of them are situated either in or adjacent to a plaza. Even the

Brewsters chain is not immune to this tendency, the brothers Lanigan having built their suburban Calgary location, the fourth in the group, in an enclosed mall near the southeastern tip of the city.

Not that the Lake Bonavista Brewsters has any reason to apologize for its location. The Lanigans have carefully protected the atmosphere of the pub from the "shopping mall restaurant syndrome" that has turned countless such establishments into roadhouse clones or fast-food joints with sit-down prices. Instead, Brewsters is what Laurie Lanigan describes as a Canadian play on the British pub theme.

Saying that the brothers are proud of the individuality of each Brewsters, Lanigan explains that the only recurring theme in the chain is that of a purely Canadian brewpub. When designing their decors, he continues, the idea was to neither borrow too heavily from the British pub tradition nor fall back on the American roadhouse/sports bar concept.

The result is a comfortable combination of several styles that weighs each in different proportions at every location. The Lake Bonavista Brewsters, for example, trades more heavily on the old English pub theme than the others, but not at the expense of a few television screens and background music.

The man in charge of the brews at the shopping mall is Michael Tymchuk, a former Spinnakers (see separate entry under British Columbia) brewer whose name also crops up in a consulting capacity with a few other western brewpubs. The stability of a permanent position over the uncertainty of consulting seems to agree with Tymchuk and, although he says he could use a little more room, he is very happy with the new brewery he has at Lake Bonavista.

He also enjoys a little friendly rivalry with another Spinnakers alumnus, downtown Brewsters brewer Cliff Aukland. While Tymchuk says that he or Aukland will occasionally make the 20-minute drive to help the other brewer out, it is obvious that the two men also enjoy keeping track of the each other's brews and comparing them to their own.

Apparently, there is nothing like a little healthy competition to help keep the beer flowing properly in Calgary.

SCOREBOARD

(Note: To provide points for comparison but also avoid over-duplication, the Hammerhead Ale, Original Lager and Stout were reviewed at all four locations while the other brands and specialties were tasted in only one location each.)

Big Horn Bitter (5% vol.)

Amber-coloured with a nutty, sour orange aroma. The soft and lightly roasted caramel front precedes a strongly woody and bitter body with pronounced nuttiness (Brazil nut, hazelnut) developing through the taste to a bitter nutshell finish. ★★½

Hammerhead Red Ale (5% vol.)

Light amber in colour with a spicy caramel nose holding faint saline notes. The light and slightly appley start leads to a thinnish, fruity (plum, cherry pit) body and a dry and woody finish. ★★

Original Lager (5% vol.)

Pale gold in colour with a sweet-and-sour, citric grain aroma. The carbonic start is light and faintly citric while the body turns rather grainy but retains the citrus notes along with a light sourness. The finish sours further with cereal grain notes. ★½

Palliser Pale Ale (5% vol.)

Medium gold to light amber in colour with a lightly floral, strong toffee nose. A slightly buttery and lightly fruity (peach, apricot) start leads into an earthy body with woody hopping rising throughout to a faint hint of lime in the dry, woody finish. ★★

Shaughnessy Stout (5% vol.)

Dark chocolate in colour with a baker's chocolate, woody hop and coffee aroma. The roasted and burnt malt start heads into a bittersweet mocha body and a clean, coffee finish. ★★

Brewsters Brew Pub and Brasserie

LOCATION:	*8 Main Street North, Moose Jaw, Saskatchewan S6H 3J6*
PHONE:	*306-694-5580, (fax) 306-694-5580*
OWNERS:	*The Lanigan Group*
MANAGER:	*Victor Dormuth*
BREWER:	*Stan Gerlach*
CONSULTING BREWER:	*N/A*
CAPACITY:	*550 hl*
TOURS:	*On request*
BRANDS:	*Big Horn Bitter, Blue Monk Barley Wine, Bow Valley Brown Ale, Continental Light Lager, Ernest Bay Premium Pilsner, Flying Frog Lager, Hammerhead Red Ale, Original Lager, Palliser Pale Ale, Shaughnessy Stout, Specialties, Wild West Wheat*

Given that the three Lanigan brothers who form The Lanigan Group got their start in the hospitality trade through the buying and selling of hotels, it comes as no surprise that one of their four brewpubs is housed in a hotel. Even a hotel in Moose Jaw.

The Moose Jaw location is not odd for the Lanigans because, in many ways, Moose Jaw is the brothers' second home. It was there, after all, that Michael bought his second hotel and involved his brother Laurie in his business. It was also in Moose Jaw that the third brother, Marty, got himself into the growing family industry through the purchase of a second hotel.

The historic inn which houses the third of the four Brewsters brewpubs is the Cornerstone Inn, situated on Main Street across from the train station in the heart of the city. Built in 1889, the Cornerstone has been called many names including the Maple Leaf Hotel and the Churchill Hotel, but it is now simply known as "The Stone."

For a decade prior to its new life, the bar in The Stone was named Lanigan's and was a prairie hotel bar like so many others of its ilk across Saskatchewan. In October 1991, however, Lanigan's became Brewsters and Moose Jaw became the only city on the Prairies outside of Saskatoon, Regina and Calgary to have its own brewpub.

While the Lanigan brothers knew from their history with brewpubs that they were due for a tough time selling the concept, the decision was made to expand the chain to their hotel anyway and the brewing equipment was purchased. And some curious equipment it was, indeed.

Unlike their other breweries, the Moose Jaw brewery was outfitted with used rather than new brewing and fermenting kettles, including some vessels that were rescued from a bankrupt dairy. The resulting brewery, kept running by brewer Stan Gerlach, is as interesting as it is unusual.

As the brothers suspected, selling their own beer has been a trial at times in tradition-strong Moose Jaw but, by 1993, their house beer accounted for a full 70 percent of their beer sales. It makes one wonder if the popularity of the Brewsters beer has been partially forged by some of the longtime Moose Jaw residents who may well remember the days of Moose Jaw Brewing in the 1930s and are proud to see beer being made in their hometown once again.

If nothing else, the Moose Jaw Brewsters proves that an age-old tradition like brewing can fit comfortably into a century-old hotel.

SCOREBOARD

(Note: To provide points for comparison but also avoid over-duplication, the Hammerhead Ale, Original Lager and Stout were reviewed at all four locations while the other brands and specialties were tasted in only one location each.)

Continental Light (4% vol.)
Light gold in colour with a sweet and very caramelly malt nose. The slightly bitter start has notes of sweet grain leading to a thinnish, grainy body with grassy hop bitterness and a slightly buttery, bitter-sweet finish. ★★

Flying Frog (5% vol.)
Medium gold to light amber in colour with a candied malt aroma that is sweet and somewhat flowery. The bittersweet, woody start leads into a nutty body with faint caramel malt and a lightly bitter, earthy and somewhat astringent finish. ★½

Hammerhead Red Ale (5% vol.)
Deep rust in colour and sweet in the plummy malt aroma. A mild start with very light sweetness leads to a full, plummy and mildly alcoholic body with notes of nutty hop. The bitter finish carries dry, nutty notes. ★★

Original Lager (5% vol.)

Light gold-coloured with a soft and sweet grain aroma holding a few sour, rooty notes. A soft, sweet grass start precedes a bittersweet and very grainy body holding notes of hay and grassy hop. The dry and fairly neutral finish holds some hints of bitter, dried-leaf hop. ★½

Qu'Appelle Valley Brown (5% vol.)

Copper-coloured with a sweet, butterscotchy and mildly floral nose. An off-dry start with very faint, sweet chocolate notes heads into a sweet and fruity body of apple, light chocolate and woody hop with a bitter and earthy hop finish. ★★

Shaughnessy Stout (5% vol.)

Deep plum-coloured with a sweet chocolate toffee aroma carrying some light, sweetened coffee notes. A soft, mildly chocolatey start with nutty notes precedes a bittersweet body of roasted malt and light, earthy hopping with soft coffee notes and a bitter, espresso finish. ★★

Brewsters Brew Pub and Brasserie

LOCATION:	*1832 Victoria Avenue East, Regina, Saskatchewan S4N 7K3*
PHONE:	*306-761-1500, (fax) 306-761-0863*
OWNERS:	*The Lanigan Group*
MANAGER:	*Laurie Lanigan*
BREWER:	*Mike Gamblin*
CONSULTING BREWER:	*Cask*
CAPACITY:	*1,040 hl*
TOURS:	*On request*
BRANDS:	*Big Horn Bitter, Blue Monk Barley Wine, Bow Valley Brown Ale, Continental Light Lager, Ernest Bay Premium Pilsner, Flying Frog Lager, Hammerhead Red Ale, Original Lager, Palliser Pale Ale, Shaughnessy Stout, Specialties, Wild West Wheat*

When the Saskatchewan government allowed brewpubs in its province in the late 1980s, it decided that a grand total of four licences—two in Regina and two in Saskatoon—were to be awarded among all of the applicants. Fortunately for the Prairies, the three Lanigan brothers were chosen to receive one of those licences. "Fortunately" because The Lanigan Group now owns four of the six full grain brewpubs in Alberta and Saskatchewan.

Of the four Lanigan pubs, all named Brewsters, the Regina location in the east end of the city was the first and, says Laurie Lanigan, was also where the brothers learned a lot about the brewpub business.

To begin with, says Lanigan, they did not know the full effect of the choice they had to make between grain or malt extract brewing. In fact, he admits, they did not know much about the brewpub business at all, a situation they partially remedied through visits to several Ontario and British Columbia brewpubs.

Research notwithstanding, the Lanigans still ended up with a malt extract brewing system when they opened in May 1989 and became Saskatchewan's first modern brewpub.

A great deal of customer education went on in the early days, says Lanigan, because they had to convert the domestic bottled lager drinker into a specialty draught ale and lager drinker. The situation was further complicated by the fact that, by Lanigan's count, there were no more than a half dozen imports available at the time.

Regardless of its handicaps, however, Lanigan says that the Regina Brewsters survived through a combination of persistence, the constant attention given to the food and their focus on serving the neighbourhood as a pub. Also, according to Lanigan and his brother Marty, they learned more about brewing quality beers as the pub developed and, soon enough, were looking to changing the system to a full grain one.

Like all of the Lanigan brewpubs, the Regina one is now full grain and, in retrospect, the brothers are almost embarrassed by the extract brews they served in the first year or two. In contrast, the two men are so proud of their brews now that, as of the spring of 1993, Laurie and Marty were investigating the possibility of bottling their beers for sale in their attached cold beer off-sale store.

SCOREBOARD

(Note: To provide points for comparison but also avoid over-duplication, the Hammerhead Ale, Original Lager and Stout were reviewed at all four locations while the other brands and specialties were tasted in only one location each.)

Big Horn Bitter (5% vol.)

Copper-coloured with a brewhouse aroma containing notes of lightly sweet malt and nutty, perfumey hop. The bitter and mildly caramel start leads into a full body with a strong, leafy hop over a lightly sweet and fruity (orange, apricot) malt. The bitter and woody finish holds faint touches of sweet molasses. ★★★

Blue Monk Barley Wine (7.5% vol.)

Port-coloured with a sour and vinous nose. The thick and chewy body has a jammy start leading to a sweet-and-sour cherry body with sugar and coffee notes and an alcoholic edge approaching that of a fortified wine. The sweet and alcoholic finish is reminiscent of grape jelly. ★★

Hammerhead Red Ale (5% vol.)

Deep copper-coloured with a roasted grain, floral hop and light toffee nose. A roasted butterscotch start leads into a full, plummy body with some woody hop. The bitter and well-hopped finish carries hints of coffee. ★★$^{1}/_{2}$

Original Lager (5% vol.)

Light gold in colour with a caramel grain nose holding some spicy hop notes. The sweetish, carbonic start with candied lemon peel notes leads to a bittersweet and grainy body holding rooty hop and extremely light citric notes with a bitter, earthy finish. ★$^{1}/_{2}$

Shaughnessy Stout (5% vol.)

Dark burgundy in colour with a medium to light coffee and licorice aroma. The sweet and slightly yeasty chocolate start precedes a full body of anise, bitter coffee and nearly burnt grain. The finish is bitter with baker's chocolate notes. ★★$^{1}/_{2}$

Wild West Wheat (5% vol.)

Light gold in colour and very fresh in the new hay aroma. A light, grainy, sweet-and-sour start leads into a slightly clovey body of grain and grassy hop notes with a dry and lightly bitter finish holding faint notes of citrus. ★$^{1}/_{2}$

Bushwakker Brewing Company

LOCATION:	*2206 Dewdney Avenue, Regina, Saskatchewan S4R 1H3*
PHONE:	*306-359-7276, (fax) 306-359-7750*
OWNERS:	*Bev Robertson, family members & silent partners*
MANAGER:	*Elaine Robertson*
BREWER:	*Scott Robertson*
CONSULTING BREWER:	*Brad McQuhae*
CAPACITY:	*1,650 hl*
TOURS:	*On request*
BRANDS:	*Granny's Bitter, Last Mountain Lager, Northern Lights, Palliser Porter, Regina Pale Ale, Rotated specialties, Stubblejumper Pils*

One of the more elusive connections in the Canadian brewing business is the link between cross-country skiing and beer. The answer is the Bushwakker Brewing Company, named after a term used to describe skiing through the dense brush and whacking at it with one's poles.

While many home brewers have taken their passion into the commercial brewing field, few have done it as successfully as Bev Robertson, the owner of Bushwakker. And few have done it as unconventionally.

A prizewinner in Canadian Amateur Brewing Association contests past, Robertson was working with a sophisticated, full-grain brewing system at home when the call came from the Saskatchewan government to enter applications for brewpub licences. Despite his lack of experience in the hospitality trade, Robertson figured that, if he was going to brew anyway, he might as well be brewing commercially. After arranging a franchise agreement with Victoria's Spinnakers (see separate entry under British Columbia), Robertson submitted his application and sat back to wait for the results.

Unfortunately, he was not successful the first time out in 1988 and had to wait until the government decided to issue further licences. In the interim, Robertson says that other brewpub owners who had been licensed approached him to brew in their establishments but he refused unless they agreed to turn them into full-grain operations. His proposal was not accepted.

His second application for a licence was approved and Robertson was soon searching for a home for his brewpub. Although he originally considered a downtown location for the Bushwakker, Robertson says that he decided on the uptown site mainly due to its extensive available parking. Construction of the new brewpub—Regina's first all-grain operation—began in August 1990 and was completed and opened by January of the following year.

The beer is taken very seriously at the Bushwakker and, although Robertson has handed the brewing chores over to his son, he is still fiercely proud of the beer that he serves to his customers. So proud, in fact, that he keeps one major brewery beer on tap only because he is forced to by law and carries no domestic bottled beer at all, save for three Big Rock brands.

This total devotion to brewing has apparently been successful. Robertson boasts that 95 percent of all beer sales and 50 percent of the pub's total sales come from the house taps, truly impressive numbers for any brewpub. Furthermore, Robertson adds that his regular customers are equally serious about their beer.

If there is a reason for the Bushwakker's good health beyond the beer, Robertson says that it probably lies in the valuable experience he has gained from his various volunteer activities. Working with such groups, he says, has been instrumental in his development of a sound managerial style and likely makes up for his lack of a bar and restaurant background.

As of the summer of 1993, Robertson was negotiating a deal that would place a second Bushwakker in Winnipeg as a franchise partnership with a local businessman from that city. Ironically, Robertson, who was once in search of a franchise himself, is now in a position to offer one.

SCOREBOARD

Granny's Bitter (4% vol.)
Medium gold in colour with a leafy, bitter aroma holding a little sweet nuttiness. Nutty (walnut) bitterness begins a round, leafy body with medium bitterness and a faint hint of maple before a strongly bitter and earthy finish. ★★¹/₂

Last Mountain Lager (5% vol.)
Light copper-coloured with a wet hay nose that has a light floral character. The soft and sweet molasses start leads into a mild body containing floral notes with butterscotch malt. The taste bitters slightly in the faintly sour and woody finish. ★¹/₂

Northern Lights (4.5% vol.)

Light gold in colour with a faintly sour, rooty hop nose carrying light notes of grain and sweet grass. The lightly acidic, grainy start with sugary notes leads to a bittersweet body mixing strong, grassy hopping with a sweet and slightly caramel grain leading to a cereal finish holding a touch of sugar. ★★

Palliser Porter (5.7% vol.)

Ebony in colour with a strong mocha nose holding burnt sugar and alcoholic notes. The semisweet, chocolatey start precedes a full, dark chocolate and milk chocolate mix in the body with very mild earthy hopping and a slightly acidic, bitter coffee finish. ★★★

Regina Pale Ale (4.5% vol.)

Rust-coloured with a full and fruity aroma holding notes of raisin, plum and cherry. A soft, raisiny start leads to a balanced, bittersweet fruit-and-nut body with a finish of medium bitterness and nutshell notes. ★★¹/₂

Stubblejumper Pils (5.% vol.)

Light gold-coloured with a sweet, floral and slightly butterscotchy aroma. A sweet and vaguely buttery start precedes a full, bitter hop body buoyed by flowery notes. The finish is strongly bitter and rooty with nutshell notes. ★★¹/₂

Clark's Crossing Brewpub

LOCATION:	*3030 Diefenbaker Drive, Saskatoon, Saskatchewan S7L 7K2*
PHONE:	*306-384-6633, (fax) 306-384-3322*
OWNERS:	*Gord McCormick & Dave Dunn*
MANAGER:	*Greg Taylor*
BREWER:	*Monty Wood*
CONSULTING BREWER:	*Custom Brewing*
CAPACITY:	*520 hl*
TOURS:	*On request*
BRANDS:	*Golden Spring Ale, Great Northern Lager, Prairie Pilsner*

The second wave of brewpub licences in Saskatchewan in 1990 produced rather varied results. In Regina, a home brewer was pursuing his dream of bringing his beer to more people while, in Saskatoon, an entrepreneur was busy trying to simply bring beer—any beer—to an expanding area of that city.

That businessman was Gord McCormick, a restaurateur who, according to co-owner Dave Dunn, was attracted to the brewpub world by the possibility of the provincial government's extending permits to sell beer for home consumption to the rest of the brewpubs in Saskatchewan. The off-sale permits, as they are known, had proven to be extremely profitable for the first quartet of brewpubs in the province and the thinking was that the government was ready to give the same opportunities to the new brewpubs.

With his new brewpub licence in hand, McCormick enlisted the assistance of one of the few people in the province who had experience in setting up a brewpub, namely Dave Dunn. One of the co-owners of Regina's Barley Mill Brewing Company, Dunn agreed to consult with McCormick on the new establishment and the setup was well under way by the fall of 1990.

As construction on the brewpub was coming to an end, a calamity occurred: McCormick began to run out of money.

Faced with a decaying financial position, McCormick asked Dunn if he would be interested in buying into the enterprise. The way Dunn tells the story, he agreed to the idea of purchasing a small share of the company with the full intention of selling out once the business got on its feet. The problem was, it never did.

As of the summer of 1993, according to Dunn, Clark's Crossing was still wavering between success and failure. In addition to the fact that the much-anticipated off-sale licence had not come through, he says the reason for the brewpub's unsure condition is that it failed to establish a strong pub identity from the start and continues to be seen as something between a restaurant and a bar. For a brewpub, Dunn adds, that's like having one foot in the grave.

The Clark's Crossing grave digger can rest easy, though, for the decision was made in early 1993 to do something to help the beleaguered brewpub. Once the crew is finished on the construction of the Dunns' newest brewpub in Regina (see Last Straw in Coming Soon listing), Dunn says that they will be travelling up to Saskatoon to engage in the redesign.

The refurbished Clark's, he adds, will be very much a pub rather than a restaurant and will be given a new name (unknown at the time of writing).

SCOREBOARD

Golden Spring Ale (5% vol.)
Medium gold in colour with a sweet, apricot aroma containing some maple notes. A slightly salty and lightly sweet, plummy start precedes a soft body of fruity malt and woody hop carrying raisin notes to a quick, grassy finish with sour root notes. ★½

Great Northern Lager (5% vol.)
Light to medium gold in colour with a sweet and fruity nose (peach, apricot) holding a hint of ginger. The sweet but tangy start leads into a slightly sour, malty body with a grapefruit-like tang and some rooty hopping. The sour and bitter finish is weedy with a few vinous notes. ★

Prairie Pilsner (5% vol.)
Medium gold-coloured with a flowery hop aroma cut by icing sugar notes. The largely neutral start has a touch of kelp and roast malt before heading into a full body with leafy and grassy hop notes on a medium sweetness with a touch of orange. The bitter finish has notes of fresh hay and confectioner's sugar. ★½

Fox & Hounds

FOX & HOUNDS

PUB & BREWERY

LOCATION:	#11—7 Assiniboine Drive, Saskatoon, Saskatchewan S7K 1H1
PHONE:	306-664-2233, (fax) 306-664-2267
OWNERS:	John & Angie Cunningham
MANAGER:	John Cunningham
BREWER:	Monty Wood
CONSULTING BREWER:	Cask
CAPACITY:	520 hl
TOURS:	On request
BRANDS:	American Light Lager, Continental Pilsner, Occasional seasonal specialties, Old English Ale, Original Lager

One of the original four brewpubs in Saskatchewan, and the very first in Saskatoon, was the Miners Brewpub in the Canarama Shopping Centre at the city's north end. It was appropriately decorated in a rustic, mining motif and was also reportedly very unsuccessful. The Fox and Hounds is nothing like the Miners.

John Cunningham and his wife Angie bought the Miners after less than a year of its existence and changed the theme within four months. Reborn as a semi-British-style pub with more than a bit of a nod to the sports enthusiast, the Fox is, according to Cunningham, doing much better since its facelift.

Cunningham first got interested in the brewpub side of the hospitality business while working for his father-in-law, Dave Dunn, in Regina. (Dunn and his brother Perry own or have interests in Bonzzini's, Clark's Crossing and the Barley Mill brewpubs—see separate entries.) Although he was not enraptured by the brewing end of things, Cunningham was impressed with the other potential moneymaking aspects of the original four brewpubs and so, when the Miners came up for sale, he and his wife made the move.

The other moneymaking possibilities Cunningham was attracted to in connection with the original four brewpubs are the off-sale beer licences that accompanied the brewpub licences. In Saskatchewan, beer is sold only through government liquor stores or off-sale premises, the latter traditionally located in hotels. The exceptions to that tradition, however, came when the government decided to add off-sale privileges to the four brewpub permits it originally issued. According to Cunningham, that privilege alone is worth the cost of keeping the brewery running.

Since he and his wife purchased the brewpub, Cunningham has added a full-sized store to maximize his take-out beer sales as well as increase the profile of the pub. As of the summer of 1993, the pair were investigating the possibility of further renovating the bar to add more seats to the 150 for which they are currently licensed.

They do not sell a great percentage of house beer at the Fox and Cunningham admits that they do not push the products in any great way, either. In fact, Cunningham says that if it were not for the fact that the brewery has to be operational in order for the off-sale licence to continue, he would, in all probability, close down the malt extract brewery altogether. It comes as no great surprise, then, that he also has no intention of bottling the house beer for sale in the store at any time in the future.

Although beer might not be the emphasis at the Fox, Cunningham says that the neighbourhood night life most definitely is and he adds that they do roughly three-quarters of their business after the dinner hour. Do not expect a nightclub theme with dance music and strobe lights, though, for the Fox is still first and foremost a pub, and Cunningham says that what music they do play is kept at a level to allow for easy conversation.

Although it sounds as if not a lot of that conversation is about the house beer.

SCOREBOARD

American Light Lager (4% vol.)
Very pale gold in colour with a sour, acidic grain nose holding some lime notes. The very thin body starts with a light lemony taste before moving to a sour citrus and grain middle and a sharp, dry and sour finish holding some green apple notes. ¹/₂

Continental Pilsner (5% vol.)
Light to medium gold in colour with a bittersweet and lightly floral aroma. The thin straw start leads into an orangey body with icing sugar and flowery hop notes. The mildly sweet finish carries some acidity. ★

Old English Ale (5% vol.)
Amber-copper in colour with a soft, caramelly nose carrying orange and peach notes. A very soft, sweet-and-sour orange start precedes a bittersweet body of caramel malt and light leafy and woody hop notes. The finish is of bitter, woody hop and confectioners' sugar. ★

Original Lager (5% vol.)
Light gold in colour and lightly sweet in its caramel malt aroma. The soft, semisweet butterscotch start precedes a bittersweet, rooty and grassy body with the bitter second half of the taste turning sharply sour in the finish. ★

Saskatoon Brewing Company/ Cheers Roadhouse

LOCATION:	*2105—8th Street East, Saskatoon, Saskatchewan S7H 0T8*
PHONE:	*306-955-7500, (fax) 306-955-8144*
OWNERS:	*Ross Turner, 4 small-interest partners*
MANAGER:	*Ross Merideth*
BREWER:	*Randy Uytterhagen*
CONSULTING BREWER:	*Mike Tymchuk, Brad McQuhae*
CAPACITY:	*1,000 hl*
TOURS:	*On request*
BRANDS:	*Big Sky Pale Ale, Blackstrap Bock, Classic Lager, Occasional specialties (Octoberfest, Pilsner, Light), Prairie Dark Ale*

The outlying residential neighbourhoods of Saskatoon are dotted with strip malls, most of them containing the expected assortment of shops and restaurants. In one particular mall on 8th Street, however, lies something decidedly unexpected: the Saskatoon Brewing Company and Cheers Roadhouse.

Like so many other brewpubs scattered across Canada, Cheers was inspired by Victoria's Spinnakers (see separate entry under British Columbia). Ross Turner, the owner, is a former resident of Vancouver Island and, when the opportunity came to apply for one of the Saskatchewan government's four available brewpub licences, he jumped at the chance to follow the path laid by one of his favourite pubs in his native province.

Or perhaps "jumped" is not quite the right word: "strolled" may actually be closer to the case. By the time that the other three of the original Saskatchewan brewpubs had opened for business, Turner had still not begun work on the renovations that would make the former government liquor store into Cheers. And even then, the construction took nine months to complete. The man was obviously not in a huge hurry.

According to manager Ross Merideth, when the two men were scouting for sites to house the brewpub, they decided that it made a lot of sense to put as much distance as realistically possible between themselves and Miners, currently known as The Fox and Hounds (see separate entry) and, at the time, the only other Saskatoon brewpub. They accomplished that goal when they ended up on the other side of the city.

Distance from the competition, the first all-grain brewpub brewery in Saskatchewan and a pair of respected consultants in Mike Tymchuk and Brad McQuhae (both former Spinnakers brewers) were apparently not enough to ensure instant success for Cheers. According to Merideth, the Saskatoon Brewing Company opened in November 1990 to a fairly luke-warm response. Not that people did not like the large pub and attached restaurant of Cheers, says Merideth, but convincing the patrons to opt for the house beer over their normal brew was another matter entirely.

Eventually the persistence of the Cheers staff and brewers paid off and, according to Merideth, the percentage of house beer sold compared to all other brands doubled over the first year and a half. In fact, the popularity of the brews had soared so much that, although the Cheers brands were not being sold in the attached cold beer store as of the summer of 1993, the brewer and management were considering the move as an option for the future.

And if the reputation of their own lagers, ales and bocks continues to grow at that rate, it will be a very sweet future indeed.

SCOREBOARD

Big Sky Pale Ale (5.2% vol.)
Light to medium gold in colour with a bitter, wet straw nose. The soft and lightly orangey start precedes a bitter and very grassy body with roasted barley notes and a bitter, woody hop finish. ★★

Blackstrap Bock (6.5% vol.)
Amber-coloured with a sweet, malty aroma holding tomato notes. The flowery start precedes a sweet, caramel and toffee body with mocha and earthy hop notes. The bittersweet, woody hop finish carries light alcoholic and saline notes. ★★$\frac{1}{2}$

Classic Lager (5.5% vol.)
Medium gold in colour with a light aroma of soft grain mixed with woody hopping. A slightly bitter grain front leads to a bitter and sour, grassy body with medium woody hopping and light medicinal notes. The bitter finish possesses some slightly burnt notes. ★★

Prairie Dark Ale (5.8% vol.)
Deep amber-coloured with a burnt toffee aroma holding some coffee notes. The slightly sweet and candied start with very light apricot notes leads to a bittersweet, somewhat plummy body with roasted grain and woody hop over faint sugar notes. The bitter and slightly sour finish continues with woody hop and roasted malt flavours. ★★

Ontario

Amsterdam Brasserie and Brewpub

LOCATION:	*133 John Street, Toronto, Ontario M5V 2E4*
PHONE:	*416-595-8201, (fax) 416-595-0646*
OWNERS:	*1019777 Ontario Inc.*
OPERATING PARTNER:	*Rick Montgomery*
GENERAL MANAGER:	*Rick Colli*
BREWER:	*Harley Smith*
CONSULTING BREWER:	*Cask*
CAPACITY:	*1,200 hl*
TOURS:	*On request*
BRANDS:	*Eagle Lager, Redtail Lager, 16 rotating specialty brews, Non-Alcoholic Lager*

Were it not for a reflective second look, Toronto's first brewpub might well have ended up as a parking lot.

For a parking lot was exactly what real estate investor Roel Bramer had in mind when he purchased the property in the fall of 1985. The building, says Bramer, was in disastrous condition and, before the opening of the Skydome and the rebirth of the King Street West neighbourhood, there seemed little value to keeping the structure upright.

When he went by his new investment for a second look, however, Bramer reconsidered his views and chose to clean up the old warehouse and put in a restaurant. Considering that there was little else than empty warehouse space south of Queen Street in those days, it was more than a bit of a gamble on Bramer's part.

Hardly a stranger to the restaurant trade, Bramer had owned several bars and eateries in the Toronto of the 1970s before he sold practically all of them (save the Gasworks) in 1977 to go sailing around the world for over a year. When he returned to the city with his new wife, he opted for the then-booming real estate market over the service industry and sold his one remaining bar interest.

Then came that property on John Street.

The building that now houses the Amsterdam was in such poor shape that it took Bramer a full year to prepare it for restaurant use. That was perhaps a blessing in disguise for Bramer, though, as the new legislation allowing brewpubs came down about halfway through the construction. When he discovered the possibility of brewing in-house, Bramer suddenly realized why he had been holding back on making use of the building's basement and decided that it would be home to the brewery.

The reaction to Bramer's minimalist decor, *prix fixe* menu, café furnishings and, most of all, house-brewed beer was immediate and enthusiastic. The Amsterdam had large crowds and lineups almost from day one.

Since its opening, the Amsterdam has gone through a few brewers (including Joel Manning who now brews at Bramer's other brewpub, the Rotterdam—see separate entry), switched from malt-extract to full-grain brewing, revised its menu several times and added a small, adjoining bar called the Little Amsterdam.

In the fall of 1993, Toronto's oldest brewpub changed hands as the owners of the nearby Loose Moose and Alice Fazooli's restaurants and bars cemented their hold on the area with the purchase of the Amsterdam. Their plan was to make minor changes to the pub and stay open for the remainder of the year before closing for an expected six weeks to effect extensive renovations. Although the new owners do plan to change the name of their acquisition, they will cotinue the tradition of freshly brewed beer on John Street.

SCOREBOARD

Eagle Lager (5% vol.)
Light to medium gold in colour with a thick, sweet and caramelly aroma containing light notes of spice (cinnamon, nutmeg) and a faint nuttiness. The start is rather mild with a sour graininess and traces of fresh hay leading to a moderately bitter and earthy body containing notes of caramel malt, sour grain and faint florals. The finish adds a pleasant hop bitterness to the remaining earthiness of the body. ★½

Redtail Lager (5% vol.)
Light copper-coloured with a subdued aroma of toasted grain carrying some nutmeg and floral notes. The start is fresh and slightly sweet with red apple notes mixing with butterscotchy malt. The body bitters with woody hop notes and a very light hint of clove before an earthy and bitter finish with burnt wood notes and a very faint, yeasty tang. ★½

Barb's Union Station

LOCATION:	*4396 Kennedy Road, Markham, Ontario L3R 9W1*
PHONE:	*905-940-3131, (Fax) 905-940-8097*
OWNER:	*Barbara Stitt*
MANAGER:	*Owner*
BREWER:	*John Lippert*
CONSULTING BREWER:	*Cask*
CAPACITY:	*900 hl*
TOURS:	*On request*
BRANDS:	*Canadian Ale, Canadian Lager*

Every once in a while, the brewing business takes the most unlikely of candidates and pulls them into the industry, whether they want to go or not. At Barb's Union Station, that is exactly what happened.

The "Barb" is Barbara Stitt, a tiny woman who just happens to also be a human dynamo. Up until she took over the Union Station brewpub, she did not even drink beer, much less expect to find herself in the middle of the industry.

The brewpub itself was conceived by two restaurateurs near the end of 1989. The two men reportedly built the place from the ground up and had it open by the end of November of that year. They subsequently sold the Markham location to a numbered company in January 1992 and thereby began the cycle that was to see Stitt enter the business.

The numbered company was a family operation known to the Stitts (Barbara and her husband Charley) through relatives; therefore, when the family came to them seeking financing, the Stitts had no problem lending the company funds on a first-lease basis. Thus the Stitts became creditors of Union Station.

The business, like so many in the recessionary Toronto of the time, encountered numerous difficulties until finally, on November 12, 1992, the landlord of the strip mall that housed the brewpub locked out the owners. When she heard this, Barbara Stitt came down to the location to see if there was any way that the owners could be let back in. Instead, she walked away the proud owner of a restaurant and brewpub.

Not that the Stitts were complete novices to the restaurant business. Charley had been in the trade for most of his life, having owned numerous spots, and Barbara, in her own words, had "done a bit of everything."

The couple's first intentions were simply to fix up the restaurant-pub, run it for a while and then sell it off as a viable business. They certainly had no intention of keeping it and even fewer thoughts of brewing beer.

Public demand intervened in their plans, however, and soon the Stitts found themselves looking for a brewer, namely John Lippert, the contract brewer who had run the beer operations at the Station previously.

What's more, Barbara found herself enjoying the challenge of running the 371-seat pub and restaurant.

Since reopening Union Station in February 1993, Barbara says that she has placed a great deal of emphasis on running the place with the same level of quality she would expect were she a patron rather than an owner. To this end, she says, she continually stresses quality, cleanliness and service to her staff and makes a point of personally greeting everyone who comes into her establishment.

And the toy train, which has circled the ceiling of Union Station since its opening, still runs its route.

SCOREBOARD

Canadian Ale (6% vol.)

Light to medium gold-coloured with a sweet and lightly fruity (plum) nose holding petrol aromas. The very sugary start is full and slightly orangey, leading to a very sweet body of brown sugar with fruity (orange, faint bing cherry) and plastic notes. Strong refined sugar finish. ★

Canadian Lager (6% vol.)

Medium gold to bronze colour with a sweet, cardboardy aroma containing date notes. The raisiny body holds some woody hop and roasted sugar notes. The quick finish is of lightly bitter hop touched with roasted, refined sugar. ★

Blue Anchor

LOCATION:	*47 West Street, Orillia, Ontario*
	L3V 5G5
PHONE:	*705-325-7735*
OWNER:	*Barry Neil*
MANAGER:	*Rick Neil*
BREWERS:	*John Lippert/Rick Neil*
CONSULTING BREWER:	*Continental*
CAPACITY:	*500 hl*
TOURS:	*On request*
BRAND:	*Blue Anchor Pub Brew*

Orillia is a small, cottage-country community like many other small, cottage-country communities: it has a picturesque main road dotted with small businesses; its population increases dramatically during the summer and the residents possess a strong sense of community.

What does set Orillia apart from other such towns and cities, however, is that it has its own brewpub.

Situated just a few doors from the Orillia Opera House on the city's main drag, the Blue Anchor has been an operating brewpub since early 1988 and was purchased by owner Barry Neil in December of that year.

Neil, a former Toronto trucking operator, viewed the acquisition as a nice way to remove himself from the city to a relaxed life of semi-retirement. He is still waiting for the relaxed part.

Running the pub, says Neil, is a lot more work than he anticipated, even with the managerial help of his son Rick. With a strong reputation as a neighbourhood pub and considerable business from summer cottagers and boaters, Neil says that the running of the pub keeps him hopping far beyond any concept of semi-retirement would warrant.

What's more, he continues, the recession of the early 1990s did nothing to make his job any easier. The Orillia economy, says Neil, was battered quite badly by the tough economic times and it took a lot of work and perseverance to keep the bar afloat.

However, despite the tough financial times, Neil says that the pub has a good regular clientele from which to draw and, in turn, he tries his best to give back to the community everything that it gives to him. One example of this spirit is the snowmobile that Neil raffles off for the local Kinsmen organization every winter from his front window.

Brewing operations at the Anchor have long been handled by Toronto contract brewer John Lippert, but Neil and his son are being trained to take over that aspect of the pub, as well.

Of the 16 domestic, micro, imported and house draughts available, the pub's own, malt-extract beer is surpassed in sales by only Molson Canadian. Despite that fact, Neil allows that local people would probably patronize his pub at the same rate even if it did not have the house brew.

With a heavy emphasis on sports provided by the bar's satellite dish, five television screens, two dart boards and pool table, the Anchor conveys a male, blue-collar atmosphere and, admits Neil, can occasionally get a little rowdy late at night. The warm, roadhouse-style motif, however, can also be extremely comfortable and inviting for anyone interested in enjoying a casual drink or meal.

The same "small town" qualities that drew Barry Neil to Orillia in 1988 are still apparent to anyone willing to make the drive up Highway 11. What's more, even if they do not always drink the house brew, it is evident that this tight-knit community has wholeheartedly embraced its brewpub.

Perhaps this is a sign for other, not-so-large locales to follow Orillia's lead and strive for their own resident brewery.

SCOREBOARD

Blue Anchor Pub Brew (5.5% vol.)
Pale gold colour with a sweet-and-sour, malty grain aroma. The light and slightly bitter start leads to a sugary body with sour grain notes rising through to the finish. A strong confectionery sugar taste mixes with notes of orange rind in the finish. ★

CC's Brewpub

LOCATION:	*#1—6981 Mill Creek Drive, Mississauga, Ontario*
PHONE:	*905-542-0136*
OWNERS:	*John & Frank Pucci*
MANAGER:	*John Pucci*
BREWER:	*Murray Voakes*
CONSULTING BREWER:	*Murray Voakes*
CAPACITY:	*750 hl*
TOURS:	*On request; reserve for groups*
BRAND:	*CC's Brew*

Acigar-smoking cat in a trench coat and carrying a violin case àla Chicago gangster is not exactly your average brewpub symbol. Then again, CC's is not exactly your average brewpub.

One of a family-run chain of six bars and restaurants, the CC's in the Streetsville neighbourhood of Mississauga is the only brewpub of the lot. It is also one of the largest and most active locations in the group.

The idea behind CC's developed in 1980 or 1981 when the original family business—a fine-dining restaurant in the Toronto suburb of Mississauga—fell on hard times as people eschewed formal meals for the casual comfort of neighbourhood bars and pubs. Rather than make small changes to the dining room, the family chose to radically alter the concept and turn it into a "Chicago-style" bar.

The name was pulled from a popular brand of rye whisky and the "cool cat" cartoon adopted as the calling card for the new bar. According to John Pucci, the reinvented establishment was in the black within months.

Nearly a decade later, the Pucci brothers were ready to open their third location and, in anticipation of this, one of their landlords took them to see the Streetsville site. The two men were impressed with what they saw and signed a long-term lease to take over the 300-plus seat room.

Having visited the Amsterdam in Toronto and the original Mississauga Luxembourg (now defunct) and seen the rising popularity of the brew-pub concept, the Puccis decided to put a brewery into their new CC's and reportedly spent more than a million dollars designing and building their newest operation.

What they had when they were finished was an establishment that is flexible enough to serve casual, roadhouse-style meals in the afternoon and present live bands, dancing or karaoke at night.

The brewing operations, like those of so many of Ontario's smaller-volume brewpubs, are handled on a contract basis. The brewer at CC's, Murray Voakes, was recommended by the brewing system installer and has been with the operation ever since.

Using a modified malt-extract system, Voakes brews with an all-grain mash containing 30 percent corn adjunct. In 1993, he was planning to add a light beer and a Rickard's Red-style dark to the light-tasting CC's Brew.

In the spring of 1993, CC's made Ontario brewpub history by becoming the first brewpub to advertise on television, the chain having bought commercial time on Toronto's CITY-TV.

Expansive and reliant on promotions and gimmicks, CC's is not necessarily the place for a quiet, relaxed pint in the evening. Then again, if your vocal chords are up to some karaoke . . .

SCOREBOARD

CC's Brew (5% vol.)

Very pale gold in colour, this lager has a light, sour, citric grain nose. The body is weak, thin and very much in the national style. It has a soft start and a sweet, heavily acidic and grainy character. The finish is sour and rooty. ★

CEEPS & Barney's

LOCATION:	*671 Richmond Street, London, Ontario N6A 3G7*
PHONE:	*519-432-1425, (fax) 519-432-1426*
OWNERS:	*CEEPS—Barney's Ltd.*
PRESIDENT:	*Rick Tattersall*
MANAGER:	*Rick Tattersall*
BREWER:	*Charles MacLean*
CONSULTING BREWER:	*Charles MacLean*
CAPACITY:	*520 hl*
TOURS:	*On advance request*
BRANDS:	*CEEPS Lager*

When Rick Tattersall speaks of the old tavern he operates in London, Ontario, it is obvious that he believes he is talking about more than a bar. For Tattersall, running the CEEPS is as much about the maintenance of a cultural legacy as it is about managing a business enterprise.

That is because there is a whole lot of history behind the CEEPS and, in his 28 years with the tavern, Tattersall has made every effort to document as much of it as possible. The result is a man, and a tavern, with a great sense of the past.

The Grand Pacific Hotel opened, according to Tattersall, in 1890 but changed its name shortly thereafter to the C.P.R. Hotel. The renaming came about as a result of the construction of the Canadian Pacific station adjacent to the hotel and, despite the fact that Canadian Pacific has never owned so much as a piece of the building, that name stuck with the hotel for the better part of the last century.

Although it is difficult to tell exactly how long the hotel has had a beer-serving tavern, Tattersall says that it must date back to at least the early 1900s because he knows through his research that the second owner, Eli Griffith, was fined $20 back then for having a draught beer line running up to his apartment. And no, it was not because Griffith was a closet alcoholic that he had the line; rather, according to Tattersall, it was there so that Griffith could continue to sell beer in his home outside of licensed business hours.

The hotel and tavern were sold again both before and after Prohibition and were in the hands of a woman known only as Mrs. Richardson by 1934. By then, of course, liquor licensing in Ontario was going through its post-Prohibition restructuring and, according to Tattersall, Mrs. Richardson was able to obtain one of the first licences to serve alcohol issued under the new system.

Mrs. Richardson sold the hotel in 1948 and it changed hands once more in 1956, finally becoming the property of the company that would become CEEPS–Barney's Ltd.

Although the bar was still named the C.P.R. Tavern up until 1970, it had for all intents and purposes been the CEEPS for many years prior to that, the nickname coined by the generations of students who had frequented the watering hole. As for the Barney's part, that is the name of the bar and restaurant adjoining the tavern.

When the brewery was finally installed in the CEEPS in early 1991, Tattersall says that he was of a mind to handle the brewing operations himself. He soon realized that many more hours of work would be required than he had the time for and the brewing services of their consultant, Charles MacLean, were enlisted.

Although the brewpub element of the 100-year-old tavern does lend it a uniqueness in London, Tattersall admits that they have done little to market that aspect of the business and he adds that there has been very little change in the tavern's business since the brewery went on-line. As before, he says, the clientele is a loyal one made up of older folk during the day and students after 8:00 p.m.

By Tattersall's estimation, the one lager that MacLean brews at the CEEPS sells at a rate of about 25 to 30 percent of all the draught beer sold at the tavern. Considering that both the groups that form the customer base of the CEEPS generally tend toward mainstream, commercial brands, that can be considered a significant percentage, despite the fact that it falls far short of the 60 to 80 percent marks set by some other brewpubs.

Then again, the CEEPS is far more of an old Ontario tavern than it is a new Ontario brewpub and, as Tattersall says, there will, or should, always be room for historic old taverns in this province.

SCOREBOARD

CEEPS Lager (5% vol.)
Light gold in colour with a faint aroma of sweet grain. The sweet, grassy and sugary start leads toward a slightly less sweet but still grassy body with a light rooty sourness creeping in the second half and dominating the finish. ★

Charley's Tavern

LOCATION:	*4715 Tecumseh Road East, Windsor, Ontario N8T 1B6*
PHONE:	*519-945-5512, (fax) 519-945-5512*
OWNERS:	*David Cooper*
MANAGER:	*Gord O'Keefe*
BREWER:	*Mike Dumechelle*
CONSULTING BREWER:	*Continental*
CAPACITY:	*350 hl*
TOURS:	*On request*
BRANDS:	*Ale, Lager*

Like most of Canada, Ontario is speckled with taverns that date back to the early years of this century. These beverage rooms are generally rich in character and short on creature comforts; the tables are wobbly, the benches and barstools are rough and wooden and the smell of decades of drinking is pervasive.

Nonetheless, these old taverns have a charm all their own and it is a shame that many of them are being forced by financial considerations to change into something for which they are definitely not suited.

To keep afloat, some have tried experimenting with that scourge of the 1990s, karaoke, while others have played with open stages, country line-dancing and revamped food menus. And a couple, like Charley's, have even tried brewing their own beer.

Charley's Tavern, located in the east end of Windsor, has been around since the 1920s and under David Cooper's ownership since 1951. In that time, little has apparently changed in the tavern.

Rough-hewn on the outside, the interior of Charley's is similarly basic with its drinking-hall atmosphere and shadowy lighting. In one corner, however, over near the entrance, the gleaming copper kettles of the brewery hold sway behind large windows, dominating that particular section of the bar.

The brewery was installed in 1987, making Charley's one of the earlier brewpub operations in the province. The hope at the time was that, with the interest generated by the new industry and the prospect of unique— and cheaper—draught, new life would be bestowed upon the old tavern.

According to manager Gord O'Keefe, that never happened. Despite brewer Mike Dumechelle experimenting with a dozen or so recipes throughout the years, O'Keefe says that Windsor people have never really adjusted to the idea of house-brewed beer. While the brewery does not cost the ownership a great deal to operate, neither has it ever really taken off in the community nor generated any great profits.

Instead, the surprisingly large tavern with a capacity of 320 patrons— 445 with the patio open—has cruised along much the same way it has for the better part of the century, providing a haven for the predominantly blue-collar residents of the neighbourhood.

Each week, Charley's plays host to two live bands on their small stage and, on the other five days, a deejay takes charge of the sounds. On a lazy spring Saturday afternoon, though, Charley's Tavern is simply a quiet place to have a beer and watch the game on television.

SCOREBOARD

Ale (5.5% vol.)
Light to medium gold in colour with a faint (to the point of being almost indiscernible), sweet, malted-grain aroma. Strongly citric start to a candied lemon-lime body mixed with some sweet grain and bitter, woody hop. Sweet and sour, malty and thick finish. ★

Lager (5.5% vol.)
Light gold in colour with a light, sour and grainy aroma. The citric start leads into a thick and creamy body that has sour root mixing with syrupy molasses on more citric undertones. Sour-bitter and acidic finish. ★

Denison's Brewing Company

(incorporating Growlers Pub, Conchy Joe's Oyster Bar
and Crazy Louie's Brasserie)

LOCATION:	*75 Victoria Street, Toronto, Ontario*
	M5C 2B1
PHONE:	*416-360-5877*
OWNERS:	*Consortium of 10 owners*
MANAGER:	*Len Little*
BREWER:	*Michael Hancock*
BREWING CAPACITY:	*2,000 hl*
BRANDS:	*Filtered Lager, Royal Dunkel,*
	Seasonal specialties, Unfiltered Lager

Occasionally, the beer world offers up a near-perfect symmetry of brewing operations. Denison's Brewing is one half of one such instance.

With its fine dining room, upper-class bar, oyster and seafood annex and lager brewing, Denison's is the perfect *yin* to the British pub-style *yang* of the Granite Brewery uptown (see separate entry). Where the Granite is all ale, wood grain and country charm, Denison's is lager, soft light and urban polish. No two bars in the city make more perfect bookends.

The principal in the Denison's operation is Prince Luitpold, a descendant of Bavarian royalty and the owner of the Kaltenberg Brewery located in his family castle just outside of Munich, Germany.

In 1984, Luitpold and representatives of Molson and Coors met to form a distribution partnership in Georgia. While the business itself did not work (the plug was pulled in a mere three months), Luitpold's interest in the North American beer scene was cemented and he began to examine ways in which he could obtain a foothold on this continent.

By early 1987, Luitpold's quest had been fulfilled and the site of the old Sheldon Tavern in downtown Toronto was chosen as the future location of Denison's Brewing Company.

The brewer who came under contract with Luitpold was Michael Hancock, a veteran of Molson who left that company with the understanding that he would soon be the brewing partner of the new venture. The Molson connection, however, did not stop at Hancock's resignation letter. No less than Eric Molson himself took a small interest in the project due to the combined factors of a love of brewing and a friendship with Luitpold that dated back to the failed distributorship.

In fact, according to Hancock, all ten partners in the business came together through friendship and an interest in brewing, with not a restaurateur among them.

As early as the spring of 1989, the brewery was operational and test brewing had begun. However, because there were no walls surrounding the beer tanks at that time, test brewing was soon suspended at the request of a beleaguered foreman who could not keep his construction workers from engaging in a little testing of their own.

By November of that year, both levels of the bar–restaurant were open and the light and dark lagers, with both filtered and unfiltered versions of each available, were ready to pour.

Much to Hancock's surprise, the filtered Royal Dunkel lager was much ignored in favour of its unfiltered brother and, consequently, was soon dropped in favour of rotating specialty brews, although the filtered light lager remains to this day.

In the years since its opening, Denison's has experienced two significant transformations: the first being the conversion of some of its formal dining space into an oyster bar named Conchy Joe's, and the most recent being the fall 1993 metamorphosis of the rest of the upstairs dining space into Crazy Louie's Brasserie.

Today, the three restaurants housed in this little corner of the city are invariably full at lunch and, in the evening, become predominantly populated by the businesspeople of the area.

Why, it's enough to make even a prince happy.

SCOREBOARD

Filtered Lager (4.7% vol.)

Light gold in colour with a light, slightly grainy, fresh hay nose. The creamy body begins sweet and finishes bitter with a rooty, bittersweet body in the middle. The finish is grassy with a sour edge. ★★

Royal Dunkel (4.9% vol.)

Medium brown and edging toward rusty in colour with light aromatics of floral hop and caramel malt. The sweet, perfumey and floral start leads to a balanced mix of malt and earthy hop in the middle with a touch of acidity. The finish is bittersweet with raw sugar and woody hop notes. ★★¹/₂

Unfiltered Lager (4.7% vol.)

Since this is the same beer as the filtered lager, it has a similar taste profile but is neither as sharp nor as extreme in its flavours. A touch of yeastiness enters into the profile in the second half and finish. ★★

The Granite Brewery

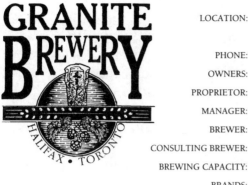

LOCATION:	*245 Eglinton Avenue East, Toronto, Ontario M4P 3B7*
PHONE:	*416-322-0723, (fax) 416-322-0117*
OWNERS:	*Ron & Kevin Keefe*
PROPRIETOR:	*Ron Keefe*
MANAGER:	*Ron Keefe*
BREWER:	*Ron Keefe*
CONSULTING BREWER:	*Alan Pugsley*
BREWING CAPACITY:	*2,000 hl*
BRANDS:	*Best Bitter,*
	Best Bitter Special,
	Keefe's Irish Stout,
	Peculiar,
	Summer Ale (alternates seasonally with the stout)

When the beer-poor Maritimes exports a brewpub to cosmopolitan Toronto, it certainly merits some heavy-duty consideration!

So, when the Granite Brewery was readying itself to open in August 1991, there was much speculation among the city's beer lovers as to how the kid brother to Halifax's well-known Granite would fare in the jungles of the Toronto's merciless restaurant and bar scene. Co-owner and proprietor Ron Keefe, however, was not worried.

Unostentatiously housed in the base of an office building at the corner of Eglinton Avenue and Mt. Pleasant Road in uptown Toronto, the Granite Brewery was Toronto's fourth brewpub to open and, as it turned out, the first of three to commence operations in the hustle and bustle of the Yonge and Eglinton area within a year.

The story of the Toronto Granite's origins is, oddly enough, a tragic one. Its roots are found in the dream of a third Keefe brother, Wilfred, who succumbed to cancer at the age of 41 after building a successful portfolio of buildings and businesses in Nova Scotia. The unattained goal of Wilfred, however, was to open a restaurant in Toronto. After their brother's death, Ron and Kevin decided to fulfil Wilfred's dream by building a Toronto version of Kevin's Granite Brewery.

A year later, after scouting numerous locations, including one on Danforth Avenue in the middle of the Greek district, the uptown location was settled on and work began.

It was slow going for the brothers as the preparation of the site took over half a year to fully complete. The preparation of the brewer, however, took considerably less time.

The brewer in the Maritimes was Kevin, a successful graduate of the highly rigorous Peter Austin and Partners brewers training course at the Ringwood Brewery in England. Rather than Kevin's trying to teach his brother everything he knew about brewing, it was decided that Ron would take the equally intensive course offered by Austin's president, Alan Pugsley, at the Wild Goose Brewery in Maryland. So, for two weeks, the younger Keefe endured the dawn-until-night regime of Pugsley who, according to his pupil, is a tireless brewer.

The result, though, was a successful graduate and the central Canada Granite was ready to go.

A favourite stop for many of the city's brewers, both professional and amateur, the Granite is neatly divided into pub, library, dining room and snug sections, each serviced efficiently with a full food and drink menu. While the front pub and library sections are by far the most popular, attracting the majority of the establishment's business both day and night, the dining area at the rear, with its roaring fireplace in the winter, offers an equally relaxed setting.

The Granite has managed to do the impossible: as well as importing its ales, it has imported the soothing pace of a Maritime afternoon to its hectic Toronto surroundings.

SCOREBOARD

Best Bitter (4.5% vol.)
Light brown with a slight orange colour and a soft, fruity malt nose. The slow and lightly leafy start develops into a true and full-bodied middle with slight bitter orange notes. The bitter and faintly sour finish turns slightly metallic toward the end. ★★★

Best Bitter Special (4.5% vol.)
The same as the Bitter but dry-hopped to a wonderful result. The pronounced, fresh aroma of the hop leaf is almost reminiscent of a walk in the autumn woods and the body is gently hopped up to a bitter, earthy and slightly perfumed character. ★★★¹/₂

Peculiar (5.6% vol.)
Reddish mahogany colour with a sweet, malty nose holding coffee notes. The bitter body is not too strong or imposing, with a touch of licorice and a strong, bitter finish. Full-bodied and somewhat earthy. ★★¹/₂

Stout (4% vol.)

Deep purple in colour, it has soft aromatics with sweet licorice and fresh tobacco notes along with some light smokiness. The body is somewhat thin and characterized by a touch of candied licorice at the front leading to a slightly vinegary, coffee-with-brown-sugar body and a light, smoky and slightly sour and acidic finish. ★½

Summer Ale (4% vol.)

Medium gold and slightly coppery in colour with a leaf and wet hay aroma holding notes of orange rind. The soft and lightly spicy (nutmeg, very faint clove) start holds hints of tangerine and precedes a bitter and leafy body with a touch of butterscotch and peach. The finish remains bitter and adds some woody notes. ★★½

The Kingston Brewing Company

LOCATION:	*34 Clarence Street, Kingston, Ontario K7L 1W9*
PHONE:	*613-542-4978*
OWNERS:	*Richard Cilles, Paul Debbenham*
MANAGER:	*Van Allen Turner*
BREWER:	*Roger Eccleston*
CONSULTING BREWER:	*Alan Pugsley*
BREWING CAPACITY:	*570 hl*
BRANDS:	*Dragon's Breath Pale Ale (contract-brewed by Hart), Dragon's Breath Real Ale, Regal Lager, Various specialties*

In 1986, as the new era in pub brewing was finally opening up in Ontario, two establishments were racing for the title of the province's first operating brewpub—Welland's Atlas Hotel and the Kingston Brewing Company (KBC). The problem for the government's public relations people, however, was how to choose which would be the first *official* licensed brewpub.

This issue was further complicated by the fact that the Welland location housed a rough-and-tumble club, hardly the preferred location for a historic moment. The solution lay in a compromise: Welland got licence number one and Kingston received the status of the first official brewpub of the modern era in Ontario.

While the Atlas is no longer with us as a brewpub, the Kingston Brewing Company has thrived and recently made another mark in their brewing history by having Hart Breweries in Ontario produce a contract-brewed, bottled beer on the market under the brewpub's own name.

When they first opened their doors in 1986, such grandiose achievements were not even a glimmer in the eyes of the proud but nervous new owners.

The KBC was largely built from the ground up over the fall and winter of 1985 as the location, formerly home to two retail shops, had to be completely redesigned and the brewery and kitchen added on. The owners did much of the labour themselves, Cask Brewing provided the tanks and Alan Pugsley came on later as a consultant.

Even when all the work was completed, there was still the herculean task of getting the government to complete the licensing procedure so that they could sell the lager that was sitting in their conditioning tanks. Governments being governments, the Kingston Brewing Company opened in February with no beer of their own for sale.

The paperwork finally came through in April, and the four tanks of beer that the owners thought would last for two weeks vanished in one flurry of a weekend as customers drank the brewpub dry. The KBC appeared to be on the road to success.

In their first year, the Brewing Company accomplished a near impossibility in the Ontario restaurant trade and actually turned a profit, a feat they have duplicated every year since. Their mixture of house-brewed beer, "pub grub" menu and congenial atmosphere has proven to be a success with both tourists and locals alike.

Their mainstay brews—the Cask Brewing Equipment-constructed lager and the Pugsley-invented ale—are both extract beers as are their specialties. In the winter of 1992, the KBC contracted Hart Breweries and their old friend Pugsley to assist in the development and brewing of the Pale Ale. Both bottled and draught versions of the Pale are brewed entirely at Hart with a full-grain mash.

Another feather in the Kingston Brewing Company cap is the production of their own wine, an undertaking they commenced in the spring of 1991. While neither red nor white will receive high accolades from oenophiles, each adequately fills the role bar manager Van Allen Turner describes as "chicken wings and nachos wine."

SCOREBOARD

Dragon's Breath Pale Ale (4.5% vol.)

(Although this contract-brewed draught is available elsewhere throughout the Kingston area and is reviewed as a bottled beer under the entry for Hart Breweries, I thought it appropriate to review it at its point of inspiration, if not origin.) The unfiltered draught has much higher aromatics (hop and Scottish marmalade notes) than the bottled version. Its body, while rounder than its filtered brother, is strong and forceful with a fruity start of peach and pear notes and a strong hop presence combining with the fruit for a bittersweet middle. The finish, although a touch astringent, is pleasantly bitter and earthy. ★★★

Dragon's Breath Real Ale (6% vol.)

A cask-conditioned beer served on a gravity pump, it is orangey-brown with a very light aroma of appley molasses. The apple carries into the soft start which, in turn, changes to a full-bodied middle of tannic, woody hop and light lime and fruit. A strongly bittering finish with a hint of confectionery sweetness from the extract completes the taste. ★★½

Regal Lager (5% vol.)

A medium-to-light gold beer with a thick, perfumey nose holding lots of floral notes and a distinct sweetness. Round-bodied if a touch thin toward the finish, it has a soft, grassy start, which moves to a slightly astringent middle with bittering hops battling the sweetness of the extract. Woody notes with a hint of lime give way to a bitter and rooty finish. ★★

Lighthouse Brewpub

The **Flying Dutchman** *Hotel*

LOCATION:	*143 Duke Street, Bowmanville, Ontario L1C 2W4*
PHONE:	*905-623-3373*
OWNER:	*Fred D'Silva*
MANAGER:	*Christopher Mendes*
BREWER:	*Christopher Mendes*
CONSULTING BREWER:	*Continental*
CAPACITY:	*520 hl*
TOURS:	*On request*
BRANDS:	*Lighthouse Lager, Newcastle Lager*

Driving along the 401 Highway between Toronto and Kingston, one spies a large hotel looming to the north by the name of the Flying Dutchman. It is safe to say that countless commuters have driven right by the Bowmanville lodgings without ever once thinking that it just might be home to its very own brewery.

The brewpub that so many drivers speed by is the Lighthouse Brewpub, a fairly large restaurant and dance club owned through an investment company by Fred D'Silva. Also the owner of the Flying Dutchman Hotel, D'Silva made his money in the construction industry and, according to Lighthouse manager and brewer Chris Mendes, has about a dozen other businesses on the go.

When D'Silva purchased the Dutchman in 1986, it is doubtful that he had the dream of installing a brewery in the hotel restaurant. However, after a few years of ownership, says Mendes, they realized it was time to renovate the lobby eatery and they considered several options, including a franchised roadhouse, before they decided that their best bet was to build a brewpub.

The main factor behind that decision, says Mendes, was that the hotel drew much of its business from salespeople and managers on their way from one meeting to another. The added attraction of a unique concept like a brewpub, it was thought, could increase the volume of trade they drew from that sector by appealing to sophisticated tastes. The addition of a dance floor and thrice-weekly deejay would help make sure that entertainment-oriented customers could be enticed into the Lighthouse, as well.

The Continental malt-extract system was installed near the end of 1989 and, early the next year, Mendes began to learn how to brew beer.

Although Mendes had no brewing experience whatsoever, he did possess what he calls "the will to learn." That will must have served him well because, after six brews with Continental representative John Downing, he was ready to go it alone.

Mendes has been brewing at the Lighthouse ever since, and has only once tampered with the existing beer recipes, when he experimented with making a "dry" beer. It was an experience he says he would not want to go through again, even though he considered the experiment a success. The construction of a new recipe was simply, in his words, "too hard."

While there have been reports that the Lighthouse is frequently out of one or the other of their house brews, that may simply be a case of coincidences and bad timing. There was a confirmed lack of house beer during the winter of 1992–1993 though, as Mendes took advantage of a slow period to shut down the brewery completely and effect some needed maintenance on the kettles. It was a successful practice, says Mendes, one he vows will never happen again—a bit of news thirsty travellers will no doubt greet with a sigh of relief.

SCOREBOARD

Newcastle Lager (5% vol.)

Amber-coloured with a slightly sweet and hoppy aroma. The leafy start with evident hopping leads into a bittersweet and somewhat metallic body containing lemon-lime notes and minimal carbonation. The fresh hay finish carries light acidity and lingering citric notes. ★

Lion Brewery (in the Huether Hotel)

LOCATION:	*59 King Street North, Waterloo, Ontario N2J 2X2*
PHONE:	*519-886-3350, (fax) 519-886-0761*
OWNERS:	*Bernie Adlys & family*
MANAGER:	*The Adlys family*
BREWERS:	*Kelly & David Adlys*
CONSULTING BREWER:	*Cask*
CAPACITY:	*1,500 hl*
TOURS:	*On request*
BRANDS:	*Adlys Ale, English Ale, Huether Premium Lager, Lion Lager*

Every so often in Ontario, one gets lucky enough to come across a genuine piece of brewing history. The Huether Hotel is one such bit of breweriana.

As long ago as 1842, there was beer being brewed in the Huether (pronounced HEE-ther) by a man named William Rebscher, a German brewer who set up the property as a brewery and inn. Fourteen years later, the first Huether bought the property and christened the operation the Lion Brewery. Nine years later, Christopher Huether took over from his father, Adam, and installed the final piece of the inn's legacy in the form of a sign proclaiming "C. Huether's Hotel—Lion Brewery".

Over time, the brewery closed and the inn became the Hotel Ewald and, later, the Hotel Kent before it was sold to John Adlys in 1953. The Adlys family still owns the Huether with John's son Bernie and his wife, Sonia, sharing the majority of the title, and their children splitting the rest.

It was under the Adlys ownership that the brewing traditions of the building were brought back to the fore with the construction of the brewery in the basement of the hotel. After Bernie Adlys had taken over the operation from his father, it became evident to the new proprietor that there were numerous, much-needed repairs and renovations to be done to the grand old building. As cash became available, Bernie and company— especially sons David and Kelly—made improvements to the establishment including turning the hotel into a dorm for 22 students and adding a licensed pool room to the complex.

Along the way, it was discovered that it would be technically possible to dig out the basement, which had been filled in years earlier, and restore the brewery to the Huether.

The process was long and arduous, but eventually the project was completed and, on June 4, 1987, the Lion Brewery was brought back to life and the hotel renamed the Huether to commemorate the occasion. The attached pub, replete with brewing memorabilia covering the walls, was further enlarged in 1990 by the discovery and subsequent excavation of a malting room beside the brewery.

The entire complex, which now stretches to the better part of a block, includes the brewery and attached pub, the pool room, a sports bar (the Penalty Box) and entertainment room (the Kent Lounge), a party room on the second floor for special events, the dorm, a top-floor cinema that is leased to outside interests and an attached brew-on-premises (BOP) location where, under the guidance of Kelly or David, satisfied customers can try their own hands at brewing beer.

This is not to imply that the Adlys family is finished with their renovations. Kelly and David plan to move the brewery to an underground space between the pub and the BOP so as to enlarge their brewing capacity and more easily accommodate tours. After they complete that project, it is hard to say what the two enterprising young men will try next.

It is unlikely, though, that it will have anything to do with relaxing.

SCOREBOARD

Adlys Ale (5% vol.)
Rust-coloured with a chocolate-toffee aroma holding slight apple notes and a hint of yeast. The lightly mocha front carries some astringency before a body of semisweet chocolate. McIntosh apple and faint molasses with some smokiness evident in the second half. The still slightly smoky finish is mildly yeasty and astringent and holds strong apple notes. ★ 1/2

English Ale (5% vol.)

Deep chocolate colour with a very malty, chocolate molasses nose. A light-bodied ale, it has some surprising depth of flavour. Coffee notes begin the taste, leading to a slightly bitter, chocolate middle with woody hop notes. The finish, which continues the lightly hoppy bitterness, adds mocha notes. ★$\frac{1}{2}$

Lion Lager (5% vol.)

Medium gold in colour with light aromatics containing some sweet grain, caramelly malt and a hint of floral hopping. The very creamy body has a slightly sour character throughout the taste. Beginning with a sweet, grainy and almost orangey start, the body bitters somewhat with the hopping in the middle before turning rather grassy with sugar evident in the finish. ★

Marconi's Restaurant

LOCATION:	*262 Carlingview Drive, Etobicoke, Ontario M9W 5G1 (below Journey's End Suites)*
PHONE:	*416-675-6854, (fax) 416-675-5911*
OWNERS:	*Larry & Lisa Marconi*
MANAGERS:	*Owners*
BREWER:	*Alda Slater*
CONSULTING BREWER:	*Gord Slater*
CAPACITY:	*520 hl*
TOURS:	*On request*
BRANDS:	*Dry Lite, European Lager, Occasional seasonal specialty brews*

Since 1979, residents of Sudbury have been dining on the selection of steaks and pasta at the original Marconi's Restaurant. Unfortunately for the northerners, however, it was in Toronto that the brewpub was born.

Larry Marconi explains that the move to Toronto was calculated mainly to work on the development of his packaged-food line. Of course, the opportunity to open his own brewpub was not something he looked at lightly, either.

Marconi's first move out of the "Big Nickel" was to open a non-brewpub restaurant in Mississauga. The suburban location, he says, enabled him to test-market his new, supermarket food lines in a dining situation, thus reducing the risk associated with bringing a new product to the market.

While the Mississauga situation was a positive one, along the way Marconi had become convinced that the trend in the 1990s was to beer and wine. Consequently, he decided to open a brewpub closer to Pearson International Airport and sell his other area restaurant.

The site that he settled on for the brewpub was the main floor of the Journey's End Suites hotel, a locale Marconi says works symbiotically for the two businesses. The family atmosphere of the restaurant portion of Marconi's is perfectly suited to a hotel situation, he says, and the malt-extract brewpub acts as a draw for out-of-town visitors who may end up staying in the hotel.

The extract brews available on tap sold so well, says Marconi, that he approached the Algonquin Brewing Company near the end of 1990 to have them produce a bottled version of his beer. The result was the first brewery-brewpub licensing venture in Canada and the full-grain Algonquin-brewed lager, in addition to being sold at beer stores around the province, has since joined the house brands on the draught taps at the brewpub.

The summer of 1993 saw Marconi remodelling the bar portion of his establishment to turn it into a brewing museum. That same area is also home to a dance floor, weekend karaoke nights and a seasonal theme that is changed every month or two.

As for Larry Marconi, he hopes to open more hotel-based brewpubs in the southern Ontario region in the future and he still sees bright things on the horizon for the industry.

SCOREBOARD

Dry Lite (4.2% vol.)
Light gold in colour with low aromatics of sweet, slightly floral malt. The sweet, lightly hopped front leads to a light body of sweet lemon and sour grain with a touch of flowers. A dry and acrid finish complete the taste. ★

European Lager (4.8% vol.)
Medium gold in colour with a light nose holding sweet hay notes. The body begins sour and leafy before becoming moderately creamy, sweet and grassy with a balance provided by some light, woody hopping. The finish is bittersweet and grassy. ★$^{1}/_{2}$

Master's Brew Pub & Brasserie

Master's Brew Pub & Brasserie

LOCATION:	*330 Queen Street, Ottawa, Ontario K1R 5A5*
PHONE:	*613-594-3688*
OWNERS:	*Tom Barton & Jean-Paul Taillfer*
MANAGER:	*Kelly Littlemore*
BREWER:	*Martin Ruddy*
CONSULTING BREWER:	*N/A*
CAPACITY:	*652 hl*
TOURS:	*On request*
BRANDS:	*Ale, Lager*

Many breweries and brewpubs the world over have been conceived over a few beers in a bar or pub, and Master's, Ottawa's only brewpub, is no exception.

Former Carling O'Keefe brewer Peter Cantelon and hotel manager Rick Willan were reportedly frequent imbibers at a popular Ottawa watering hole and, one afternoon in early 1987, they happened to grab the ear of Tom Barton. The subject matter was the brewpub concept and all three men agreed that the idea would likely work well in the nation's capital. Barton then enlisted his friend Jean-Paul Taillfer and the ownership group was formed.

Barton, who had become enamoured of various brewpubs through his travels, led the way to the founding of Master's when he and Cantelon left for a road trip to visit some existing Ontario locations. After seeing Toronto's Amsterdam, the Kingston Brewing Company, Welland's Atlas (since closed) and the Olde Heidelberg (for all, see separate entries), the pair was convinced that they too could open a brewpub.

Due to Willan's hotel connections, the group thought it a good idea to locate in what was then part of the York-Hanover chain of hotels. Unfortunately, the York-Hanover group were reportedly experiencing serious financial difficulties at the time and it took the partners several months to convince the company to give them a lease. They were eventually successful, however, and the brewing equipment was ordered from Cask in November 1987.

The first brew at Master's new brewery was completed in December of that same year and the owners then had to wait three to four weeks to get their licensing approval from the Liquor Board of Ontario. The permit arrived and the doors opened at 4:00 p.m. on January 20 of the next year.

With his Carling background, it made sense that Cantelon would be the brewer at Master's but his new wife did not agree with that logic. Tired of the late nights and long hours, she suggested that Cantelon would be better off being a full-time husband than a full-time brewer and he had to agree. By St. Patrick's Day, 1988, both Cantelon and Willan had left the group.

After some advance training by Cantelon and Toronto brewer Gord Slater, Barton took over the brewing duties at Master's by himself until a young man by the name of Martin Ruddy showed up in the pub some two months later. An enthusiastic home brewer, Ruddy was interested in getting involved with larger-scale brewing and asked if he could sign on with the brewpub. Figuring that he could always use extra help, Barton trained Ruddy on the system and the two men became a brewing team.

That first road trip that he and Cantelon had taken had convinced Barton of the usefulness of business trips to other brewpubs and, over the next year, he and Ruddy visited a dozen or so brewing establishments in Quebec, Ontario and the northeastern United States. At one point in the summer of 1991, the two men dropped by the Lion d'Or in Lennoxville, Quebec (see separate entry under Quebec and the Maritimes) and, on the basis of what they saw, decided to introduce some grain to their malt-extract system.

Barton claims that Master's has regularly used 60 percent grain in their mash ever since they made the conversion and adds that he thinks they have much better products for the effort. Of course, the effort is not something he has to be overly concerned about anymore since he passed all of the brewery work over to Ruddy in 1991.

Given Barton's propensity for research junkets to various brewpubs, it is appropriate that Master's is located in Canada's capital city. After all, what better place for a brewpub that has drawn inspiration from breweries across the country?

SCOREBOARD

Ale (5% vol.)

Light rust-coloured with a spicy (nutmeg) nose carrying some light fruitiness. The fairly flat body begins slightly fruity (orange, apricot) before developing a sour, yeasty edge in the body with a trace of earthy hop. The finish becomes quite sour, almost to the point of mouth-puckering, with strong yeasty flavours. ★

Lager (5% vol.)
Medium gold in colour with a strong clove spicing carried in the aroma with traces of orange. The equally spicy and clovey body begins lightly fruity and sweet before some bitter hopping begins to rise through the taste to a somewhat sour and rooty finish. ★½

Olde Heidelberg Restaurant & Brew Pub

LOCATION:	*2 King Street, Heidelberg, Ontario*
	N0B 1Y0
PHONE:	*519-699-4413*
OWNERS:	*Bob Oberholtzer Sr. & Jr.,*
	Howie & Bob MacMillan
MANAGERS:	*Howie & Bob MacMillan*
BREWERS:	*Howie & Bob MacMillan*
CONSULTING BREWER:	*Continental*
CAPACITY:	*365 hl*
TOURS:	*On request*
BRANDS:	*Olde Heidelberg Draft*

Driving along Highway 15 just northwest of Waterloo, the last thing you would expect to find among the small towns and Mennonite farms that dot the area is a brewpub. Thanks to four men and a historic building, however, that is exactly what meets you on the main street of Heidelberg.

The Olde Heidelberg Brewery and Restaurant dates back to the mid-nineteenth century and, like many inns of its time, has a solid, historic connection to the brewing business. In this case, the ties are found with the old Kuntz Brewery of Waterloo which had the deed to the building from 1917 to 1929, when it presumably began its career as a tavern.

In its later life, the tavern and adjacent 16-room motel came to be owned by the father-son team of Bob Oberholtzer, Sr. and Bob, Jr., until, in the summer of 1986, a hockey game in the nearby town of St. Clements brought a new pair of partners to the ownership group.

After playing in that hockey game, Howie MacMillan dropped by the tavern for a beer. At the time, MacMillan, a retail and restaurant management veteran, was in the middle of seeing his Army and Navy store sold to the Ontario discount giant Bi-Way and knew that he would soon be looking for new employment. Weary of working for others, he happened to engage in a conversation with Oberholtzer, Sr., and quickly developed an interest in buying into the business.

A short time later, MacMillan and his then partner joined the Oberholtzers in the ownership of the Olde Heidelberg and the plans that the latter pair had developed to install a brewery in the historic inn were put into action.

The brewery was up and running by September 1986 and, according to MacMillan, it made an immediate impact on the amount of tourist trade the small town bar and restaurant received. Only the third pub to begin brewing in the province, the Heidelberg's malt-extract brewery was enough of an anomaly, says MacMillan, that the radius from which they drew their customers expanded significantly following its installation.

A mere six months later, MacMillan and the partner with whom he had bought into the Heidelberg had unresolvable business differences and MacMillan convinced his younger brother, Bob, to buy out the partner's shares. In the years that followed, while the Oberholtzers have remained involved in the ownership of the hotel and brewpub, the day-to-day operations of the facility have been passed to the MacMillans.

Both MacMillans say that the brewpub is still an important tourist attraction and, to make things even more attractive in a Bavarian way, they present sing-along nights every Friday and Saturday with the corner, upright piano leading the tunes. As well, the brothers have introduced a do-it-yourself steak pit for customers who are so inclined.

While they might not be leading the sing-along on Friday night, the local Mennonites are apparently fond of the Olde Heidelberg, as well, making it the one brewpub in Canada where you never know whether the next group of customers will arrive by car or horse and buggy.

SCOREBOARD

Olde Heidelberg Draft (4.5% vol.)
Medium gold in colour with a candied malt aroma carrying orange toffee notes. The thin, sugary grain start leads to a thick, sweet-and-sour body holding heavy sugar notes on a sour, vegetal malt base with perhaps a touch of floral hop behind it. The finish is sour and grassy with hints of the remaining sugar. ★

Pepperwood Bistro

LOCATION:	*1455 Lakeshore Road, Burlington, Ontario L7S 1B5*
PHONE:	*905-333-6999*
OWNERS:	*Mike Dine*
MANAGER:	*David Whale*
BREWER:	*Geoffery Mallard*
CONSULTING BREWER:	*N/A*
CAPACITY:	*350 hl*
TOURS:	*On request*
BRANDS:	*Cream Ale, Victoria Red Ale*

Occasionally, a brewery will get a second chance in the same location, more frequently one will be reborn in a different locale, but almost never does a brewery receive a third shot at survival in the same spot.

Unless, apparently, that brewery happens to be located on Lakeshore Road in the Toronto/Hamilton suburb of Burlington.

The Pepperwood Bistro originally came to life as the Suds International brewpub. Once that business failed, the location was reborn as the Burlington member of the ill-fated Luxembourg brewpub chain. Finally, after the chain and, later, the pub itself went bankrupt, current owner Mike Dine moved in and the Pepperwood was born in the early spring of 1993.

A chef with a small but successful restaurant in Tottenham, Ontario, Dine had been looking for a new, slightly larger spot for over a year when he found the Pepperwood, and even then it was not his ideal choice. Over the course of his search, Dine had actually settled on three different restaurants on three different occasions and each deal had eventually fallen through. The frustration of his search was beginning to make Dine suspect that his plans might never see fruition.

All that changed when he received a call from the proprietor of Burlington's Sonoma Valley Bistro, a man Dine knew from the industry who was also the owner of the building that held the closed Luxembourg. Through frequent conversations with the restaurateur, Dine became convinced that he could do something with the brewpub and a deal was struck.

One thing that both Dine and his new landlord agreed upon was the need for a fresh concept if the restaurant was ever going to work. One of the problems that had plagued the site was the cavernous feel of the room, something not suited to a pub atmosphere. To address this difficulty, Dine separated the bar at the front from the restaurant at the back, thereby creating a much cozier environment and altering completely the look of the restaurant.

Working with friends and family, Dine effected all the renovations himself and, after waffling about whether to reopen the brewery or not, brought in Tottenham resident and Canadian Amateur Brewers Association vice-president Geoffery Mallard to brew his beer.

Mallard's first challenge was to cope with the fact that the brewery had been constructed for malt-extract brewing. Not at all pleased with that style, he eventually managed to turn the operation to full-grain by constructing portable mash tuns (vital to full-grain brewing) that he could maneuver about in the brewery. The result, according to initial reports, has enjoyed a positive response by the community.

Mallard would like to eventually have house brews on all eight taps at the Pepperwood, but it's questionable whether the brewery's limited capacity will allow him to do that. Regardless of his success in such lofty pursuits, it seems enough that he and Dine have put craft brewing back into Burlington.

For the third time.

SCOREBOARD

Cream Ale (4.9%)
Light to medium gold in colour with a very spicy (cinnamon) aroma holding orange toffee and light rye bread notes. The soft start blends cinnamon and nutmeg notes in the malt on the way to a mildly hoppy body with some light nuttiness and sour orange flavours. The fairly quick, dry finish has a few sour orange and light petrol notes. ★★

Victoria Red Ale (4.8%)
Light, coppery colour with a faint smokiness in an otherwise fruity (cherry, apricot) and caramelly aroma. The creamy start has a mild sweetness and orange notes before entering a bitter and woody body with a hint of lingering cherry flavour and a touch of rootiness. The dry finish is also bitter and woody. ★★¹/₂

(Note: At the time of writing, it was not determined which brands were to be permanent at the Pepperwood. However, the two reviewed are considered the most likely candidates for residency and were the only brews on tap when the Bistro was last visited.)

Port Arthur Brasserie and Brewpub

LOCATION:	*901 Red River Road, Thunder Bay, Ontario P7B 1K3*
PHONE:	*807-767-4415, (fax) 807-767-4140*
OWNERS:	*Fraser Dougall*
MANAGER:	*Ron Lemarquand*
BREWER:	*John Tilbury*
CONSULTING BREWER:	*Cask*
CAPACITY:	*375 hl*
TOURS:	*On request*
BRANDS:	*Arthur's Lager, Specialty brands*

S tepping into the tile-and-chrome surroundings of the Port Arthur Brasserie and Brewpub, one notices only the slightest evidence that the premises formerly housed one of the Kelsey's chain of roadhouse restaurants.

And, likely, that is exactly the way owner Fraser Dougall wants it.

A man who, by all accounts, owns a good deal of Thunder Bay, including real estate, television, and print and radio interests, Dougall also owned that city's two Kelsey's franchises before he decided to go it alone and leave the chain in 1987. While he renovated one of his locations into a family restaurant, Dougall wished to do something a little different with the other site.

Basing his decision on the recent closing of Northern Breweries' Thunder Bay operations and the popularity of the since-closed Conners/ Renegade brewery in the city, Dougall selected the brewpub option as the way to go. He felt that the area would embrace the new concept and saw the restaurant on Red River Road—one of the main spokes out of downtown—as the ideal place to try his idea.

Evidently Dougall was not completely confident that the brewery would draw all on its own, because he incorporated a sports bar/dance club motif into the mix, as well. The mélange produced a final concept that was initially a little hard for the neighbourhood to accept.

Brewer John Tilbury admits that the Port Arthur struggled a bit at first, although he hastens to add that the bar has risen from its early trials after the late 1987 opening and is now doing much better.

Tilbury himself joined the company in August 1991 and learned all he knows about brewing while on the job. The young brewer admits that he is still naive about some of the complexities of brewing, but he also demonstrates an enthusiasm for his vocation that can be matched by only a handful of brewers in Canada.

The malt-extract, "German-style" lager does not sell a lot in the Port Arthur—Tilbury explains that northerners' beer prejudices are very hard to break—but that does not prevent Dougall from promoting the brew in all of his advertising. Although he has a lot to promote with the nation's only brewpub volleyball court, a deejay seven nights a week and numerous activity and theme nights (including an early spring hot tub party on the patio), Dougall never forgets to push the brewery in the process.

Perhaps, one day, he may even succeed in lifting some of those prejudices.

SCOREBOARD

Arthur's Lager (5% vol.)
Light gold in colour with a fresh, sweet aroma of very slightly sour grain, light florals and candied citrus peel. The light, creamy and slightly lactic start holds a bit of grassiness and leads to a grassier body with slight yeasty and rooty sourness on a sweet, caramelly base. The finish is sweet and sour with a trace of sour root. ★

Rotterdam Brewing Company

LOCATION:	*600 King Street West, Toronto, Ontario M5V 2E4*
PHONE:	*416-868-6882, (fax) 416-977-5214*
OWNER:	*Roel Bramer*
COMPTROLLER:	*Adele Espina*
GENERAL MANAGER:	*Andrew Hussey*
BREWER:	*Joel Manning*
CONSULTING BREWER:	*Continental*
CAPACITY:	*5,000 hl*
TOURS:	*On request or scheduled weekly to coincide with Sunday brunch service*
BRANDS:	*Amber Weizen, Blonde Ale, Cherrywood Lager, Framboise, Lager, Light Lager, Milk Stout, Non-Alcohol Lager, Nut Brown Ale, Pilsner, Scottish Ale*
	24 rotating specialty brews for one tap

"Standing in semi-frozen mud."

That is the clearest picture owner Roel Bramer has of the construction of the Rotterdam, hardly a cherished memory of the early days of Ontario's largest-capacity brewpub.

But, truth be known, the origins of the Rotterdam are anything but glamorous, beginning as it did in a shallow, garbage-filled basement in an old building on a forgotten stretch of King Street West. Then again, transformations from the unglamorous into something decidedly more hospitable are a Bramer specialty.

The owner of Toronto's first brewpub, the Amsterdam (see separate entry), Bramer has twice bought buildings he thought of as disasters and twice converted them into brewpubs almost as an afterthought. To say he operates unconventionally is an understatement.

When Bramer purchased the Rotterdam building in late 1987, his evaluation was that it would be best used as a brewpub. This assessment, of course, came following the signing of the purchase and, as he did with the Amsterdam, Bramer says that he let the building define its use rather than vice versa.

The semi-frozen mud part came after Bramer's crew had cleared "several tons" of garbage out of the basement only to find a dirt floor. Undaunted, Bramer turned adversity into opportunity and dug the floor down to accommodate the restaurant while he situated the brewery on a second-level terrace, thus reversing the Amsterdam's basement brewery/main floor restaurant approach.

Designing the brewpub as he went along, Bramer says that he sought not so much to duplicate the look of his other brewpub (although the similarities are undeniable) as he was guided by his personal tastes and the physical structure of the building. Regardless of his motivation for the decor, there can be no doubting his reasoning behind the installation of a micro-sized, full-grain brewery.

The large brewery was fitted on the gamble that Ontario liquor legislation would soon be altered to allow brewpubs to bottle and sell their own beer for home consumption. Bramer took the chance in 1989 and he is still waiting.

The positive side to Bramer's misplayed roll of the dice is that brewer Joel Manning has a lot of room in which to brew, age his beer and experiment with beer styles. He also has space in which to make the .5% alcohol All Night Lager, the first draught "non-alk" in Ontario (available at both of Bramer's establishments).

In the past couple of years, Manning has been one of the more innovative Ontario brewers, having put such eclectic styles as cherry wheat and smoked beer on tap and bottle-conditioning his Christmas bock.

And who knows? Someday he may even be allowed to sell those bottles to take home.

SCOREBOARD

Amber Weizen (5% vol.)
Amber-gold coloured with a very spicy (clove) aroma carrying light hints of sweet grain and banana. The soft start has some notes of clove and lightly toasted grain leading into a spicy (more clove) and slightly creamy body of faintly sour grain with hints of plastic. The finish is bitter with lingering clove and woody hop notes. ★★

Framboise (6.5% vol.)
Medium to dark red in colour with a strong raspberry aroma. The sour and slightly yeasty raspberry juice start sweetens in the body with more of the pure fruit emerging along with a note of raw grain. The finish bitters considerably while carrying some acidity and notes of the fruit skin. ★★¹/₂

Lager (5% vol.)
Light to medium gold in colour with a moderately sweet and caramelly aroma carrying traces of earthy hop. The slightly bitter and woody start carries hints of sweet grain prior to moving to a creamy and bitter body holding woody hop, very light spice (clove) and sour grain flavours. The finish holds more sour grain and bitter, earthy hop in equal proportion. ★¹/₂

Light Lager (3.5% vol.)
Light gold in colour with a toasted cereal grain aroma holding light caramel and woody hop notes. The slightly carbonic start is very grainy but balanced between sweet and bitter while the toasted grain body holds some bitter and woody hop, a hint of leafy hop and a touch of sourness before moving into a bitter hop and grain finish that borders on sourness. ★★

Milk Stout (6% vol.)
Extremely deep brown in colour and lightly sweet in its mocha aroma with soft notes of anise. The faintly acidic start has notes of coffee and plum before the pronounced and bitter espresso body holding hints of burnt sugar and black licorice. The coffee continues in the slightly burnt and very bitter finish. ★★¹/₂

Pilsener (5.5% vol.)

Medium gold-coloured with a sour grain aroma holding notes of earthy hop and petrol. The sweetish start has toffee and plastic notes combining with earthy hopping before the creamy body of bitter and earthy hop, very faint florals and sour, burnt grain. It finishes with a very rooty and sour taste carrying some woody hop notes. ★½

Scotch Ale (5.5% vol.)

Deep burgundy in colour with a soft and sweet aroma of toffee and coffee. The light start carries molasses and very faint earthy hop notes before a bittersweet body of baker's chocolate, sweetened coffee, faint plum and extremely faint saline. The finish tastes strongly of espresso with a trace of demerara sugar. ★★½

The Spruce Goose

LOCATION:	*130 Eglinton Avenue East, Toronto, Ontario M4P 2X9*
PHONE:	*416-485-4121, (Fax) 416-485-4158*
OWNERS:	*John Wilkins, Tony Florsham*
MANAGER:	*John Wilkins*
BREWER:	*Charles MacLean*
CONSULTING BREWER:	*Charles MacLean*
CAPACITY:	*520 hl*
TOURS:	*On request*
BRANDS:	*Spruce Joose*
	Canuck Joose

Like the owners of the two other brewpubs in Toronto's Yonge and Eglinton area (Vinefera and the Granite—see separate entries), John Wilkins and Tony Florsham did not know that they were about to enter a very competitive situation when they decided to build their brewpub in that popular region.

Opened within two months of the Granite, the Goose was a concept which, according to Wilkins, was virtually tailored to fit the location rather than vice versa. While the two owners of the Yonge and Sheppard area bars Maxwell's Mix and the Victoria and Albert pub were indeed looking to start a brewpub, their intent in moving to the trendy uptown district was to open a dance bar rather than a brewery. In the end, they did both.

The space that hangars the Goose had, in previous years, been home to several concepts, none of which had made any money. So, when the partners closed the purchase of the spot in a whirlwind 36 hours, they knew that they had to take a very close look at the location before deciding on a course of action.

The two men had examined the possibility of installing a brewery in their Yonge-Sheppard pub, concluding that it was an impractical move. Instead, they thought, why not combine a dance club, which they felt was what the Yonge-Eglinton area lacked, with a brewery, which, at the time, the area also lacked. Given the curious, two-level layout of the premises, they theorized that the "brew club" concept might work well in a site notorious for its restaurant failures.

Soon after renovations to the Goose had begun in April 1991, Wilkins brought contract brewer Charles MacLean in to supervise the brewing end of things. The two men had met through the woman with whom Wilkins was living and, as MacLean carried some impressive credentials, including the opening of the Wellington County Brewery, the match seemed logical to the partners.

Due to the design of the building, the brewery of the Spruce Goose is stuck in a back corner of the upper level, a factor that may partly explain the low percentage (30 percent) of house beer sold in comparison to the other ten taps at the Goose. Wilkins, however, maintains that the youth of his clientele relative to that of other brewpubs accounts for the low ratios. Either way, it is clear that the Goose is not an average brewpub and, as such, does not follow standard brewpub trends.

Thursday through Saturday nights inevitably yield lineups at the Goose these days, a sure sign that the partners were correct about the dance club aspect of the operation, and Wilkins says that lunch and dinner crowds are improving steadily as are the house beer sales.

It looks as if the Spruce Goose will be flying for some time to come.

SCOREBOARD

Canuck Joose (5.5% vol.)
Light gold in colour, it has the sweet, fresh grain aroma one identifies with the national style, albeit in a more aromatic, fresh hay format. The sweet, creamy start sours in the middle with notes of sour root and grass and finishes with high acidity. ★

Spruce Joose (5.5% vol.)

An amber ale that is closer to medium gold in colour, this beer has a sweet, perfumey and lightly fruity malt nose. The taste starts off very malty with notes of slightly caramelized brown sugar and faint candied fruit before developing a light, woody bitterness in the second half. The finish is bitter-sour with evident acidity. ★½

Tracks Brewpub

LOCATION:	*60 Queen Street East, Brampton, Ontario L6V 1A9*
PHONE:	*905-453-3063*
OWNERS:	*Jimmy Floris, Chris Minos*
MANAGER:	*Owners*
BREWER:	*John Lippert*
CONSULTING BREWER:	*Alan Knight*
CAPACITY:	*190 hl*
TOURS:	*No, brewery visible from bar*
BRANDS:	*Old Mill Lager*

In the mid-to-late 1980s, a lot of Ontarians were caught up in the micro-brewery/brewpub craze of the day. Two such men were Henry Maag and Mark Cruden, the owners of Houstons Restaurant and Tracks Bar in the Toronto suburb of Brampton.

Beer drinkers themselves, the two men were very interested in the brewpub concept and, when they factored in the originality of the idea (the industry was still fairly young), the temptation to turn their small bar into a brewpub proved to be too great to resist.

Brewing had begun by the end of 1987 and, reportedly, the patrons of the bar took very kindly to the idea of drinking house beer. It was not long before Maag and Cruden knew that they had a hit on their hands and, perhaps, were regretting not having opted for a brewery that was a bit larger than the small, malt-extract operation they had selected.

Evidently, the owners eventually tired of the rigours involved with running a restaurant, pub and brewery and decided to sell first Houstons and, subsequently, Tracks to two different parties. The purchasers of the latter operation were current owners Jimmy Floris and Chris Minos.

While Floris admits that he is not a beer drinker himself, he is very happy to have the brewery on the premises and feels that the uniqueness of the concept keeps people coming to his bar. It probably does not hurt that he has Hanwell's Brewing Services' Alan Knight in charge of his beer.

Knight came to Tracks in relief of former contract brewer Charles MacLean in late 1989, shortly before the ownership change. By lasting until 1993, he has become the most enduring of Tracks's four brewers who included, for a short time, the establishment's chef.

The Knight years were not to last, however, as Tracks's longstanding brewer left for New Zealand in the summer of 1993. The new proprietor of Hanwell's, Doug Warren, proved to be too busy to keep the beer flowing at Tracks and he soon handed the reins to John Lippert, brewer at Barb's Union Station in Markham (see separate entry). Like Warren and Knight before him, Lippert's most daunting task is to maintain a supply of house beer at a bar where demand frequently outstrips the capacity of the brewery.

Although Floris also bemoans the capacity problems, he says that despite his lack of brewpub experience prior to the purchase of Tracks, he has thoroughly enjoyed his time as owner and is considering a Newmarket location for his second brewpub. The community, he says, has really adopted the pub as their own local brewery and the resultant support and loyalty have been very encouraging.

SCOREBOARD

(Note: The beer reviewed here is the full-grain creation of Knight. Lippert plans to brew in a similar style but will be using malt extract.)

Old Mill Lager (4.7% vol.)
Medium gold-coloured with a slightly sour, grassy nose holding faint raw sugar notes. The rich and somewhat creamy body has a confectionery start with a bit of caramel leading into a bittering body with sweet hay and bitter grass notes. The finish turns slightly sour and rooty. ★★

Vinefera

LOCATION:	*150 Eglinton Avenue East, Toronto, Ontario M4P 1E8*
PHONE:	*416-487-9281*
OWNERS:	*Der Chia Lin, Shou Teng Lin*
MANAGER:	*Der Chia Lin*
BREWER:	*Fred Wegner*
BREWING CAPACITY:	*350 hl*
BRANDS:	*Vinefera Lager*

Der Chia Lin is not Ontario's most experienced brewpub owner, but he may very well be the most persistent.

Since taking ownership of Vinefera in May 1991, Lin and his wife, Shou Teng, have endured setbacks that would crush the spirits of most people. They, however, simply keep on going with smiles and an enthusiasm that is refreshing in the beleaguered world of the restaurant trade.

While Shou Teng Lin does come from a service industry background, it is not one which you would naturally associate with brewpub ownership. For seven and a half years, she ran an ice cream shop in Toronto's massive Eaton Centre shopping mall and, when rent there got to be too high, she and her engineer husband chose to enter the cutthroat world of the city's bar and restaurant trade.

Once the commitment had been made to take over the failed premises of a former singles bar in the restaurant-dense Yonge and Eglinton district, Lin decided that, for reasons of appeal and profit, it made sense to operate the spot as a brewpub. What Lin did not know was that, by the time he had opened his establishment, his would be one of three brewpubs within a very short distance of one another. He also didn't know the first thing about brewing beer.

At about the same time as Lin signed for his new premises, he also signed a contract with a popular brewery supply firm for them to design, install and start up the brewery. After a delay of six months caused by problems with the receivership proceedings of the former tenants, renovations were begun and the brewery was installed . . . sort of.

While the man with whom Lin had signed the contract did indeed follow through with the delivery of the brewery, that was about all he did. After insisting on, and receiving, a certified cheque for the specified sum, the contractor, according to Lin, was out the door before the last piece of equipment was even put down. Lin was now left with a partially installed brewery and no one to run it.

Fortunately for Lin, the brewing industry is by and large a friendly one and he was soon able to find assistance in the form of Michael Hancock, brewer and part-owner of Denison's Brewing Company in Toronto (see separate entry). Although too busy to help out himself, Hancock recommended that Lin contact John Downing, a brewing consultant who was formerly with the company that supplied Lin's brewery.

While the restaurant had been open since March 1992, it was not until the end of May that Downing was able to get the brewery up and running. During that time, one of Lin's managers made contact with John Lippert, brewer at the Union Station brewpub, who was then contracted as brewer for Vinefera.

After two false starts due to bad yeast problems, Lippert was finally able to get a house lager on tap in June. Unfortunately, quality problems continued to dog Lippert and, by the fall of that year, Lin was in the market for a new brewer.

Enter once again Michael Hancock. This time, Hancock suggested that the solution to Lin's problems lay at the feet of Alan Knight of Hanwell's Brewing Services. Never one to pass on good advice, Lin negotiated a dissolution to Lippert's contract and Knight began brewing for Vinefera just before the Christmas of 1992.

Although Knight's lager received generally good reviews, Lin was searching for a new brewer within less than a year, as Knight left the country to pursue other interests. Through a mutual acquaintance, he met John Wegner, the proprietor of the Create-A-Brew BOP in Mississauga, and the third brewer of the pub's short history was at work by the fall of 1993.

When I asked about the tremendous adversity he had faced in his first year, Lin countered with the statements that he had never failed at anything, and that it was not in his nature to give up.

SCOREBOARD

Vinefera Amber Lager (5.5% vol.)

Light rust in colour with a full and very sweet, candied orange aroma. The thin start is fairly neutral but for light fruit sugar notes, and the body mixes dried hay flavours with a fruity (orange, apricot) sweetness and a slight nuttiness. The fruit dries out in the finish with more nutty notes but serves up a sour-grain taste, as well. ★¹/₂

Vinefera Light Lager (4.5% vol.)
Light gold-coloured with a sweet and sugary aroma carrying a light, grainy sourness and notes of freshly cut grass. The start is thin and fresh with strong cereal grain notes leading into a thin, sour body with grassy and citric flavours. The finish bitters slightly with notes of wood but retains the sour, grainy edge. ★

Quebec and
the Maritimes

Bar La Cervoise

LOCATION:	*4457 Rue St. Laurent, Montreal,*
	Quebec H2W 1Z8
PHONE:	*514-843-6586*
OWNERS:	*Jean Pierre Trepanier, Claire Lavallée*
MANAGER:	*Mario Sevegny*
BREWERS:	*Shawn Tordon, Thomas Robson*
CONSULTING BREWER:	*Jamie Gordon (Cask)*
CAPACITY:	*720 hl*
TOURS:	*On request; call in the morning*
BRANDS:	*La Fûtée Lager, La Main Ale*

In the estimation of owner Jean Pierre Trepanier, at least half of the patrons of La Cervoise have no idea that there is a brewery housed in the deep recesses of the bar. And, as long as they keep drinking the La Cervoise brands, he doesn't particularly mind whether they know it is house-brewed or not.

The lack of a strong brewpub identity is completely understandable in the case of La Cervoise. The word "micro-brasseur" (micro-brewery) is only present on the front sign in very small letters and the brewery, normally dark during business hours, is not exactly front and centre in the establishment. Nonetheless, says Trepanier, the regular customers know about the brewery and they will let the staff know if there are any undesirable changes in the house brews.

Trepanier did not start out to get into the brewpub business, though he did have the idea of capitalizing on the popularity of premium beers.

After selling his two Montreal taverns, Trepanier searched for a year to find a bar and a concept that would get him back into the local hospitality business. The idea came fairly quickly when he noticed the success a beer bar by the name of the Fûtenbulle was enjoying through its sales of specialty beers. Using the same concept on the busy strip of St. Laurent near Mont Royal seemed a promising proposition to Trepanier, but that was before he visited the Cheval Blanc.

The Cheval (see separate entry) was the city's first brewpub and had been very well received in the downtown area. The concept of brewing his own beer intrigued Trepanier and struck him as a step up from merely specializing in other people's brews. Before long, La Cervoise was on its way to becoming Montreal's third brewpub.

In his quest to build a brewery, Trepanier met Jamie Gordon through Gordon's Cave à Vin, a home-brewing and wine-making shop. In addition to running the shop, Gordon was also working for Cask at the time and, in his capacity with the latter company, he agreed to act as a consultant on the brewery for Trepanier.

While Trepanier now says that he would purchase a full-grain brewery if he were to do it again, he adds that there was little choice when he was setting up in the summer and fall of 1988. So, a malt-extract brewery was installed at La Cervoise during its non-operating hours—the bar itself opened in March 1988—and brewing began on September 5 of that year.

La Cervoise is a bar in the most literal sense of the word. It is open from 3:00 p.m. to 3:00 a.m. seven days a week, the only available foods are the hot dogs and popcorn that come from behind the bar, the vast majority of its sales come through draught beer and the tables are small and square with just enough room for a few glasses of ale. While this motif is to be expected given Trepanier's tavern background, equally unexpected is the garage door that rolls back to open the bar to the street and the regularly changed art that covers the walls.

As well, for the 50 percent of the patrons that do not know, there is the matter of that little brewery nestled in the back.

SCOREBOARD

La Fûtée Lager (4.7% vol.)
Light to medium gold in colour with a caramel and butterscotch aroma holding sour and sulphurous yeast notes. The sugary and slightly tart front is cut by sour root notes before leading into an appley body with oaky hopping and a touch of sour yeast. The finish bitters with leafy and woody hop along with some remaining caramel sugar. ★½

La Main Ale (4.7% vol.)
Reddish amber-coloured with a soft, green apple nose holding petrol notes. A bitter but lightly fruity (cherry, strawberry) start precedes a full, sweetish body balancing very bitter and earthy hopping with sweet, candied apple malt. The finish is bitter with earthy hop and a slight chalkiness. ★★

Le Cheval Blanc

LOCATION:	*809 Ontario Street East, Montreal, Quebec H2L 1P1*
PHONE:	*514-522-0211*
OWNERS:	*Jerôme Denys*
MANAGER:	*Jerôme Denys*
BREWER:	*Jerôme Denys*
CONSULTING BREWER:	*N/A*
CAPACITY:	*832 hl*
TOURS:	*Not encouraged, but part of the brewery is on display in the bar.*
BRANDS:	*Ambrée (Amber Ale), Blonde (Pale Ale), Brune (Brown Ale), Rotating specialties, Scotch Ale (alternates with the Brune), Wheat*

Most brewpubs that are converted from existing bars or taverns have to add some expected equipment like a brewing kettle, fermenters, extra plumbing and draught-dispensing lines. When Jerôme Denys changed the Cheval Blanc into a brewpub, he had to add a women's washroom!

The reason behind the curious renovation was that, in the early 1980s, the Cheval Blanc—the name means white horse—was not exactly what one would call a terribly progressive bar. It was, in the most traditional and male-oriented sense of the word, a tavern.

Time had passed the Cheval Blanc by, though, and Denys reports that the tavern was not doing very well when he took it over in 1981, thereby becoming the third generation of his family to run the bar. Over his family's grumblings, says Denys, he dragged the tavern into the modern age and began to attract a new crowd, including younger people and students. Then he went to New York City.

It was in the Big Apple that Denys first became interested in the brewpub concept. A visit to the Manhattan Brewing Company brewpub got his mind to wandering and, upon his return to Quebec, he began to informally investigate the possibility of doing such a thing at the Cheval. Then, when the Lion D'Or began brewing in 1986, Denys's intentions became serious.

By the end of 1986, Denys was learning all he could about brewing, getting his Continental brewing system installed and, by early the next year, he had begun to brew. But it was not without a little help that this all came to pass.

Denys's ally in his affairs was Pierre Rajotte, a well-known beer connoisseur and brewing consultant Denys knew through the Campaign for Real Ale (CAMRA) consumer group. Rajotte helped him quite a bit in the start-up, says Denys, adding that he still consults occasionally with Rajotte on a casual basis.

The first brewpub in the city was, according to Denys, an instant success. A new clientele was drawn by the original concept and, says Denys, has grown with the brewpub in its knowledge and appreciation of beer. If something is not right with a brew, he adds, they will let him know it.

The most curious features of the Cheval are the kettle tops sticking through two of the tables at the back of the pub. One might expect that this was a planned curiosity designed to bring the drinker closer to the brewing process but that is simply not the case. In reality, it was an accident of measurement that introduced the kettles to the decor.

Denys had planned to put his brewery in the basement of the pub back when he was setting up, but had neglected to make sure the kettles would fit there. They did not, so rather than redesign the pub, Denys cut holes in the floor and raised the tanks on stilts so that they would protrude well into the tavern. Several days later, after he had noted that the customers were playing with the seals on the kettles, protective plexiglass domes were added to the look.

Over time, Denys has developed a unique theory of brewing and it is one that flies in the face of conventional commercial brewing norms. If we do not expect the same wine from a single winery year after year, he proposes, why should we demand consistency from our breweries? With that in mind, Denys regularly alters the recipes of his brews so that the Blonde you taste this spring will differ from the one you sample in the fall. This philosophy also drives Denys to experiment with esoteric specialties such as smoked and fruit beers.

When you enter the Cheval Blanc, you do not have a lot of choice in what to drink. You select from whatever Denys has on tap of his own and one commercial draught; no bottled beer, no wine, no liquor. That is one tradition Denys is happy to continue.

SCOREBOARD

Brune (5% vol.)
Deep plum in colour with a strong espresso bean aroma. A sweet and carbonic mocha start heads into a body that tastes strongly of coffee with hints of anise, burnt sugar and a yeasty tang. The finish is moderately astringent with bitter coffee flavours. ★★

Scotch Ale (5.5% vol.)

Dark copper-coloured with a soft, toffeeish nose carrying light, burnt chocolate notes. A sweet and plummy flavour starts a rich and malty body with a slight roastiness and bitter, chalky chocolate notes. A hint of tanginess appears in the second half and leads to a mildly alcoholic finish with baker's chocolate and molasses notes. ★★

Wheat (4.5% vol.)

Light brown in colour with an earthy aroma holding sharp clove and yeast notes. The tangy, spicy and slightly woody orange start precedes a lemony body of lightly bitter grain with yeast and clove notes. The soft finish contains a touch of woodiness and citric astringency. ★★

Crocodile Gatineau

LOCATION:	*5414 Gatineau Street, Montreal, Quebec H3T 1X5*
PHONE:	*514-733-2125, (fax) 514-733-6304*
OWNERS:	*Le Groupe Crocodile*
PRESIDENT:	*Bernard Ragueneau*
MARKETING DIRECTOR:	*Marie Lamarre*
MANAGER:	*Jean Luc Ruis*
BREWER:	*Guy Meilleur*
CONSULTING BREWER:	*N/A*
CAPACITY:	*550 hl*
TOURS:	*No*
BRANDS:	*Crocodile Ale*
	Croco Pale Ale (bottles contract-brewed by the McAuslan Brewery)

As witnessed, brewpubs across Canada have many strange points of origin. Some were born out of beery conversations in local watering holes, some were inspired by other brewpubs and some arose simply because the owner wanted a good glass of beer. The two Crocodile brewpubs, perhaps strangest of all, originated from a discotheque.

In 1973, a smallish bar and dance club by the name of Thursday's opened on Montreal's notorious Crescent Street strip. Fifteen years later, that disco was a huge success, had expanded several times and was ready to move further out into the hospitality market. The result was the Crocodiles.

There were several reasons for moving into the Crocodile line of bars, says marketing director Marie Lamarre, not the least of which was the disappointing performance of the first expansion facility, Friday's, a spin-off of Thursday's that was later sold. So when that experiment was abandoned, it was decided that the next step would be into a brewpub concept with, as a sop to the language difficulties in Quebec, a name that was readable in French or English.

The idea behind the entry to the brewpub market was the same as with numerous other brewpubs across the continent, namely the lure of having something different to offer the customer. The fact that the beer would help establish the name of what the company hoped would become a chain of establishments likely did not hurt the project, either.

The Gatineau site was chosen for the first Crocodile and construction began in 1986 so that the new brewpub was open by January 1987. The Thursday's example of combining a bar, restaurant and dance club under one roof was followed and, according to Lamarre, the reaction was positive.

Not that there were not a few confused faces around the bar at first. The Thursday's customers who wanted to check out the new spot were not, after all, the standard brewpub patrons and, says Lamarre, the house brew came as a bit of a surprise to many of them. A domestic draught was kept for the diehards, though, and the Crocodile soon caught on in the tradition of Thursday's.

And the Thursday's tradition is about the only one that the Crocodile did follow, for it is decidedly not an average brewpub. As if the discotheque/bar/restaurant concept was not enough to set the Crocodile aside from the rest, the designers added a mass of steel and chrome to the outside that positively announced the Crocodile's presence to the street. Subtle it was not.

Well equipped, on the other hand, it most definitely was. The brewery, though perhaps not as spacious as brewer Guy Meilleur would like, is of a good size and one wonders if, given the will to do it, full-grain brewing would not be impossible at the Crocodile. That decision, however, will have to wait as Lamarre and Meilleur are unanimous in saying that the conversion is not in the cards for the immediate future.

While the Gatineau Crocodile, or any Crocodile for that matter, is not a typically British-style brewpub, at least the three floors of variety offer a choice that few other brewpubs can match and it is likely that at least one of them will appeal to any given customer. Even if that customer is not a Crescent Street regular.

SCOREBOARD

Crocodile Ale (5% vol.)
Light to medium gold in colour with a very soft aroma of lightly per-fumey florals. The mildly sweet and carbonic start is soft with touches of caramel and sour orange leading into a bittersweet, creamy and grassy body with hints of flowers and orange. The finish is bitter, faintly acidic and rooty. ★½

Croco Pale Ale (5% vol.)
See Crocodile St. Laurent

Crocodile St. Laurent

LOCATION:	*4238 Rue St. Laurent, Montreal, Quebec H2W 1Z3*
PHONE:	*514-848-0044, (fax) 514-848-0183*
OWNERS:	*Le Groupe Crocodile*
PRESIDENT:	*Bernard Ragueneau*
MARKETING DIRECTOR:	*Marie Lamarre*
MANAGER:	*Jean-Pierre Abdul*
BREWER:	*Guy Meilleur*
CONSULTING BREWER:	*N/A*
CAPACITY:	*1,200 hl*
TOURS:	*No*
BRANDS:	*Crocodile Ale, Croco Pale Ale (bottles contract-brewed by the McAuslan Brewery)*

When a concept works in the restaurant trade, the immediate incli-nation is to elaborate and expand upon it. That being the case, the first Crocodile brewpub must have worked fairly well because, when the second Crocodile on St. Laurent opened in September 1989, it was certainly elaborate and expansive.

Playing on the same bar/restaurant/discotheque theme that had worked so well for the ownership group at their Thursday's club on Crescent Street in downtown Montreal, the St. Laurent Crocodile comprises three massive floors of very extravagant decor and comfortable surroundings. It is also home to a substantial malt-extract brewery.

Guy Meilleur, who was formerly an assistant brewer at Carling O'Keefe before joining the Crocodile chain, handles the brewing chores at both Crocodiles. He suggests that the size of the two breweries—more than either location really requires—was based on the premise that the Crocodiles might some day be able to sell their keg beer to other bars, thereby increasing production rather dramatically. For the time being, however, that remains an unrealized dream.

The underutilized brewing capacity may also have something to do with the fact that Crocodiles three and four were built without breweries, although marketing director Marie Lamarre says that the decisions taken in those cases had more to do with the recession of the late 1980s and the size of the buildings that were chosen as sites than anything else. She also adds that, when the next Crocodile is built, it will likely have an attached brewery.

Lamarre says that, despite there being breweries at only half of the Crocodiles, the brewpub concept has been very good to the company. The staff at the brewpubs sell the house beer because they are all very fond of it, she says, and the company features the brewpub aspect in their advertising and point-of-sale merchandise because they have found it to be a great draw for the establishments.

The lack of breweries at the two locations has, in fact, yielded an unexpected bonus for the Crocodile chain: a contract-brewed bottled beer by the name of Croco Pale Ale.

According to Lamarre, the decision to contract the McAuslan Brewery (see separate entry under Quebec and the Maritimes) to produce Croco Pale Ale was made because the company wanted a house beer that they could serve in all of their locations. Since they could not legally take their own brew from one Crocodile to another, Croco was born.

McAuslan was chosen, says Lamarre, because the brewery had a good reputation and was a local operation. The relationship debuted on Valentine's Day, 1990, and has been going strong ever since, she says.

The St. Laurent Crocodile represented a small departure for the company; where the Gatineau location kept on a domestic draught, there is only the house beer represented on tap at the St. Laurent establishment. This choice, say both Lamarre and Meilleur, has not had any ill effect on the business, and the bar staff say they rarely receive any complaints regarding the draught selection. After all, they say, that is the way a brewpub should be.

SCOREBOARD

Crocodile Ale (5% vol.)

Light to medium gold in colour with a lightly sour, orangey aroma carrying some sweet toffee notes. The very soft start is carbonic and slightly sweet with candy sugar and caramel malt flavours. It heads into a sweet-and-sour body of light caramel, root, fruit (apricot) and very faint florals before coming to a bitter, grassy finish. $\bigstar^{1/2}$

Croco Pale Ale (5% vol.)

Light to medium gold in colour with a mapley malt aroma holding orange notes and a slight hint of cinnamon. The mildly sweet and spicy (nutmeg, cinnamon) start moves into a body of moderate woody hop and sour orange malt with some caramel notes and a bitter hop and toffee finish. $\bigstar\bigstar$

Granite Brewery

LOCATION:	*1222 Barrington Street, Halifax, Nova Scotia B3J 1Y4*
PHONE:	*902-422-4954, (fax) 902-423-2793*
OWNERS:	*Kevin Keefe*
GENERAL MANAGER:	*Nadine Halliday*
BREWER:	*Kevin Keefe*
CONSULTING BREWER:	*Alan Pugsley*
BREWING CAPACITY:	*835 hl*
BRANDS:	*Best Bitter, Keefe's Irish Stout, Peculiar*

Kevin Keefe says that he does not think of himself as a Canadian brewing pioneer. He is much too modest.

Keefe may be accurately called the East Coast version of British Columbia's John (Horseshoe Bay Brewing, Spinnakers) Mitchell, the man largely responsible for the introduction of legislation allowing for brewpubs and the resurrection of traditional beer styles in this country. What Mitchell accomplished out West, Keefe similarly achieved in the Maritimes; there can be no doubt that every small brewer in Canada owes at least a small debt of gratitude to these two men.

Unlike Mitchell, however, Keefe was not a brewing pioneer by choice so much as by circumstance.

In the early 1970s, Keefe and his brother Wilfred were making their livings by purchasing and redeveloping buildings in and around Halifax. As chance would have it, the Gainsborough Hotel came into their possession in 1975 and the two brothers made the fateful decision to spruce up the old building and enter the hospitality trade. In November of that year, Gingers was born and the future of the Keefes was forever altered.

Kevin Keefe explains that, at the time, there were only about 20 taverns, lounges and cabarets in Halifax, so it did not take long for Gingers to make a mark on that city's night life. Within two years, Keefe says, Gingers was a landmark tavern serving 70 to 80 kegs of beer a week and hosting live entertainment nightly.

For the remainder of the decade and into the 1980s, the Keefes acquired other bars and restaurants, thus expanding their operations and contributing to what Keefe describes as "too much time spent yelling on the telephone." By the time he read about the Horseshoe Bay Brewing Company in British Columbia (see separate entry under British Columbia) in a magazine, Keefe was ready for the resumption of a more active role in the business.

Within a matter of weeks at the start of 1984, Keefe had his brother investigating breweries in England (where the latter was on vacation), requested information from the British consultancy Peter Austin & Partners and registered for a two-day introductory course at the Newman Brewery in Albany, New York. A short time later, he began lobbying the government for a law to allow brewpubs to exist.

Keefe's rationale was based on more than the urge to brew beer. He knew that, in the highly competitive Halifax licensed trade, the brewpub concept was one that other bar owners would have a hard time copying. He also knew, however, that he would be facing an uphill battle in trying to convert Maritimers to British-style ales.

When Keefe began to receive positive signs that the government was going to allow him to proceed with his brewery, he took off for a two-month course at Peter Austin's Ringwood facility in England and, by January 1985, was setting up the first Granite Brewery in Gingers.

As Keefe expected, initially there was resistance to the new ales, Haligonians eventually did come around and Gingers became famous all over again, this time as a haven for English ale in the East. The old building was beginning to decay rather badly, though, and it wasn't long before Keefe was out sourcing a new home for his brewery.

The home he found was the Henry House, the original residence of one of the Fathers of Confederation, William Alexander Henry. After a public hearing to allow for a tavern to be located in the historical land-mark, the Granite Brewery was moved, the name "Gingers" dropped and the focus of the establishment changed to that of a relaxed pub and restaurant rather than a raucous drinking and entertainment hall.

Opened in April 1988, the new location has served him well, says Keefe, and he has made few changes since he first unlocked the doors. As well as being a brewer and pubowner, Keefe is apparently also a champi-on of Halifax history.

SCOREBOARD

Best Bitter (4.5% vol.)
Light brown and slightly coppery in colour with a dried leaf and wood aroma holding just a hint of caramel malt. The soft, leafy and lightly bitter front leads to a hoppy, full and woody body with light bitter orange notes and an enduring, bitter and slightly biting finish. ★★★

Peculiar (5.6% vol.)
Reddish mahogany colour with a lightly roasted coffee aroma holding notes of burnt sugar. The sweet and (slightly) sour start heads to a malty body of moderate sweetness with coffee and light chocolate flavours alongside earthy hopping and a touch of lingering astringency. It is bittersweet in its mild finish with notes of raisin and a light espresso tang. ★★½

Stout (4% vol.)
Deep purple-coloured bordering on black with an espresso and licorice nose. A light, sweetish start with plum and sugar notes precedes a mildly astringent body with coffee and baker's chocolate flavours. The finish is of sweetened coffee with a slight, sour citrus tang. ★★

L'Inox

LOCATION:	*37 St-André Street, Quebec City, Quebec G1K 8T3*
PHONE:	*418-692-2877*
OWNERS:	*Pierre Turgeon, Roger Roy, André Jean*
MANAGER:	*Pierre Turgeon*
BREWER:	*Pierre Turgeon*
CONSULTING BREWER:	*Jerôme Denys*
CAPACITY:	*600 hl*
TOURS:	*On request*
BRANDS:	*Transat Light Ale, Trois de Pique Bock, Trouble Fête Ale*

Pierre Turgeon and Oakland A's manager Tony La Russa have something in common.

Like the A's skipper, Turgeon is a trained lawyer who chucked in his profession to pursue a decidedly different career. Unlike La Russa, it was not the baseball diamond that lured him from his practice. In Turgeon's case, that call came from the brewing kettle.

Like his two partners, urban geographer André Jean and engineer Roger Roy, Turgeon was a home brewer with a passion. That shared passion eventually grew to the point that the three professionals began to seriously consider discarding their careers and involving themselves directly in the brewing industry. Their first concept was to begin a "brewing club" where members could come to make their own beer, much like today's brew-on-premises establishments.

When that idea was discarded due to its impracticality at the time, the three turned to the fledgling brewpub industry that seemed to be receiving an enthusiastic response in the province. Following research tours of several Quebec and Vermont businesses, they came to the conclusion that a brewpub would work in Quebec City and set about to make it happen.

Since none of them had any idea how to brew on a comparatively large scale, they approached Jerôme Denys of the Cheval Blanc brewpub in downtown Montreal (see separate entry) to ask him if he would train them. Denys agreed and the business was under way.

The location the trio chose for their new brewpub was strategically sound at the time but seems a little out-of-the-way in the 1990s. Turgeon explains that the area that is home to L'Inox was supposed to be the next big development in the city, but that progress in the sector has been painfully slow. In an odd turn of fate, he adds with a chuckle, it is L'Inox which now draws people specifically to the area.

Construction began in August 1987 and the carpet was still being laid 30 minutes before the bar opened in November of that year. Although it was not until December that the brewery was fully functioning, they were still able to greet the new year with glasses of L'Inox's house brew.

From the start, Roger Roy chose to stay out of the day-to-day operations at L'Inox, leaving Turgeon and Jean to split the duties of running the pub. While both men had been equally trained by Denys, the general division of work left Turgeon with the management end of things and Jean with the brewing chores. That situation lasted until November 1990 when Jean came to the conclusion that the operation was a lot more difficult than he had expected and passed the torch to Turgeon with both Jean and Roy becoming silent partners in the business.

The former lawyer now wears many caps at L'Inox, not the least of which is brewer. His secret to the quality of his extract beers, he says, lies in the custom-made malts he purchases in bulk from British Columbia. Insofar as he does not have the room to go to full-grain brewing, Turgeon adds, he feels that he should at least get the finest available extracts.

L'Inox—the name is short for "inoxydable" or stainless—has expanded to double its size over the years and Turgeon was hoping to get three new tanks in the brewery by the end of 1993. The positive initial reaction the brewpub received, says Turgeon, has translated into a solid customer base and a good amount of trade for the establishment.

It is clear that Turgeon is one lawyer who has not only passed the bar, but successfully run one, as well.

SCOREBOARD

Transat (5% vol.)
Light gold in colour with a lightly sour, rooty aroma holding petrol notes. The soft and malty start holds some vegetal notes before a sour and slightly woody body with grapefruit and orange notes. The finish is very sour and vegetal. ★¹/₂

Trois de Pique (6.5% vol.)
Copper-coloured with a rooty nose holding strong plastic and faint sugar notes. The soft, sweet and malty start turns very woody and whiskyish in the body with pronounced bitterness leading to a strongly alcoholic and oaky finish. ★★

Trouble Fête (5% vol.)

Light brown and hazy from its unfiltered state. The muddy nose has sour yeast notes over a slightly caramelly malt with light floral and spice notes. A sharp, tangy and spicy start with evident yeast leads into a sour grain body punctuated by faint plastic and light cinnamon notes before a tangy and earthy finish. ★$^{1}/_{2}$

La Brasserie Lion D'Or

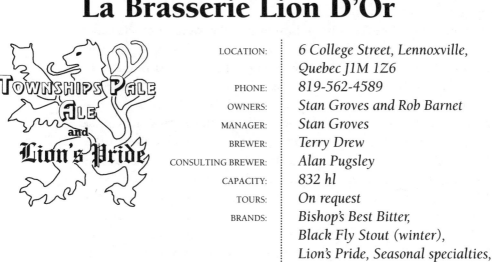

LOCATION:	*6 College Street, Lennoxville, Quebec J1M 1Z6*
PHONE:	*819-562-4589*
OWNERS:	*Stan Groves and Rob Barnet*
MANAGER:	*Stan Groves*
BREWER:	*Terry Drew*
CONSULTING BREWER:	*Alan Pugsley*
CAPACITY:	*832 hl*
TOURS:	*On request*
BRANDS:	*Bishop's Best Bitter, Black Fly Stout (winter), Lion's Pride, Seasonal specialties, Township's Pale Ale*

S tan Groves has a new spin to put on the traditional freshman, sophomore, junior and senior year classifications of college and university students. His parallel categories are Pale Ale, Lion's Pride, Best Bitter and Stout. It is a program from which he says more than a few students from nearby Bishop's University have graduated.

Lion D'Or was one of the first two small breweries to start the renaissance in Quebec in 1986. Oddly enough, the other one, Massawippi Brewing (now operating as Unibroue; see separate entry), was located a short distance away in North Hatley, thus causing some confusion as to which brewery was which and where. This situation was further confounded when Massawippi became a bottling micro rather than a brewpub and moved its operations to Lennoxville, causing Groves to joke that, for a time at least, Lennoxville had the highest ratio of breweries to population anywhere in North America.

Groves was, and is, the man behind the Lion. It was Groves who became interested in the craft-brewing business when he heard about

British Columbia's Horseshoe Bay Brewing (see separate entry under British Columbia) while he was residing in Edmonton; it was also Groves who originally approached the Quebec government about the idea when he returned to the province in 1984.

At the time, Groves's father was a part owner in the Lion and had no problem involving his son in the business so that the younger Groves could pursue his brewing interest. The bar was well established (since 1973) and the garage building that would eventually house the brewery was standing, so there seemed to be little between Groves and pub brewing, except for the government.

In cooperation with the Massawippi interests who were after the same objective, Groves says that he lobbied the legislators intensely for the better part of two years. The only time he stopped was to go to England to take part in the four-week brewers training course offered by Alan Pugsley of Peter Austin & Partners.

Groves says that he became good friends with Pugsley during the course and was keen to have him help set up the operation in Lennoxville. At this point, the legislature was preparing to pass the necessary laws, so Groves contracted Pugsley and the brewery went into construction in early 1986.

The Lion D'Or opened on Canada Day of the same year with the Township's Pale Ale and soon added the Lion's Pride. According to Groves, the response was encouraging, especially from the university students at Bishop's, although some prodding and education were necessary.

The next Lion brew is noteworthy because it was invented by accident! While Groves was teaching his brothers how to brew, one of them accidentally threw in six kilograms of hops rather than six pounds. The disaster turned fortuitous when the trio tasted the finished beer and the recipe was added to the beer menu.

The Lion benefits from an early quirk of the Quebec brewing laws that allow it to sell keg beer to other bars. While it is not something they engage in to a great degree, says Groves, the outside sales are helpful when the university is closed for the summer and sales decline rather dramatically.

Of course, the down time of the summer is also beneficial for Groves. After all, every professor needs time to prepare his instruction materials for the next year's students.

SCOREBOARD

Bishop's Best Bitter (4.5% vol.)

Light copper-coloured with a soft, woody nose holding strong leafy notes and a hint of charcoal. The leafy start shows a faint fruitiness before yielding to the dry and bitter body flavoured by strong woody and leafy hopping. The finish has a touch of sour, roasted grain in a still-bitter hop character. ★★½

Lion's Pride (4.5% vol.)

Copper-rust-coloured with a very light molasses aroma. The fruity (canned peach and orange) and sweet start leads into a slightly bitter, caramelly body carrying faint floral notes before finishing with a light bitterness and floral butterscotch notes. ★★

Townships Pale Ale (4.5% vol.)

Light gold in colour with a sweet, floral and caramelly nose. A slightly candied and carbonic start precedes a creamy body with butterscotch notes, a bitter, woody hopping and a touch of rooty sourness. The finish holds dried leaf notes in a lightly bitter character. ★½

Brasserie Mon Village

LOCATION:	2760 Côte St. Charles Road, St. Lazare, Quebec J0P 1V0
PHONE:	514-458-7006, (fax) 514-458-4615
OWNER:	David Crockart
BREWER:	Ken Hodeson
CONSULTING BREWER:	Cask
CAPACITY:	416 hl
TOURS:	Wednesdays on request
BRANDS:	Como Pale Ale, Mon Village Gold

There is an age-old question among beerophiles which asks whether bread or beer came first in the natural order of the world. No such mystery prevails at Mon Village, however; bread was definitely first. Of course, that is only because the building which now houses the brewery was formerly a bakery.

Technically speaking, Mon Village is a micro-brewery rather than a brewpub because, among other things, it brews beer for three different licensees in the St. Lazare/Hudson area outside of Montreal. Of course, by that definition, the Lion D'Or (see separate entry) is also a micro, but there is something a little different about Mon Village. Part of that difference is David Crockart.

To hear Crockart talk about his brewery, one almost gets the impression that he built it purely as a hobby. He explains that he owned the Mon Village Restaurant at the time, saw a story about Massawippi Brewing on television, drove out to visit that brewery and decided to build one of his own.

Naturally, it was not quite as simple as that, but Crockart did seem to go through a lot less stress and strain than the average micro-brewer or brewpub owner and some of that ease can be neatly traced to the man's political connections.

Crockart says that he had good access to the "right" people through his local Member of the National Assembly who was the provincial Minister of Trade and Commerce at the time. The Minister directed him to the correct agencies and, says Crockart, he had his licence within three months. After that, it was simply a matter of completing the renovations on the old bakery and installing the malt extract brewery before, in the spring of 1987, the Brasserie Mon Village was in operation.

Brewer Ken Hodeson was, and still is, a bartender at Crockart's Willow Hotel in Hudson; he had an interest in home brewing and wanted to take a shot at the commercial game. Having no training in brewing himself and little time to devote to such things, Crockart went along with Hodeson and the bartender has been brewing ever since.

Although Crockart says that there were some horrible beer batches at first, including many that went down the drain, the Cask-constructed Mon Village Gold and Hodeson-created Como Pale Ale were eventually worked out according to the memory of the brews Crockart recalls drinking in his youth.

Crockart eventually sold the restaurant in order to focus his attention on his hotel, but he kept control of the brewery. While it is not something he concerns himself with too intensively, Crockart evidently enjoys owning a brewery and serving his own beer at the hotel. In 1990, he even toyed with the idea of converting to a full-grain system, but those plans were waylaid by the economic downturn and Crockart now says that he has other, higher-priority projects ahead of any brewery renovation.

The Mon Village brewery now brews beer for the Willow, the local branch of the legion and the Mon Village Restaurant where Crockart pays his rent for the old bakery building in kegs of brew. It seems unlikely that this customer list will grow in the near, or even not-so-near future, but that prospect does not appear to worry Crockart one bit.

SCOREBOARD

Como Pale Ale (4.5% vol.)

Deep reddish-brown in colour with a sweet caramel and light chocolate aroma carrying a few faint floral notes. The body begins sour and carbonic before becoming bitter and somewhat sour with baker's chocolate notes and evident yeastiness. The finish is bitter, earthy and astringent. ★

Mon Village Gold (4.5% vol.)

Light to medium gold in colour with a sweet caramel and butterscotch nose. The soft, sweet and slightly tangy start leads to a creamy body with grassy sourness and a husky sweetness. A little yeast rises in the body before the bitter, slightly leafy and astringent finish. ★

CHAPTER EIGHT

Coming Soon...
or Going Soon

As of October 1993, the following breweries were either just beginning operations, preparing to start up or stuck in limbo due to financial or other considerations.

Alberta

Strathcona Brewing Company
7921 Coronet Road, Edmonton, Alberta T6E 4N7
Phone: 403-465-0553, (fax) 403-465-0554

- A micro-brewery founded in late 1986 which produced bottled and draught ales. At the time of writing, it was in receivership awaiting a court-appointed sale.

Saskatchewan

The Last Straw
127 North Albert Street, Regina, Saskatchewan S4R 3B8
Phone: 306-543-3331

- Located in the premises that was formerly home to the Regina Luxembourg, this is an all-grain brewpub set up by the Dunn brothers, owners of the Barley Mill Brewing Company in Regina and parts of other brewpubs. It opened in July 1993.

Manitoba

Bushwakker Brewpub
location not yet known, Winnipeg, Manitoba

- A spin-off of the successful Regina brewpub created under the direct supervision of the owner of the original Bushwakker, Bev Robertson. It was scheduled to open by the end of 1993.

Ontario

Angel Brewing Company
6 Queen Street West, Mississauga, Ontario L5H 1L0
Phone: 905-274-9662

- A micro-brewery to be housed in the original Conners Brewery in the old Port Credit district of the Toronto suburb Mississauga. It will brew ales and lagers on draught and in bottles (sold from the brewery only) and was slated to start business in the fall of 1993.

Canada's Finest Beers
5th Concession, Mersea Township, Wheatley, Ontario N0P 2P0
Phone: 519-825-3785, (fax) 519-785-0184

– Housed in the former Wheatley Brewing location, this regionally oriented micro-brewery is expected to concentrate mainly on draught lager sales but plans also to sell bottled beer from the brewery. It began production in August 1993.

Hometowne Brewery
1 Adelaide Street North, London, Ontario N6B 3P8
Phone: 519-432-1344, (fax) 519-432-1381

– A small, draught-only micro-brewery that began brewing in the fall of 1993. The intent is to brew five styles of beer including Canadian ale, lager, brown ale, stout and light lager and focus on the regional market.

Jolly Friar Brewpub
320 Bay Street, Sault Ste. Marie, Ontario P6A 1X1
Phone: 705-945-8888

– A northern Ontario brewpub that closed its doors due to financial pressures in the fall of 1993 after five years of operation. It is currently in limbo as the owners of the bar/restaurant space try to find someone willing to continue running it as a brewpub.

Taylor and Bate Brewing Company
55 Mill Street, Elora, Ontario N0B 1S0
Phone: 519-846-2965

– A very small-production micro-brewery creating a traditional pale ale for draught sales in the local area and bottle sales from the brewery. It opened its doors in September 1993.

Trafalgar Brewing Company
760 Pacific Road, Unit 9, Oakville, Ontario L6L 6M5
Phone 905-844-0937

– A small brewery spinning off of the successful Brew Perfect BOP business in this Toronto suburb. The focus will be on a Czech pilsner but plans are also in place for a British-style best bitter. Opening scheduled for December 1993.

Quebec

Brasserie Bas Saint-Laurent/Lower St. Lawrence Brewing Company
5600 Hochelaga Street, Montreal, Quebec H1N 3L7
Phone: 514-696-9177

– A micro-brewery specializing in custom-brewed, premium draught beers created for individual restaurants. The plan is for the brewery to produce up to 42 different beers in different styles and startup was expected in late 1993.

La Brasserie Portneuvoise
125 Hardy Street, St. Casimir, Quebec H3V 1A1
Phone: 418-339-3242

– An on-again, off-again micro-brewery located outside of Quebec City. At the time of writing, it had again been resuscitated only to fall into financial problems once more and was contemplating a change in location or closure.

CHAPTER NINE

And Now What?

S ince completing my beer-tasting journeys across Canada, dozens of people have asked me the same question: What was your favourite?

As simple and innocent as that query appears, it opens a Pandora's box of possible answers, none of which I relish the thought of giving. My standard response, therefore, is to rattle off the names of six or so good beers and hope that my questioner will be satisfied with that. The alternative, the long answer, is simply too complicated to pursue.

The truth is I have no particular favourite. Or, more accurately, I have a particular favourite for no longer than an hour or two. My preference for any given brew varies dramatically according to the time of day, whether or not I am eating, what I have or have not already consumed, my mood at the time and even what the weather is like. Although that may sound like a weak excuse, it is, and should be, the reality of beer appreciation.

I am constantly amazed at how people react to beer in comparison to, say, wine. Few people I know would even think of asking noted wine writers Tony Aspler or David Lawrason which of the multitude of dramatically different wines in the world is their favourite. Yet it is a question I get all the time. Similarly, I do not think that either Tony or David has to continually defend the fact that they do not have a large gut. Ah, but such is the row a beer writer has to hoe.

There is no doubt that there are some great beers brewed in Canada, even some approaching world-class level (and one which was there for a time but slipped). However, the biggest problem these breweries have lies in convincing people to try them. For that reason, my final comment focuses not on myself or the brews of this country, but on you, the reader.

Canadians used to be proud beer drinkers, but over the last several decades, we have become a nation of lager swillers. The overwhelming majority of us have been raised on national beer styles which, for reasons explained earlier, have become increasingly bland over the years. The result has been that we have come to see beer as a cold whistle-wetter or worse yet, a simple intoxicant.

As I have stated numerous times over the course of this book, beer is a noble and complex beverage. With this in mind, I would like to encourage all those who read this to go out today and try a new style of beer, perhaps even a brand listed in the reviews. Give it a chance and do not judge it immediately on what you see, smell or taste. You may not like it at first but you may grow to appreciate its qualities.

Once you have done that, you are well on your way to reclaiming a part of your heritage.

Selected Further Reading

While the field of beer journalism cannot be said to have exactly exploded in the last few years, it has certainly taken off as never before. The following is just a starter list of works for the beer enthusiast; there are many more quality sources of information that are but a brief search away.

BOOKS

Aidells, Bruce and Denis Kelly, *Real Beer and Good Eats*. Alfred A. Knopf, New York, 1993.

Bowering, Ian, *The Art and Mystery of Brewing in Ontario*. General Store Publishing, Burnstown, Ontario, 1988.

D'Eer, Mario, *Le Guide de la Bonne Bière*. (published in french) Editions du Trécarré, Ville Saint Laurent, Québec, 1989.

Erickson, Jack, *California Brewin'*. Red Brick Press, Reston, Virginia, 1993.

Jackson, Michael, *The Simon & Schuster Pocket Guide to Beer*. Simon & Schuster Inc., New York, 1991.

Jackson, Michael, *Michael Jackson's Beer Companion*. Reed Consumer Books, London, 1993.

Jackson, Michael, *The New World Guide to Beer*. Running Press, Philadelphia, 1988.

Johnson, Steve, *On Tap: Guide to North American Brewpubs*. WBR Publications, Clemson, South Carolina, 1993.

MacKinnon, Jamie, *The Ontario Beer Guide*. Riverwood Publishers, Sharon, Ontario, 1992.

Papazian, Charlie, *The New Complete Guide to Home Brewing*. Avon Books, New York, 1991.

PERIODICALS

All About Beer, Chautauqua Inc, Durham, North Carolina.
American Brewer, American Brewer Inc., Hayward, California.
Beer Magazine, Mario D'Eer Creations, Ottawa, Ontario.
Beer: The Magazine, Owens Publications, Hayward, California.
BiéreMAG (published in french), Mario D'Eer Creations, Ottawa, Ontario.
Celebrator Beer News, Celebrator Publications, Hayward, California.

Index of Beers Reviewed